I0406658

MIKHAIL SERGEEV

THE CRUCIFIXION IN PAINTING

FROM THE MIDDLE AGES TO POST-MODERNISM

With a Foreword by Rev. Michael A. Meerson

BOSTON · 2023

MIKHAIL SERGEEV

The Crucifixion in Painting:
From the Middle Ages to Post-Modernism

Copyright © 2023 by Mikhail Sergeev
Copyright © 2023 by M•GRAPHICS

All rights reserved. No part of this book may be reproduced or
utilized in any form or by any means, electronic or mechanical,
including photocopying, recording, or by any information storage and
retrieval system, without the written permission of the copyright holder.

ISBN 978-1-960533081 (pbk)
ISBN 978-1-960533401 (hardcover)
Library of Congress Control Number: 2023941793

Cover Image: *Cross and Sickle (Pseudo-Messiah)* by Vitaly Komar
Tempera, oil on canvas, 72 × 66 inches, © 2010-2023
From the author's collection. Used per V. Komar's permission

Published by M•GRAPHICS | Boston, MA
  🖵 www.mgraphics-books.com
  🖂 mgraphics.books@gmail.com

Printed in the United States of America

TABLE OF CONTENTS

It seems to me that the contemporary expressive style gives, and has already given, new possibilities for religious art... To say it in <terms of> religious symbolism, the subject matter is man crucified, not God-Man resurrected.

Paul Tillich

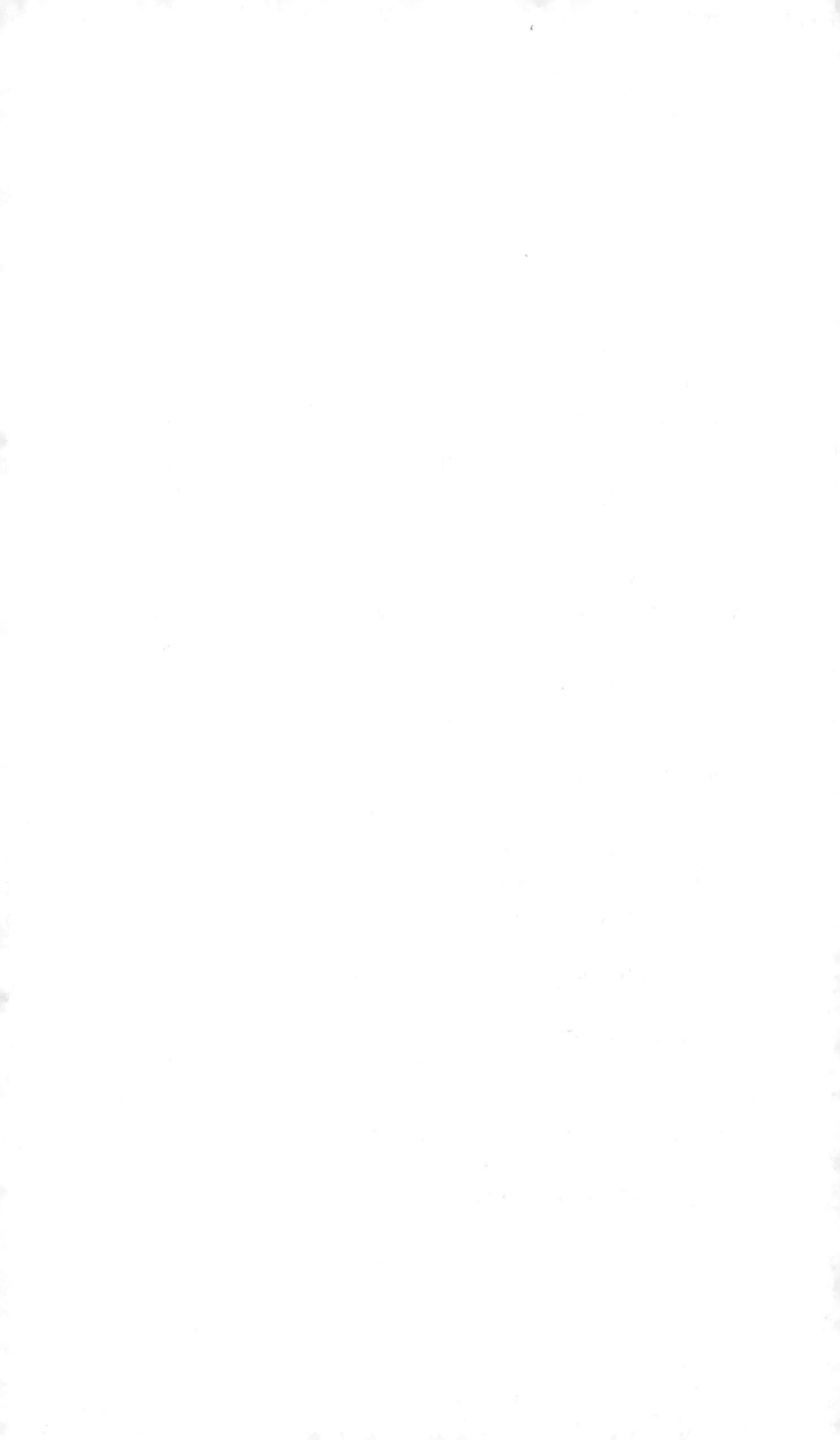

*To my dearest mom and dad
with filial love and
spiritual affection*

Acknowledgments

The author would like to express his deep gratitude to the University of the Arts leadership for providing me with financial support throughout the years for the research and writing of my book. In 2004–2005, I received a Venture Fund Grant to proceed with the initial stages of my work on conference papers about the Crucifixion. In 2007–2008, I was awarded a Faculty Development Grant to continue writing and developing conference presentations on the Crucifixion in modern art.

In 2012 I received a stipend from Dr. Peter Stambler, then the Dean of the Liberal Arts Division of the University of the Arts, which allowed me to obtain partial copyright for painting reproductions for my book. In 2015–16 I was offered a Faculty and Academic Development Grant to complete the first draft of the manuscript. Finally, in 2023 I was awarded a Creative Research and Innovation Grant through funding provided by the President's Fund for Excellence, which made the publication of my manuscript possible. I thank my home institution for this continuing support and generous help!

I would also like to thank my friends and colleagues, Mary Theis and Nancy Heller, for their invaluable help in the copyediting process of the manuscript. My most excellent thanks, however, go to my wife Alyona, who spent much time searching the Internet for information and images about the Crucifixion, significantly facilitating my study and work.

1

FOREWORD

by Rev. Michael A. Meerson, Ph.D.

*"Christ Crucified, a scandal to the Jews,
and madness for the Greeks."*

(1 Cor. 1: 23)

IN THE PRESENT BOOK, MIKHAIL SERGEEV invites us to revisit the mystery of the Cross as it is presented through the medium of modern art, specifically visual art. He also emphasizes the radically new nature of such representations. Starting in the nineteenth but mainly in the twentieth century, the genre of the Crucifixion came to keep transcending all canonical and theological boundaries. Sergeev states that following the zeitgeist and the anthropological paradigm shift of modernity, "the crucified Christ became a social emblem, a symbolic expression, and redemption applied to everybody beyond confessional difference, gender, race or social status" (26).

The most vivid horror of human pain and death, the Crucifix has grown into the icon of human suffering at large. Sergeev brings to our attention the awareness of one of the artists who understood this, a German Expressionist, Otto Dix. As recorded by the art critics, Dix shared his impression of dread at envisioning the deadly torments of a crucified person: "When you read a detailed description of a crucifixion... that is so horrible, awful. How the limbs swell up... How the person cannot breathe. How the face changes color. How he dies a horrible, utterly horrible death" (142).

3

The Expressionist master's reaction brings us to the actual reality of the cross, on which St. Paul wrote in his first letter to the Christian community in Corinth: "We preach Christ Crucified, a stumbling block (scandal) to the Jews, and madness for the Greeks" (1 Cor. 1: 23). We might add that for the Romans, this preaching amounted to a mortal insult. What reaction to the worshiping of a crucified person could be expected from the empire which introduced this most torturous death as a dreaded punishment for the enemies of its state and military power? Jesus died on the cross as a rebel against this power. Such was the accusation against him forced out from Pilate, the Roman governor of Judea, by the Jewish high priests envious of Jesus and afraid of his prophetic appeal to the people.

Roads in Judea were covered with crucifixes a generation after this event, during the stages of the Jewish war of liberation, which Rome managed to suppress by straining all its military forces. Elevated for public display, Jewish rebels expired in agony upon them. In the mind of simple Roman folks and, especially of the military or state officials, the worship of the Crucified Christ, believed to be the chief of rebels ("the King of the Jews"—according to Pilate's subscription), —revered now not merely by some marginal Jews, but even by Roman citizens of significant standing,[1]—had come to be perceived as the most insolent mockery at the Roman state power. Otherwise, it is impossible to understand the insane cruelty with which the Imperial authorities executed whole army regiments along with their commanders for their profession of faith in Christ.[2]

---

[1]   In his letter to Philippians, written about 56 C.E. during his first imprisonment in Rome, St. Paul mentioned, among Christians, some "of the Imperial household" (Phil.4: 22).

[2]   On April 23, the Orthodox Church commemorates the martyr Alexandra, the Empress and wife of Diocletian (d. 303 C.E.). There is no historical confirmation that she was executed during Diocletian's most cruel persecution of Christians, but the very fact of the

Therefore, it is not surprising that the veneration of the cross came from Judeo-Christian circles and only gradually permeated the devotion of the Catholic Church with its majority of Gentile Christians. "In Judeo-Christian literature, — stated Bellarmino Bagatti, — the cross was considered not as a wood to be thrown away after the death of Christ, but as His personified power, which will remain with Him in His passion and death, and his glorification."[3] In the apocryphal "Gospel of Peter," the cross followed the risen Jesus and two angels who accompanied Him into heaven. In the mind of the Judeo-Christians, the Cross, having ascended into heaven with the resurrection of Jesus, remains there and will return with Jesus in His second coming." Fr. Bagatti emphasized the Jewish-Christian origin of the belief in the religious significance of the cross in referring to the martyr Pionium in the second century, who "educated after the Greek manner, found these ideas strange and attributed them to the Jews."[4]

Jesus Himself had spoken not only of His imminent death at the hands of authorities but also of the most painful and shameful mode of His execution elevated for the public display: "... the Son of Man must be lifted up, so that everyone who believes in Him may have eternal life" (John 3:14–15). And again, He says it in His final address to the crowd gathered for the Passover, challenging their confidence in the unclouded eternal glory of God's Anointed One: "'When I am lifted up from the earth, I will draw everyone to me' (In saying this He indicated the kind of death He was going to suffer.) The crowd answered: We heard from the Law that the Messiah will live forever. How, then, can you say that the Son of Man must be

---

Church's commemoration reveals the wide diffusion of the faith in the Crucified Savior among various strata of Roman society.

[3] Bellarmino Bagatti, o.f.m. *The Church from the Circumcision: History and Archaeology of Judaeo-Christians*, trans. Fr. Eugene Hoade, O.F.M., Jerusalem: Franciscan Printing Press, 1971, 221.

[4] Ibid.

lifted up? Who is this Son of Man?" (John 12: 32–4) Here is set forth the paradox of the future iconographies of the cross—as the confluence of the human unbearable suffering and death on the one hand and the divine glory of eternal life on the other. In Chapter 1, Sergeev points out that Byzantine and Roman canons developed their specific versions of the Crucifixion's art. The Byzantine tradition focused more on the divine glory of the Son of God, while Roman Catholicism emphasized the Savior's humanity and His redemptive sufferings. The stress on Christ's human nature and his vulnerability has remained the most characteristic feature of Western Christian art and has passed on into its modern development.

The Byzantine canon had emerged in the same Roman Empire, which eventually surrendered, starting with Constantine the Great, to the overwhelming superiority and practicality of the new religion. It had pushed, however, the horror of its traditional tool of execution, now abolished, into the depth of the unconscious, converting it into the symbol of divine victory.[5] The Roman Church, remaining part of the same empire for centuries, followed the same canon through its early Middle Ages. As Sergeev pointed out, only Renaissance artists, aspiring to achieve historical accuracy, turned to "the exactness of its illustrative representation" and accentuated the Savior's humanity.

The Renaissance introduced and pursued the anthropological shift and the rise of subjectivity, which both came to fruition in the twentieth century. The turning point, however, was announced in the nineteenth century in the thought of Ludwig Feuerbach.

---

[5] According to tradition, the night before his decisive battle with Maxentius, Constantine "the Great," later canonized as a saint by the Church, had a vision of the cross accompanied with words: *In Hoc Signo Vinces* ("In this sign, thou shalt conquer").

FEUERBACH'S TRANSLATION
OF THEOLOGY INTO ANTHROPOLOGY

Ludwig Feuerbach (1804–1872), a German atheistic thinker, re-interpreted Christianity as a projection of human nature into the eternal realm of religion. For him, God was nothing but "the mirrored image of man."[6] Christian faith has reflected what was sacred to human beings: its ultimate foundation—the human personality. In Feuerbach's view, Christianity has mistakenly subordinated anthropology to theology. He claimed, on the contrary, that by reducing theology to anthropology, he had exalted anthropology into theology by correctly reading Christianity, which, by "lowering God into man, made man into God."[7] Having introduced the anthropological shift in theological discourse, he proceeded to interpret the teaching of the Church that God was love in strictly human terms, arguing that love was mainly a human affair. Yet, as he thought this out, true human love impelled the sacrifice of self to another; hence a human God could only be a God of love. "Who then is our Savior and Redeemer? God of love!"[8] In his chapter on the "Mystery of the Suffering God," Feuerbach pointed out the essential definition of the incarnate, or, equivalently, human God, that God's love has found its full expression in Christ's Passion. It has simply exemplified that love reveals itself in the ability to suffer for others. The image of the crucifixion, which we still find in all temples,—Feuerbach argued,—presented us not so much with the Savior, but with the crucified sufferer. This meant that God as Christ embodied all human suffering. As the highest metaphysical idea, Christ's pure suffering pierced the human heart.

---

[6] Ludwig Feuerbach, *The Essence of Christianity*, ed. & abridged by E. Graham Waring & F. W. Strothmann, (Milestones of Thought), NY: Continuum, 1989, 30.

[7] Ibid., 5.

[8] Ibid., 27.

Nothing made such a strong impression on the human soul as suffering, especially the suffering of the sinless, the innocent offering himself in self-sacrifice. So, Christ's Crucifixion came to symbolize suffering as such and expressed the capacity to suffer in general.

This anthropological dimension called for trinitarian theology, whose human content Feuerbach claimed to lay bare. "Only a being who comprised in himself the whole man can satisfy the entire man," he argued. "Man's consciousness of himself in his totality is the consciousness of the Trinity." Humanity needs God the Father as "the sum of all human perfection" and God the Son, the Christ, as "the sum of all human misery."[9] Reflecting on human nature in his "atheistic dogmatics," he pointed out two aspects of anthropocentric theology: the Incarnation is brought about from the inner necessity of God-love on the one hand and from the human need for the suffering Redeemer on the other. Humanity needs the God of mercy in addition to the God of intellect and justice. The divine love expressed in the Incarnation unites God with humankind. "Love makes man divine, and it makes God human,"[10] states Feuerbach, maintaining that only the attribution of flesh and blood to God establishes a natural bond between humankind and God. Feuerbach makes the Christian God the stronghold of humanism, insisting on the fundamental exclusive humanity of the Incarnate God.

THE TWENTIETH-CENTURY THEOLOGY OF THE CROSS

Some of the twentieth-century Christian theologians, across various denominational borders, influenced by existentialism, readily accepted Feuerbach's anthropological shift as fitting

---

[9]   Ibid., 29.
[10] Ibid., 25.

more with the anthropocentric worldview of contemporary man and consequently serving as a way to revitalize the Christian faith. Among them, and even anticipating this anthropological shift, were some Russian thinkers, of whom I single out Nicholas Berdyaev (1874–1948) in philosophy and Sergey Bulgakov (1871–1944) in theology. Both started as Russian populists and Marxists, whom Feuerbach's paradigm shift had strongly influenced. Their humanism, however, through their personal experience of human fragility, made them rethink it in Christian terms and embrace what their Russian predecessor Vladimir Solovyov called "divine humanity." Bulgakov even labeled Berdyaev's existential dialectic of human and divine as "mystical feuerbachianism." Berdyaev, however, revised Feuerbach's optimistic humanism. Having lived through the First World War, the Russian Revolution, exile, and the Nazi's occupation of France, Berdyaev had corrected atheistic humanism with its false promises that had become bankrupt in the face of twentieth-century totalitarian regimes with their total disrespect of human freedom, dignity, and life itself. Pointing—obviously—at the Crucified Savior, he uttered his famous dictum: "Man is not humane; it is God who is humane." In Berdyaev's rectification of Feuerbach, it is not God who borrows his kindness and goodness from man. It is the man who reflects the goodness of God while acting kindly and sacrificially.

Sergey Bulgakov developed the theology of the cross as the universal, both cosmic and all-human: the sacrifice God, incarnate in Jesus Christ, offered for "the life of the world" (Jn. 6:51). To be sure, he had found the basis for his theology in the Holy Scriptures, summed up in St. Paul's words: ... "Our paschal lamb, Christ, has been sacrificed for us" (cf. Cor. 5:7).[11] What Bulgakov had emphasized was "the universal instinct of sacrifice, common throughout the religious world," not solely

---

[11] Sergius Bulgakov, *The Eucharistic Sacrifice*, Trans. Mark Roosien, Notre Dame, Indiana: University of Notre Dame Press, 2021, 2.

in monotheistic faiths, but in pagan religions as well. He references, therefore, to the enigmatic character of Melchizedek, from both the book of Genesis (14:18–20) and Psalms (110:4) and to the Christian elaboration on it in the Epistles to the Hebrews, which presented him as the Old Testament icon of the eternal high-priesthood of Jesus Christ. Bulgakov observes that Melchizedek "does not emerge from the Old Covenant but appears out of the darkness of time and the nations in order to meet Abraham," the forefather of all three monotheistic religions. "The borders between the Old Covenant and pagan world fade away at the appearance of the one who bears in himself the image of the Coming High Priest."[12] So Christ, representing all humanity, sacrificed Himself on behalf of it. As Bulgakov insists, the sacrifice of Christ is not only the crucifixion but also encompasses his entire cruciform earthly life, which was a path to Golgotha beginning in the manger in Bethlehem and the flight for life from the persecution of Herod. That is the crucified body, which God, in His Incarnation, shares with all humanity. However, the crucifix of the Christian churches is venerated not only as the symbol of human suffering and expression of God-man's suffering on behalf of humanity but also as its witness to the "power of an indestructible life" (Heb.7:16) revealed in the Resurrection. Such is the meaning of the Eastern Orthodox hymn sung at the veneration of the Cross: "Before Thy Cross, we fall down and worship, o Master, and Thy holy Resurrection we glorify."

Bulgakov goes even further in his universalization of the Crucifix by applying his theological thinking to the words of St. Peter in his general address to Christians: "You were... ransomed... with the precious blood of Christ, like that of a lamb without blemish or spot. He was destined before the foundation of the world but was made manifest at the end of the times for your sake" (1 Peter 1:19–20). Christ's suffering has earthly

---

[12]   Ibid., 10.

and cosmic dimensions and points to the ontology of creation. "It is not eternity that is defined by time, but the other way around... Our conception of the sacrifice on Golgotha and of its eucharistic 'remembrance' must be raised to its Divine Prototype on the holy and immaterial (*noeron*) Altar above the heavens." It must be understood based on Trinitarian dogma. As if following Feuerbachian translation of Christian theology into anthropology and then taking it back into theological discourse, Bulgakov states that the doctrine of the Trinity implies the "sacrificial love" within the Deity. Bulgakov holds as the axiom of personal love, including the love of divine hypostases, that there is no love without sacrifice.[13] All three Persons share in the same sacrificial love, each in His proper fashion. The sacrificial character of the Father's love is expressed in His total self-negation and self-emptying in the birth of the Son. The sacrifice of the Son's love is expressed in being always born of the Father, of accepting His birth as being ever born.[14] The Holy Spirit also has *kenosis* or self-emptying. The Spirit is the very hypostatic love, deprived of any selfhood; the Spirit is entirely transparent for the other hypostases being the hypostatic "*in-between*" that connects them.[15]

Since the Three Persons of the Trinity are One God, the creation is the sacrifice of the whole Trinity, simultaneously the hypostatic and functional sacrifice specifically of the Son. Thus, the eternal *kenosis* of the Son is manifested in time. It is not the fall of Adam that calls for redemption. This fall expresses the instability of a creature that comes from nothingness. To be saved, the creature must be deified. The initial decision of God to create the world necessarily includes His decision to redeem it by uniting it with Himself. In other

---

[13] Bulgakov, "Glavy o Troichnosti," in *Pravoslavnaia Mysl'*, Paris, 1928, 2:66.

[14] Bulgakov, *Agnets Bojii*, Paris: YMCA-press, 1933, 122.

[15] Bulgakov, *Uteshitel'*, Paris: YMCA-press, 1936, 213–214.

words, humanity, from its very origin, is called to become divine humanity which is the proper foundation of creation.[16] Creation and redemption are ontologically identical. Golgotha manifests both. Each is the development of the same act of the Divine Priest in the Holy Trinity. This act has a triple structure: creation-incarnation-cross, representing the three facets of Son's sacrifice.

Bulgakov became the mouthpiece for the twentieth-century theology of the cross (Jürgen Moltmann, theologians of Liberation, etc.), claiming that the image of God dying on the cross for the sake of humanity is the response of the God of Love to the suffering of the world created by Him. With this doctrine, Bulgakov responds to the question raised by modern existentialism from Dostoevsky to Sartre: why do innocents suffer? Golgotha is the proper justification of God in the eyes of the suffering creature who wants to know the reason for its suffering. The High priesthood of God, as the sacrifice and the sacrificer in the same person, serves as God's unique justification. With it, He answers the biblical Job, who suffers from the revenge and slander of Satan without realizing it.[17]

Bulgakov's close friend, Fr. Pavel Florensky, a Russian Orthodox priest, a seminal theologian, and scientist, who died as a martyr in Stalin's Gulag,[18] had cast theology of the cross in artistic terms. At one point in his scholarly career, deprived by the Bolshevik Revolution of his positions as a professor at Moscow Theological Academy and as the editor of the leading Russian theological quarterly, Florensky taught the theory of perspective in Vkhutemas.[19] Pointing at the crucifix as an ar-

---

16   Bulgakov, *Agnets*, 374–375.
17   Ibid., 399. This passage is taken from my chapter on Bulgakov in Michael Aksionov Meerson, The *Trinity of Love in Modern Russian Theology*, Quincy, Il.: Franciscan Press, 1998.
18   Florensky was executed in 1937 at the Solovky labor camp after several years of imprisonment.
19   Vkhutemas (Higher Art and Technical Studios) was an early So-

tistic icon that combined anthropology and theology, he asserted that "the cross is the image of God in man..." He had in mind Da Vinci's *Vitruvian Man*, ranked as a universal symbol of European humanism and an archetypal representation of Renaissance art. The drawing illustrated Leonardo's concept of ideal body proportion. Endowing his theology of the cross with the artistic expression remindful of Da Vinci's model, Florensky claims that man "is created as a noumenal cross. Hence every higher manifestation of human nature is in the cruciform spread. Like a crumpled bud, shrinking, sits a man in the mother's womb. It grows and straightens like a bud blooms. The flowering of the human species is the most beautiful thing that is in a person—when he is cross-stretched."[20]

THE UNCONSCIOUS IN MODERN ART

The Vitruvian Man, cross-shaped within a circle, is "justly ranked among the all-time iconic images of Western civilization" (Carmen C. Bambach) because it refers to Christ on the cross, which Carl Jung considers one of the central archetypes of the Western collective unconscious. He is that

---

viet "educational undertaking of unprecedented scale and complexity," which served as one of the major platforms for the institutionalization of the avant-garde movement... that "translated radical experiments in art, architecture, and design into a systematized body of knowledge." http://grahamfoundation.org/grantees/6269-vkhutemas-laboratory-of-the-avant-garde-19201930. It had branches in Moscow, St. Petersburg, Vitebsk, and other cities. Such world-known artists as Alexander Rodchenko, Vasily Kandinsky, El Lissitzky, Kazimir Malevich, and Vladimir Tatlin worked at one point among its faculty. It was established in 1920 and survived until 1930, when Stalin's rising "Socialist realism" crushed it with the rest of Russian avant-garde.

[20] Pavel Florensky, "Iz bogoslovskogo nasledia", *Bogoslovskie Trudy*, Moscow Patriarchate Publ. # 17, 1977, 92.

divine, glorified Man, "after whose likeness our inner man is made, invisible, incorporeal, incorrupt, and immortal," according to Jung's quoting from Origen.[21] Christ exemplifies this archetype. After all, He occupies, in Jung's words, the "center of the Christian mandala" because He is "the still living myth of our culture, our culture hero." Therefore, "He is in us, and we in him."[22]

"From the intellectual point of view," Jung further explains, "it is nothing else but a psychological concept, a construct, which is to name the entity undistinguishable and unknowable to us because it exceeds the limits of our comprehension... With the same success, we could call it 'the deity within us.' At this very point, the origins of our psychic life begin, and all the loftiest and ultimate goals converge."[23] In Jung, this notion does not extend beyond psychology and phenomenology, but the Russian Symbolist poet and thinker Vyacheslav Ivanov endows it with theological input. Christ is the absolute unique model of the utterly divine human being, "the Son of Man who is in heaven," who "came down from heaven" (Jn.3:13), lived with men, died, and then rose and ascended to where he had been before (Mk.16:19; Lk.24:51–2). Ivanov asserts this point while explaining Christ's role as the inner center of human personality because he shares the most miserable human conditions and his descent into ontological nothingness, which is what man is. Quoting from the Nicene Creed, Ivanov states: "Compared with other religions, Christianity is the most radical affirmation of the divine *kenosis* (condescension) to the point of the interment of the God-

---

21 C. C. Jung, *Aion: Researches into the Phenomenology of the Self*, Trans. R.F.C. Hull, Bollingen Series XX, Princeton University Press, 1959, 37–8.

22 Ibid., 36.

23 C. Jung, "The Relations between the Ego and the Unconscious," in the *Collected Works*, Bollingen Foundation, Pantheon Books, V 7, Part. D. (in Russian translation p. 271).

man in the womb of the earth. 'Who... came down from heaven, and was incarnate, and became man, and suffered and was buried; and rose again, and ascended,'" "making oneself nothing ("self-emptying," cf. Phil.2:7) to the point of standing alone in the face of *nothing*, and feeling oneself, for a brief moment, equal to eternity, totally non-divine because abandoned by the Father, —such is the price of the saving resurrection and victorious return to the Spring of being." Ivanov emphasized the total compatibility of the *kenotic* descent of the Word becoming Flesh and the lowliness of the human condition. Both the incarnate Word and the human being, created by this Word, submit to this supreme law of becoming, which Ivanov finds in the testimony of the Gospel: "Unless a kernel of wheat falls to the ground and dies, it remains only a single seed. But if it dies, it produces many seeds" (Jn.12: 24).[24] By dying it becomes immortal. This also occurs in the sense that it enters each of us, making it its dwelling place.

In his study, Sergeev highlights modern art's appeal to the power of the unconscious in us. According to Jung, "The concept of the archetype, which is an indispensable correlate of the idea of the collective unconscious, indicates the existence of definite forms in the psyche which seem to be present always and everywhere."[25] These archetypes do not stay there passively. They actively suffuse human creativity, finding ever-new embodiments in various art forms. Thus, art is an ongoing improvisation of old myths and symbols that spring from the wealth of our subconscious. Since archetypes are found as artistic images and motifs, art presents one of the main fields

---

[24] Ivanov, "Discorso Sugli Orientamenti dello spirito moderno", "Razmyshleniia ob ustanovkah sovremennogo duha," ("Reflections on premises of contemporary spirit (mind)"), SS., III, 462, 465.

[25] Carl Jung, "The Concept of the Collective Unconscious," in C. G. Jung, *Collected Works*, Bolingen Series XX, Princeton University Press, 1968, Vol.9, Part I, 42–3.

of investigation for Jungian analysis, which appreciates that religion and mythology have been intertwined with art from prehistoric times to the present.[26]

Jung observes two types of the creative process, "the two entirely different modes of creation." One is wholly subordinated to the will and reason of an artist. In the other, the work of art forces itself upon the author: "his hand is seized, his pen writes things that his mind contemplates with amazement. The work brings its own form; anything he wants to add is rejected, and what he would like to reject is thrust back at him. While his conscious mind stands amazed and empty before this phenomenon, he is overwhelmed by a flood of thoughts and images he never intended to create, which his own will could never have brought into being. Yet despite himself, he is forced to admit that it is his own self-speaking, his inner nature revealing itself and uttering things he would never have entrusted to his tongue. He can only obey the apparently alien impulse within him and follow where it leads, sensing that his work is greater than himself and wields a power that is not his and that he cannot command. Here the artist is not identical with the process of creation; he is aware that he is subordinate to his work or stands outside of it, as though he were a second person; or as though a person other than himself had fallen within the magic circle of an alien will."[27]

MARC CHAGALL – AN ACROSS-THE-BOARD MODERN ARTIST

Among contemporary artists, the one who had embraced the subject of this study across the board, and to whom Sergeev, to

---

26 Aniela Jaffe, "Symbolism in the Visual Arts," in *Man & His Symbols*, 257.

27 Carl Jung, "On the Relation of Analytical Psychology to Poetry," *The Portable Jung*, The Viking Press, Penguin Books, 1971, 310–11.

be sure, dedicated a very informative chapter, is Marc Chagall. As early as 1912, he painted his cubist *Golgotha* and dedicated it "to Christ." As it was said in the introduction to the exhibition in the Jewish Museum in New York (Sept.15, 2013-Feb.2, 2014): *Chagall: Love, War, and Exile,*

> The most prevalent image Chagall used during World War II was of Jesus and the Crucifixion. For Chagall, the Crucifixion was a symbol for all the victims of persecution, a metaphor for the horrors of war, and an appeal to conscience that equated the martyrdom of Jesus with the suffering of the Jewish people and the Holocaust. While other Jewish artists depicted the crucified Jesus, for Chagall, it became a frequent theme.[28]

In his art, the crucifix symbolizes the sharing of the world's suffering by the Crucified and belongs to those archetypal images he employed throughout his painting career. Chagall confessed that he understood art "primarily as a condition of the soul" and focused on its inner life, which he magically depicts in his works full of a bright mixture of people and animals, nymphs and satyrs, flowers, birds, and fish playing musical instruments, hugging lovers, over all of which reigns the image of a Jew immersed in prayer, as well as the crucifix.

In one of his early works, he places himself on the cross. In the poem dedicated to him by his French friend Blaise Cendrars (October 1913), are the words:

He's asleep
He's awake
Suddenly he's painting
He takes a church and paints with the church
He takes a cow and paints with a cow...

---

[28] See: https://thejewishmuseum.org/exhibitions/chagall-love-war-and-exile.

He paints with all the dirty passions of a little Jewish town
With all the fired-up sexuality of provincial Russia...
He paints with his thighs
He has eyes in his back side
And all at once it is your portrait
It's you gentle reader
It's me
It's him
It's his fiancée...
Skies gone mad
Mouth of modernity...
Christ
He's Christ
He spent his childhood on the cross
He commits suicide every day...
Chagall is astonished that he is still alive.[29]

These symbols, interiorized and found within an individual soul but common to all of us, belong to the collective unconscious in Jung's terms and touch upon the domain of religion. So, no wonder "Chagall—as Sergeev emphasized—is also considered one of the most significant religious painters" of the last century" (170). According to André Breton, his art overcomes the gravity of the material world, including humans and animals, by transposing them into a paradise realm in which the human condition is somehow alleviated from the weight of the original sin. (S. cf.129) Chagall did not merely use Bible stories; he perceived the world through its prism. "I went back to the great universal book, the Bible," he wrote, "Since my childhood, it filled me with a vision about the fate of the world and inspired me in my work... For me, it is second nature. I see the events of life and works of art through the wisdom of the Bible.

---

[29] Quoted in Jacob Baal-Teshuva, *Marc Chagall 1887–1985*. Taschen, 1998, 46.

A truly great work is penetrated by its spirit and harmony... Since the spirit and world of the Bible occupy a large place in my inner life, I have tried to express it. It is essential to show the elements of the world that are not visible..." [30]

The Biblical anthropocentric world is recreated in his art: man, the mediator between God and the rest of creation, stands at its center. Archetypal images cluster around him, and angels and animals accompany him. Along with the Old Testament characters, we find the crucified Christ, who appears in the scenes of the creation of man, or Moses in front of a burning bush with the angel, hands/wings spread crosswise, addressing him from within. We see it also in contemporary subjects like the revolution, where Lenin stands upside down with an outstretched arm directly opposite the Crucifixion, as if turning over and parodying Christianity, or in *War*, where Jesus looks from the cross at the fire that has engulfed the earth. In this picture, the standing crucifix seems to be facing a murdered woman lying with her arms spread out, in front of whose body kneels a praying Jew. The lamb emphasizes the sacrifice's symbolism as if ready for slaughter, or instead symbolizing it, hanging across the painting with the burning town, its fugitives, and dead bodies.

The artist painted not just life but the essence of human existence—existence threatened by the danger of annihilation. The beauty and blessedness of life are riddled with violence and death and therefore depicted under a sign of the cross. Chagall, both as a human and as an artist, felt the incompleteness of this ontology without Christ. The presence of the crucifix in his painting is consonant with the existential and artistic themes of twentieth-century Russian religious thought, particularly with Pavel Florensky.

---

[30] *Chagall by Chagall*, ed. Charles Sorlier, New York: Harrison House, 1982, 193.

A brilliant master of space arrangement who applied the techniques of the Orthodox Vita Icon to his art, Chagall could barely manage without a crucifix as constructive support for every accurate composition. In the words of Fr. Pavel Florensky: "The cross lies at the foundation of being, as the true form of being."[31] Florensky taught at Vkhutemas (Moscow) in the same years (1920–23)[32] when Chagall organized art schools in Vitebsk and St. Petersburg, where Vkhutemas had branches, and could have known Florensky personally. The same is true about Berdiaev and Bulgakov, well-known religious thinkers and cultural figures, whom Chagall could have met in Moscow or St. Petersburg, as well as in Paris, where he and they belonged to the same Russian émigré intellectual and artistic milieu in the 1920s and 1930s. At least, Chagall painted what Bulgakov wrote about Christ, "crucified for us," "a lamb destined even before the creation of the world" (1 Peter, 1:19-20).

Although it is generally accepted that Chagall used the theme of the Crucifixion to symbolize both universal, Jewish, and, finally, personal suffering, he also preserved the Christian symbolism of the Cross, interpreting it in the spirit of modernity. As if painting Feuerbach's secular essence of Christianity, he universalizes the crucifix as the symbol absorbing all human suffering. He also returned it to the Jewish environment from where it originated. It retains, however, its Christian meaning of redemption that can be discerned in his biblical paintings, such as *Jacob's Ladder* or the *Sacrifice of Abraham*." In the second painting, we see Abraham lifting a knife over Isaac lying on the wood. In the background, Jesus carries His cross, accompanied by weeping people, women with in-

---

[31] Florensky, Op.Cit., ibid.

[32] Chagall called this period of working in Russia (1914–1922) "the most productive years of my whole career." Jacob Baal-Teshuva, *Chagall*, Benedikt Taschen Verlag, 1998, 75.

fants in their arms, and religious Jews. From the Crucifixion emanates a red bloodstream reaching Abraham and Isaac. This biblical passage is read at Vespers of Holy Saturday, after Good Friday, and before Easter. The Orthodox Church interprets Isaac's sacrifice as the prototype of Calvary. In response to Abraham's readiness to sacrifice his promised son Isaac to God, God offers His Own Son in redemption for Abraham's offspring that will embrace all humans. God had not permitted the shedding of Isaac's blood, yet the blood of Jesus, "His only begotten Son," was shed on the Cross. As if following this theology, in Chagall's painting, the scarlet stream flooding Abraham and Isaac comes from the Crucifixion. Abraham's sacrifice is performed in the gesture of Christ. The theme of Isaac's sacrifice as the prototype of the eternal offering is clearly expressed in Chagall's stained-glass window in Reims Cathedral named *Abraham and Christ*. There on the left side, Chagall depicts Abraham sacrificing Isaac. At the same time, the right one builds the ladder of the Old Testament prototypes of Calvary in the spirit of the theology of the Epistle to the Hebrews. At the bottom, we see Abraham conversing with three angels, who are depicted in Abraham's encounter with Melchizedek, "the priest of God the Most High."

Chagall charges the religious message for his painting with the existential intensity of his own time, a victim of which he had almost fallen.[33] In his canvas *Falling Angel*, there is a gigantic red figure of an angel in the center falling downward with wings spread. The figure seems to push aside the prayer images that appear on its edges. On the right, there is a burning candle with a crucifix on one side and a woman with a baby in her arms on the other. On the left, an old Jew runs away with the Torah. On everything lie fiery flashes onto which pass the blood-red wings of a falling angel. This recalls the pas-

---

[33] Chagall, with his wife and daughter, had miraculously escaped the arrest by the Gestapo in the south of France.

sage from the Apocalypse, telling of Satan cast down to earth who, in his powerless rage, pursued a woman with a newborn child.[34]

In this preface, Mark Chagall is given prominence in anticipation of the author's chapter on him because he is perceived by many as the international public artist of the modern West. His works have spilled over the walls of art museums, galleries, and private collections into the public square. Two of his huge panels, one in red, the other in blue, look at passers-by from the glazed facade of the Metropolitan Opera at the Lincoln Center in New York. With their heads up, visitors to the Paris Opera can gaze at the details of the ceiling he painted. Through his stained-glass windows, light streams on delegates from around the world in the UN building in New York and upon the worshipers at the oldest Catholic cathedrals in Europe, as well as in the synagogue of the Hadassah hospital in Jerusalem. The Israeli Knesset deliberates amidst his tapestries. His mosaics stare from the walls of the First National Bank in Chicago.

His art, along with its crucifixes, made its way to the public square because it expresses the archetypes of the collective soul of humanity in the language of modern art. It reverberates with its secular side as if echoing Feuerbach and with its unpronounced religious aspirations; with the groaning of atheistic existentialism, as well as with theology of the cross of Sergey Bulgakov and others, with the Eastern Orthodox liturgy, as well as with Hasidic spirituality. Whoever questions the validity of the Crucifix for a contemporary man may find an answer in his art. Sergeev's whole book points to the artistic import of this validity.

---

[34] The passage on Chagall is based on my article: Michael A. Meerson, "Evangelie ot Marka Shagala" (The Gospel according to Marc Chagall), published in Russian in Orthodox Almanac *Put'*, #7 (Winter 1985–86) by Christ the Savior Orthodox church in NYC.

PREFACE

THE PRESENT VOLUME RESULTS FROM MY teaching experience at the University of the Arts in Philadelphia. For a quarter of a century, I have offered courses in religion and the arts to my students, who represent various creative disciplines. My teaching responsibilities included standard curriculum courses in world religions, Asian spiritual traditions, and an introduction to the Bible. I also taught the history of modern art, which was part of a required program for all incoming freshmen. This yearly course was called Nineteenth and Twentieth-Century Modernism, and it included sections on painting, sculpture, architecture, music, literature, theater, and film.

After several years of teaching, I embarked on creating courses that would merge the study of religion and the arts. I had already used this strategy in my lectures on the Bible and world religions, which I heavily illustrated with examples from church frescoes, biblical paintings, and other sacred art forms in different faiths. I planned on developing a course about the founders of great religions through examples from music, literature, and film using a three-act opera by Arnold Schoenberg, *Moses and Aaron*, the novel by Herman Hesse *Siddhartha: An Indian Poem,* and a movie by Martin Scorsese, *The Last Temptation of Christ.* I was also preparing a course about the central story of the Christian faith and the New Testament: The Crucifixion of Jesus. Because of its frequent depiction in Christian sacred art, the idea was to study the biblical Gospels and non-canonical sources of Jesus' death and resurrection.

23

Extensive research into this topic proved problematic. Plenty of scholarly studies focused on individual painters, specific art movements, and even biblical art. But no volume covered the history of Crucifixion paintings, especially in the twentieth century. To my great surprise, I discovered there was a need for more accessible, comprehensive sources on the subject.

During the next four years, from 2005 until 2009, I made a series of presentations at the regional Mid-Atlantic American Academy of Religion annual conferences in Baltimore, MD, and New Brunswick, NJ, about the Crucifixion in Expressionist, Cubist, Surrealist, Abstract, and Postmodern painting. I also published several papers on the subject in various American journals.[35] After that preliminary research, I devoted myself to composing a book about Crucifixion art through the centuries.

The structure of this volume follows historical chronology. The introduction discusses the story of the Crucifixion, based on Christian sources and contemporary research and reconstruction by biblical scholars of this central event in the Christian faith.

The first chapter presents my theory of religious cycles, which distinguishes five stages in the evolution of Christianity—formative, orthodox, classical, reformist, and critical. In

---

[35] Mikhail Sergeev, "Crucifixion in Twentieth-Century Painting," *Transactions of the Association of Russian-American Scholars in the U.S.A.*, vol. XXXVII, New York, 2011–2012, 395–416. "Crucifixion in Twentieth-Century Art: The Paintings of Marc Chagall," *Symposion: A Journal of Russian Thought,* Vol. 15 (2010), 47–56. "Crucifixion in Painting: Historical Considerations and Twentieth-Century Expressionism," *ARTS: The Arts in Religious and Theological Studies,* vol. 18, 1(2006), 26–36. "Biblical Themes in Twentieth-Century Painting: Wassily Kandinsky's Apocalyptic Abstractions," *Transactions of the Association of Russian-American Scholars in the U.S.A.,* vol. XXXIII, New York, 2003, 323–332. Reprinted in *ARTS: The Arts in Religious and Theological Studies*, vol. 16, 2(2004), 12–18.

the history of religion, they correspond to the early Christian, Orthodox, Catholic, Protestant, and modern churches. In the next part of this chapter, I discuss traditional forms of Crucifixion art related to those phases.

In the formative church period, we discover the depiction of crosses with a figure of Christ in a small circle at the center of the cross in catacomb ceiling and wall paintings. The oldest surviving Crucifixion scene dates to the early fifth century. From the sixth through the thirteenth centuries, Byzantine Orthodoxy and Roman Catholicism developed their own unique versions of Crucifixion art. The Byzantine model portrayed the divine glory of the Son of God, who offers salvation to his obedient flock. The Catholic version of the Crucifixion emphasized the Savior's humanity and suffering for the human race's sins.

Crucifixion paintings retained their revered status in the early modern (Renaissance) period. However, the Renaissance masters paid more attention to historical facts and the accuracy of pictorial representation. The subsequent Protestant Reformation, on the contrary, removed sacred art from its churches. In their iconoclastic zeal, reformers prohibited most religious imagery, including the Crucifixion, as an act of idolatry.

This book's second chapter focuses on the eighteenth-century European Enlightenment and the burgeoning of the modern period in Western history, culture, and art. According to my theory of religious cycles, Enlightenment ideology initiated the systemic crisis of Christianity and established a rationalistic worldview based on secular values. Traditional art and artistic practices also underwent significant changes.

Neoclassicism was the first modern art movement—after the Renaissance—that sought to revive the "noble simplicity and calm grandeur" (Winckelmann) of classical Greek painting, sculpture, and architecture. The nineteenth-century succession of Romanticism, Realism, and Symbolism, on the contrary, had nothing to do with imitation. Those movements asserted modern art's originality, uniqueness, and profound impact on Western societies.

An unprecedented number and variety of twentieth-century art groups and schools marked the culmination of the Enlightenment-inspired modern art project. Contemporary artists challenged the three most vital tenets of art. They reimagined a conventional relationship between the means of representation and the object of art, reinvented the role of the author in the creative process, and reinterpreted the relationship between art and life.

In those cultural and artistic circumstances, Crucifixion painting also underwent a fundamental and profound transformation. In the nineteenth century and, especially in the twentieth, it transcended dogmatic and theological boundaries and significantly broadened its message and appeal. The crucified Christ became a social emblem, a symbolic expression of suffering and redemption applied to everybody— whether Christian or not, religious or secular, wealthy or poor, men or women, black or white, and so on.

Chapters three through seven explore in detail five twentieth-century art movements—Expressionism, Cubism, Surrealism, Abstraction, and Postmodernism. I discuss various Crucifixions created in different styles and from diverse social and ideological platforms by individual painters in these chapters. Emil Nolde (1867–1956), Georges Rouault (1871–1958), Oskar Kokoschka (1886–1980), and Otto Dix (1890–1969) represent German and French versions of Expressionism. Pablo Picasso (1881–1973), Renato Guttuso (1911–1987), and Jacques Villon (1875–1963) demonstrate Cubist explorations. Salvador Dalí (1904–1989), Marc Chagall (1887–1985), and Antonio Saura (1930–1998) exemplify Surrealist experimentations. Barnett Newman (1905–1970), Francis Bacon (1909–1992), and Graham Sutherland (1903–1980) reflect the art of abstraction. And finally, Gudmundur Gudmundsson (Erró, b. 1932), William H. Johnson (1901–1970), and Arthur Boyd (1920–1999) illustrate Pop Art and Postmodernism.

In concluding remarks, I trace the commonalities of twentieth-century Crucifixion paintings discussed in previous chapters. To sum up, the religious context and theological implications of depicting Jesus on the cross were softened, challenged, and frequently gave way to portraying the Crucifixion as the social archetype of righteous suffering. This newfound approach to this genre of painting served as the perfect instrument for expressing modern anxieties and existential crises of perhaps the bloodiest century in human history.

This book includes two sets of color illustrations. The first consists of the thirty-one most representative images from the fifth through the nineteenth centuries. They offer a systematic overview of Crucifixion paintings in classical Christian art. The second collection of twenty-four images focuses specifically on the twentieth century. It covers the avant-garde movements I explore in the corresponding chapters—Fauvism and Expressionism, Cubism and Futurism, Dada and Surrealism, Abstract Expressionism, Pop Art, and Post-Modernism. Due to the difficulties of obtaining copyrights, not every painting I discuss in my book is illustrated. In turn, not every visual example found in the volume is examined in the text. However, taken together, the illustrations and commentary provide a comprehensive summary of the evolution of the Crucifixion in painting during the first two millennia of Christian history.

Introduction:
THE STORY OF THE CRUCIFIXION

THE CRUCIFIXION IS THE CENTRAL EVENT in the life
and passion of Jesus Christ, the founder of Christianity. It was
recorded in the spirit of faith by the four Evangelists in the
Gospels they composed in the first Christian century. Those
sacred documents later became part of the New Testament's
Christian scriptures.

Biblical scholars believe that the Gospel of Mark was the
earliest to be composed. The Christian tradition ascribes its
authorship to the Apostle Peter's disciple bearing that name.
Mark finished his Gospel approximately three decades after the
Crucifixion and several years before the Jewish Temple's destruction by the Roman army in 70 A.D. His writings reflect the
crisis that enveloped the nascent community of Jesus' followers during their persecution by Emperor Nero (r. 54–68 A.D.).
Mark portrays Christ as "universally misunderstood, rejected
by his people and condemned by the Romans" and a "hidden
Messiah whose true identity is revealed only through his suffering and death."[36]

The Gospel of Mark is centered on a north-south polar-
ity, reminiscent of the biblical account of the ancient Hebrew
monarchy. After King Solomon's death around the tenth century B.C., the United Monarchy split into the Northern King-

---

[36] Stephen L. Harris, *Understanding the Bible*, 4th ed., (1st ed. 1980),
Mountain View, CA–London–Toronto: Mayfield Publishing Company, 1997, 317.

dom of Israel and the Southern Kingdom of Judah. Hebrew Scriptures portray northern Israel as rebellious and unfaithful—an antipodal state in contrast to Judah's pious and righteous Kingdom.

In an ironic reversal, Mark begins his narrative in northern Galilee, where, after being baptized by John the Baptist, Jesus begins his prophetic mission by proclaiming the glad tidings of God. He gathers his first Disciples, preaches to the crowds, heals the sick, and resurrects the dead. During his teaching, Jesus encounters enormous difficulties. Mark portrays almost everyone associated with Jesus, whether relatives or even his closest disciples, as an obstacle to his labor.

When Jesus enters Jerusalem, the city of David and the old capital of Judah, the opposition to him grows exponentially until one of the Apostles betrays him. The highest court of Jewish law, the Sanhedrin, accuses Jesus of blasphemy, and finally, the Prefect of the Roman province of Judea, Pontius Pilate, sentences him to death. Before the Sanhedrin, Jesus reveals his true messianic identity in an explicit and direct passage found only in Mark: "Again the high priest questioned him: 'Are you the Messiah, the Son of the Blessed One?' 'I am,' Jesus said; 'and you will see the Son of Man seated at the right hand of the Almighty and coming with the clouds of heaven.'"[37]

After the verdict by Pontius Pilate, Jesus was executed through Crucifixion, a punishment reserved for the worst criminals in the Roman Empire. At the end of his Gospel, Mark briefly describes the Crucifixion by focusing on what he believes are the most important details surrounding this tragic event. He begins by stating that it occurred at "nine in the morning...and the inscription giving the charge against [Jesus]

---

[37] Mark 16:61–62. All scriptural quotations, unless otherwise noted, are from *The Oxford Study Bible. Revised English Bible with the Apocrypha*, ed. M. Jack Suggs, Katharine Doob Sakenfeld and James R. Mueller, New York: Oxford University Press, 1992.

read, 'The King of the Jews'." He mentions that the "[t]wo rob-bers were crucified with him, one on his right and the other on his left." Mark also writes that the "passers-by [joined by the] chief priests and scribes" mocked Jesus for his apparent inability to save himself, which contradicted his messianic claims according to their views.

Following six hours of agony, Mark continues, "Jesus cried aloud, 'Eloï, Eloï, lema sabachthani?' which is 'My God, my God, why have you forsaken me?'" And soon after, "[s]omeone ran...soaked a sponge in sour wine and held it to his lips on the end of a stick...Jesus gave a loud cry and died." Mark ends his account of the Crucifixion by referring to another person who was present at the scene—the Roman "centurion who was standing opposite [to Jesus,] saw how he died [and] said, 'This man must have been a son of God.'"[38]

Biblical scholars believe that Mark's Gospel was a source of information for two other Gospels—by Mathew and Luke. Called the Synoptic Gospels, Mark, Matthew, and Luke share the same sequence of events and much other material in their respective narratives of the life and death of Jesus Christ.

Matthew's Gospel, which opens the sequence of Gospels in the New Testament and represents an expanded edition of Mark, was composed around 85–90 A.D. by one of Jesus' Apos-tles, a tax collector named Levi. Focusing on the continuity be-tween the Jewish and Christian religions, Matthew's Gospel re-sponds to the growing tension between the Synagogue and the Church. It portrays Jesus as a teacher deeply rooted in his Jew-ish heritage—the living manifestation and fulfillment of the Hebrew prophecies and the bridge between the Old and New Testaments.

Here are some illustrations of Matthew's approach to Je-sus' life and teachings. He begins his Gospel with the geneal-ogy list linking Jesus to King David and Abraham. Matthew's

---

[38] Mark 15:25–39.

genealogical tree confirms the Hebrew tradition, which views Abraham as the seed of prophecy and, more specifically, predicts the future Messiah to be the heir to David's throne.

In the infancy narrative of Jesus, Matthew also includes Herod's murder of Jewish infants. King Herod came to know from the wise men or magi of the birth of the Messiah and was trying to locate him. The magi found the boy and paid homage to him but were warned in a dream not to return to Herod. In the meantime, an angel appeared to Joseph and told him: "Get up, take the child and his mother with you, and escape to Egypt, and stay there until I tell you; for Herod is going to search for the child to kill him."[39] When the infuriated Herod realized that the wise men had fooled him, he ordered "the massacre of all the boys aged two years or under, in Bethlehem and throughout the whole district, following the time he ascertained from the astrologers."[40] Joseph and his family returned from Egypt to their homeland only after Herod's death.

This story is unique to Matthew. It parallels the Old Testament tale of the Passover, when the Lord would spare the firstborn of the Israelites by passing over their houses marked with the blood of the slaughtered lambs and killing only the Egyptian children. The last of the ten plagues signaled the biblical Exodus—the liberation of the Hebrews from slavery in Egypt and their consolidation as a nation under Moses's leadership. In Matthew's New Testament "remake" of the story, Joseph and his family are safe in Egypt from Herod's murders and return home so that Jesus the Messiah, as a new Moses, could liberate his followers from the 'slavery' of their sins.

The Sermon on the Mount is central to the Gospel of Matthew. Here as elsewhere, Matthew portrays Jesus as working against the background of his Jewish tradition, saying: "Do not

---

[39] Matthew 2:13.
[40] Matthew 2:16.

suppose that I have come to abolish the law and the prophets; I did not come to abolish but to complete."[41] In the Sermon, Jesus internalizes and deepens the Ten Commandments by using his famous formula: "You have heard that our forefathers were told...But what I tell you is this..."[42] By the end of his ministry, he sends his twelve Apostles to spread the glad tidings of the Kingdom of God and directs them specifically to their fellow Jews: "Do not take the road to gentile lands, and do not enter any Samaritan town; but go rather to the lost sheep of the house of Israel."[43]

Matthew's account of Jesus' Crucifixion, which follows closely that of Mark, introduces some additional features that emphasize the messianic nature of Christ's mission. The narrative begins with a rather mundane observation, that the soldiers who "had crucified [Jesus] shared out his clothes by casting lots and then sat down there to keep watch."[44] However, it concludes with a series of supernatural events that prove Jesus' messiahship. At the moment of Jesus' death, "the curtain of the temple was torn in two from top to bottom," as Matthew writes, "The earth shook, rocks split, and graves opened; many of God's saints were raised from sleep, and coming out of their graves after his resurrection entered the Holy City, where many saw them."[45]

According to biblical scholars, the Gospel of Luke is the third Synoptic Gospel, and, like the Gospel of Matthew, it also draws much of its material from Mark. The Christian tradition states that this Gospel was composed around the late 80s A.D. by the Apostle Paul's companion, Luke "the beloved," who also authored the Book of Acts chronicling the birth and evolution

---

[41] Matthew 5:17.
[42] Matthew 5:21–22.
[43] Matthew 10:5–6.
[44] Matthew 27:35–36.
[45] Matthew 27:51–53.

of the early Church. A unique vision distinguishing Luke from other evangelists is his emphasis on the universal character of Jesus' mission, encompassing both the righteous and the sinners, Jews and Gentiles.

Various parables in the Gospel illustrate Luke's emphasis on forgiveness and compassion and his portrayal of Jesus as tender and merciful. In the Prodigal Son's story, we read about the father who lost his son to a life of debauchery in distant lands. When the son had spent all his inheritance money, he decided to come home, repent, and beg his father for forgiveness. To the eldest son's disappointment, the father forgives his prodigal child without expressing any anger or disappointment, not only withholds any punishment for him but immediately prepares a feast to celebrate his return. And, moreover, to the bitter objections of his elder brother, the father responds: "My boy...you are always with me, and everything I have is yours. How could we fail to celebrate this happy day? Your brother here was dead and has come back to life; he was lost and has been found."[46]

Several chapters later, Jesus tells another parable about those pseudo-righteous people who follow the letter of the law to the detriment of its spirit. It is the tale of two men praying in the Temple. One of them, the Pharisee, proudly thanked the Lord for guiding him to abide by the law and not behave like sinners. The second one, a tax collector, is so ashamed of his transgressions that he can barely look up to heaven and only begs his Lord for forgiveness. "It was this man, I tell you," Jesus proclaims, "and not the other, who went acquitted of his sins. For everyone who exalts himself will be humbled; and whoever humbles himself will be exalted."[47]

In the same light Luke depicts the Crucifixion, when he portrays Christ as forgiving his tormentors—"Father, forgive

---

[46] Luke 15:31–32.
[47] Luke 18:14.

them; they do not know what they are doing."—and promising salvation to one of the thieves who was crucified by his side:

> One of the criminals hanging there taunted him: "Are not you the Messiah? Save yourself and us." But the other rebuked him: "Have you no fear of God? You are under the same sentence as he is. In our case, it is plain justice; we are paying the price for our misdeeds. But this man has done nothing wrong." And he said, "Jesus, remember me when you come to your throne." Jesus answered, "Truly I tell you: today you will be with me in Paradise."[48]

The fourth Gospel that portrays the Crucifixion of Jesus is very different from the previous three. As the Christian tradition asserted, it was composed by the Apostle John, son of Zebedee and brother of James, near the end of the first century in Ephesus, now in modern Turkey. In his Gospel, John provides a unique perspective on Christ as a supernatural being—the incarnation of God's Word and the embodiment of divine wisdom.

The Gospel of John differs from the Synoptic Gospels' timeline and sequence of events. It lacks the story of virgin birth or Jesus' baptism or temptations. This Gospel is also silent about exorcisms performed by Jesus or his reinterpretation of the Law of Moses. There is no tradition of the Second Coming here, either.

Instead, the Gospel opens with a unique doctrine that portrays Christ as preexistent in heaven before his incarnation on earth: "In the beginning, the Word already was. The Word was in God's presence, and what God was, the Word was."[49] John describes Christ as "God's only Son, who is nearest to the Father's heart" and who was his Father's co-worker in the creation of the world: "He was with God at the beginning, and

---

[48] Luke 23:34, 39–43.
[49] John 1:1.

through him all things came to be; without him no created thing came into being."[50] Later in the Gospel, John reinforces his depiction of Jesus as a unique mediator between God and humanity. He states that Jesus existed before Abraham[51] and is the only way to salvation: "I am the way, the truth, and the life; no one comes to the Father except by me."[52]

Focusing more on theological significance than historical accuracy, John's account of the Crucifixion similarly stresses the fulfillment of scriptural prophesies and renders Jesus' death not a humiliating defeat but a heavenly glorification. John also provided some personal details unique to his record of the tragic events. He attests that those present at the Crucifixion scene included Jesus' "mother [who] was standing with her sister, Mary wife of Clopas, and Mary of Magdala." John himself was there as well: "Seeing his mother, with the disciple whom he loved standing beside her, Jesus said to her, 'Mother, there is your son'; and to the disciple, 'There is your mother'; and from that moment the disciple took her into his home."[53]

Our discussion of the Crucifixion of Jesus, as portrayed in the Gospels, would not be complete without a reference to the event that led to his death, namely, Jesus' condemnation by the highest court of Jewish law, the Sanhedrin, and his sentencing to death by crucifixion by Pontius Pilate. Who was to blame for killing Jesus—the Jewish or Roman authorities?

The issue of accountability, which is legitimate in any legal trial, acquires particular importance in the case of Jesus. After all, in his followers' eyes, he was not only the promised Messiah and the founder of a world religion but also the Son of God, the Second Person of the Trinity. In this religious and cultural context, the tragic death of Jesus Christ amounted to

---

[50] John, 1:18, 2–3.
[51] John 8:58.
[52] John 14:6.
[53] John 19:25–27.

the crime of deicide—a unique incident in human history so far as Christians were concerned.

The Gospels describe the events leading to the conviction of Jesus as an unfolding and complex drama of the delicate balance of power between the Jewish and Roman authorities. Even before he arrived in Jerusalem Jesus was under suspicion by the Jewish leaders, who regarded the spread of his teachings and fame as threatening their legitimacy. As John reports in his Gospel, "the chief priests and the Pharisees convened a meeting of the Council." They expressed concern that, if Jesus continues to perform miracles, "the whole populace will believe in him, and then the Romans will come and sweep away our temple and our nation."

Then the high priest of that year, Caiaphas, suggested a radical solution to the problem. He said it is more in the leadership's interest that "one man should die for the people than the whole nation should be destroyed." As high priest, he prophesied that "Jesus would die for the nation and not for the nation alone but to gather together the scattered children of God. So, from that day on, they plotted his death."[54]

After his arrival in Jerusalem and Judas's betrayal, Jesus was summoned to the Sanhedrin, where he had a hearing before the Jewish religious leaders. Tradition attests that the "chief priests...tried to find evidence against Jesus that would warrant a death sentence but failed to find any." Many spoke against him, but "their statements did not tally," while Jesus held his peace and did not reply to the accusers. In the hearing's decisive episode, the high priest asked Jesus whether he was indeed the "Messiah, the Son of the Blessed One?" Matthew and Luke report that Jesus avoided a direct response by answering that they said it. However, in the earliest Gospel of Mark, as previously mentioned, we read that Jesus replied straightforwardly and unequivocally: "I am...and you will see

---

[54] John 11:48–53.

the Son of Man seated at the right hand of the Almighty and coming with the clouds of heaven." After that testimony, the fate of the defendant was sealed. Jesus was accused of blasphemy, and the "decision was unanimous: that he was guilty and should be put to death."[55]

As a court of religious law, the Sanhedrin had no authority to carry out their verdict. That was the prerogative of secular powers, in this case, the Roman governor Pontius Pilate. Pilate talked to Jesus and found nothing wrong with this man from Galilee. He sent him then to the provincial ruler Herod, whose jurisdiction covered that area. The accusation was that Jesus refused to pay tribute to Caesar and proclaimed himself the king of the Jews.

Of the four Gospels, only Luke tells us about the meeting of Jesus and Herod. He writes: "When Herod saw Jesus, he was greatly pleased: he had heard about him and had long been wanting to see him in the hope of witnessing some miracle performed by him." Herod questioned Jesus and, pressured by the Jewish priests, "treated him with contempt and ridicule and sent him back to Pilate dressed in a gorgeous robe."[56]

Then Pilate made his last attempt to avoid the decision by planning to set Jesus free during the Passover celebration. It was customary for Pilate to present the Jewish crowd with two prisoners at the feast and ask whom they would like to be released. This time it was Jesus and another by the name of Barabbas, and Pilate hoped that the multitude would choose Jesus.

However. the chief priests persuaded the crowd to pick Barabbas. In his Gospel, Matthew describes this dramatic moment as follows:

> Pilate said to them, "Then what should I do with Jesus, who is called the Messiah?" All of them said, "Let him be crucified!"

---

[55] Mark 14:55–64.
[56] Luke 23:8–11.

> Then he asked, "Why, what evil has he done?" But they shouted all the more, "Let him be crucified!" So when Pilate saw that he could do nothing, but rather that a riot was beginning, he took some water and washed his hands before the crowd, saying, "I am innocent of this man's blood; see to it yourselves." Then the people as a whole answered, "His blood be on us, and on our children!"[57]

Only then did Pilate make the final determination to release Barabbas and crucify Jesus.

What are we to make of this story? Let us remember that the issue of responsibility for the death of Christ played a crucial, often tragic, role in the problematic relationship between Judaism and Christianity. The Christian religion was conceived amid its mother faith, and Jesus, his Apostles, and other early disciples were all Jewish. By the end of the first Christian century, the two religions went their separate ways. Most Jews did not accept Jesus as the promised Mashiach but considered him a false prophet who led his people astray. Meanwhile, Christianity continued to grow due to the tremendous influx of pagans—Greeks and Romans—into their religious community. For those pagans, Jesus was the Son of God, the promised Messiah who fulfilled ancient Hebrew prophesies about humankind's salvation.

In their appraisal of Jesus' mission, Jews and Christians relied on the same collection of prophetic books in the Bible. However, they drew opposite conclusions from the Scriptures. According to scholars, classical biblical prophecy started in the eighth century B.C. with Amos's prophetic message, which notably proclaimed—"But let justice roll down like waters, and righteousness like an ever-flowing stream."[58] These were the words that Martin Luther King, Jr. famously quoted in his

---

[57] Matthew 27:22–25.
[58] Amos 5:24.

influential "I Have a Dream" speech of 1963. The era of classical biblical prophecy lasted through the fourth century B.C., giving the world many great visionaries, including Isaiah, Jeremiah, and Ezekiel.

Those prophets delivered their straightforward message to Israel in times of great turmoil for the Jewish nation. The United Monarchy King David built in the tenth century B.C. soon gave way to Israel and Judah's divided kingdoms. Both kingdoms surrendered to the same fate. In 722 B.C., Israel fell to the Assyrian Empire. The Babylonian army conquered the Kingdom of Judah in the seventh century, and in 587/6 B.C., the Babylonians destroyed Solomon's Temple—the center of Jewish religious life in Jerusalem, the capital city of Judah. Having lost their religious liberty and political independence, the Jews suffered through the first exile and its hardships, lasting more than half-a-century.

Fortunately for them, the Persians, who were more tolerant of the conquered people's religious traditions, soon eclipsed the Babylonian Empire. In his Edict of Restoration, the Persian King Cyrus II (r. 550–530 B.C.), also known as Cyrus the Great, the founder of the Achaemenid Empire, allowed the Judahites—former citizens of the Kingdom of Judah—to return to their homeland, rebuild Jerusalem and the Temple, and restore their religious community life and customs. It took several waves of diasporic Jews to return from Babylonian captivity and resettle in the land of their forefathers. Still, the repatriation was essentially complete by the end of the fourth century B.C.

In those tumultuous centuries, the Hebrew prophets delivered their message of condemnation, warning, and consolation to the Jewish nation. They criticized religious and political elites for abandoning the moral principles of their faith. They predicted the long and painful ordeal and suffering awaiting the Jewish people. They also consoled their compatriots, saying that, although their trials and tribulations would be severe, they would purify their souls, and the people would survive them.

Biblical prophets warned pagan nations that they should not be proud of their victories because their imperial supremacy was but a powerful instrument for the Almighty to punish his chosen people. They predicted that those victories would be temporary, and those nations would eventually perish in history's fires. They also foresaw the future coming of the world's savior, the Jewish Mashiach, who would restore the Jewish state's political independence and establish universal peace and brotherhood on the planet.

The Jews interpreted those predictions literally and in a forthright manner. And, since expectations for political independence and universal peace seemed utterly unrealistic in the times of Jesus, they rejected him as their Messiah. Christians, in turn, took the same prophecies symbolically—as metaphors describing spiritual rather than historical realities. According to Christian interpretations, Jesus did form a New Israel—a spiritual community of believers in him, and he did bring peace to the hearts and souls of those who followed him.

The opposition that grew between Judaism and Christianity in the first century of the Christian era reflected those differences. Still, the divergence between the two faiths was more significant and painful than a simple disagreement over scriptural exegesis. From a Christian perspective, which the Gospels confirmed, not only did the Jews reject Jesus as their biblical Messiah, but they were also guilty of his death by Crucifixion. When the Jewish crowd decided to free another man, the criminal Barabbas, over Jesus, this moment had a uniquely dramatic tone and significance. "His blood be on us, and our children!"—they shouted, suggesting a generational curse that could be transmitted from parents to their offspring for their alleged guilt in the sentencing and Crucifixion of Jesus.[59]

This understanding of the tragedy of Jesus' death became prevalent in the early Christian community that blamed the

---

[59] Matthew 27:25.

Jews for their Savior's cruel and untimely demise. The charge became even more severe after the fourth century, when Christian leaders at the ecumenical council of Nicaea in 325 A.D. settled on the doctrine of the Trinity. This doctrine became the cornerstone of the Christian faith and asserted the divinity of Jesus, who now became both fully human and fully divine.

The growing tensions between Christians and Jews, who, in the eyes of the Christians, now become guilty of no less than deicide, found multiple expressions in early Christian thought. Take the idea of the antichrist or false messiah that grew out of those tensions.

The New Testament uses the word "antichrist" only a handful of times in the Johannine epistles. In two of his letters, John speaks of Gnostic heresy that threatens the Christian Church's unity by denying the humanity of Jesus and asserting his pure divinity. In one such letter, John insists on the Savior being a man: "For many deceivers have gone out into the world, men who will not acknowledge the coming of Jesus Christ in the flesh; such a one is the deceiver and the antichrist."[60] In another letter, he reiterates the same point: "...every spirit which confesses that Jesus Christ has come in the flesh is of God, and every spirit which does not confess Jesus is not of God. This is the spirit of Antichrist, of which you heard that it was coming, and now it is in the world already."[61]

Early Christian thought conflated the Antichrist figure who would appear in the unknown future with the "lawless one" described by Paul in his Second Epistle to the Thessalonians. In this letter, Paul talks about the Second Coming and warns his fellow Christians to be watchful: "Let no one deceive you in any way; for that day will not come, unless the rebellion comes first, and the man of lawlessness is revealed, the son of perdition." He then goes on to elaborate—this evildoer "op-

---

[60] 2 John 1:7.
[61] 1 John 4:2–3.

poses and exalts himself against every so-called god or object of worship, so that he takes his seat in the temple of God, proclaiming himself to be God."[62]

The term "antichrist" also echoed another expression— false Messiah or pseudo-Christ—that Jesus himself used in his teachings: "For false Christs and false prophets will arise and show great signs and wonders, so as to lead astray, if possible, even the elect."[63] In the early Church, since the second century, to be precise, those ideas of anti- and pseudo-Christs crystallized into a concrete image of a Jewish man who would rise as the antipode to the Son of God. A Roman Christian theologian, Hippolytus (c. 170—c. 236), in his *Treatise on Christ and Antichrist*, argued that this man of rebellion and lawlessness would come from the tribe of Dan to fulfill messianic prophecies by rebuilding the Temple and making himself the king to rule the nation of Israel and the world. Hippolytus wrote:

> For the deceiver seeks to liken himself in all things to the Son of God... Christ is a king, so the Antichrist is also a king ... The Savior came into the World in the circumcision, and he will come in the same manner... The Savior appeared in the form of man, and he, too, will come in the form of a man. The Savior raised up and showed His holy flesh like a temple, and he will raise a temple of stone in Jerusalem.[64]

This identification of the Antichrist with the Jews who rejected Jesus as the true Messiah and would produce from their fold a false one who, they believed, would fulfill biblical prophecy, eventually led to and became a cornerstone of the

---

[62] 2 Thessalonians 2:3–4.

[63] Matthew 24:24. See also Mark 13:22.

[64] Hippolytus of Rome, *Treatise on Christ and Antichrist*, pgph 6, Early Christian Writings, **www.earlychristianwritings.com/text/hippolytus-christ.html.**

ideology of anti-Semitism. A distinctive form of religious racism, anti-Semitism put a dark stain on the Christian Church for centuries. And so, Judaism and Christianity, two monotheistic religions of the same Abrahamic root, not only parted ways but developed mutual animosity that would last for millennia. Jews would denounce Jesus as a false prophet who led his people astray. And Christians would believe that Jews betrayed their messianic mission and became a cursed nation that would fall prey to the satanic temptations of Jesus' nemesis, the Antichrist.

This tragic misunderstanding and misinterpretation of history resulted in anti-Semitism becoming an adjacent part of the Christian worldview and politics. Jewish communities were segregated or expelled from Christian countries; Jews were humiliated, forcibly converted to Christianity, or killed in *pogroms*. Only in the twentieth century, after the horrors of the Holocaust, were Christian churches finally able to face reality, recognize their centuries-long mistakes, and correct their ideology.

In the 1960s, at the Second Vatican Council, representatives of Catholicism, the largest among Christian confessions, issued a Declaration on the Church's Relationship to Non-Christian Religions. In it, we read about the relationship of Catholicism to Hinduism, Buddhism, Islam, and, most importantly, Judaism. The Declaration confirmed the value of diverse religions, which offer "answers to those profound mysteries of the human condition which, today even as in olden times, deeply stir the human heart."[65] But it especially acknowledged a unique bond between Christianity and the Jewish faith. "The Christian Church cannot forget," we read

---

[65] "Declaration on the Relationship of the Church to Non-Christian Religions," *The Documents of Vatican II With Notes and Comments by Catholic, Protestant, and Orthodox Authorities,* gen. ed. Walter M. Abbott, trans. ed. Very Rev. Msgr. Joseph Gallagher, Geoffrey Chapman, 1966, 661.

here, "that she received the revelation of the Old Testament through the people with whom God in his inexpressible mercy designed to establish the Ancient Covenant."[66] Even though, in the days of Christ, the majority of Jews not only did not accept but even opposed him, as the Declaration continued, "according to the Apostle [Paul], the Jews remain most dear to God because of their fathers, for He does not repent of the gifts He makes nor of the calls He issues (cf. Rom. 11:28–29)."[67]

Especially significant is what the Declaration proclaimed regarding the Crucifixion of Jesus and the theological issue of so-called "Jewish guilt." "True, authorities of the Jews and those who followed their lead pressed for the death of Christ," it said, "still, what happened in His passion cannot be blamed upon all the Jews then living, without distinction, nor upon the Jews of today."[68] The Declaration further emphasized that the "Jews should not be presented as repudiated or cursed by God as if such views followed from the holy Scriptures."[69] Finally, as the Declaration concluded, "mindful of her common patrimony with the Jews, and motivated by the Gospel's spiritual love and by no political considerations [the Church] deplores the hatred, persecutions, and displays of anti-Semitism directed against the Jews at any time and from any source."[70]

Of course, documents like this represent only the initial steps toward complete reconciliation between Judaism and Christianity. But, as we all know, it is the first step that is most difficult to take. So, the importance of this radical reversal of the Christian attitude toward the Jews and the Jewish faith is hard to overestimate.

---

[66] Ibid., 664.
[67] Ibid.
[68] Ibid., pp. 665–66.
[69] Ibid., p. 666.
[70] Ibid., pp. 666–67.

Let us come back now to the question of who killed Jesus. My personal explanation of the Crucifixion's tragedy may slightly differ from traditional views on the subject. Suppose that the death of Jesus had caused an uproar and led to a Jewish revolt. I am sure Jewish religious and Roman secular authorities considered such a possibility. After all, their shared concern was strengthening a delicate religious and political balance in the Jewish territories. But what if something went wrong?

In this scenario, the Roman authorities would have sent their emissaries to investigate the situation, find out who triggered the rebellion, and punish the guilty parties. Since the immediate cause of social disorder was the death of Jesus, they would have naturally inquired who was responsible for it. And here, they would have encountered real difficulties.

Galilee's ruler, Herod Antipas, would have replied that he had found nothing wrong with Jesus and had nothing to do with his demise. Jewish religious authorities of the Sanhedrin would have said that they did condemn Jesus for blasphemy but had nothing to do with his death, since their decisions lacked any civil power. And Pontius Pilate would have justified his sentence by appealing to Jewish leadership and their backers. In other words, the blame game would have had no winners or losers—a perfect bureaucratic setup. That seems to have been the plan, and the Gospels described it perfectly.

To sum up, the four canonical Gospels of Mark, Matthew, Luke, and John provide a unified and historically reliable record of the Crucifixion of Jesus. Biblical scholarship attests to the certainty and historicity of Jesus' Crucifixion. Furthermore, we know from the references to crucifixion in literary sources that "it was considered the appropriate punishment for slaves and the most hardened criminals."[71] The remains

---

[71] Pheme Perkins, *Reading the New Testament: An Introduction*, 2nd rev. ed., (1st ed. in 1978), New York, N.Y. / Mahwah, N.J.: 1988, 72.

of a Jewish man named Yehohanan rediscovered and dug up by modern archeologists, bear witness to the horrors of death on the cross. Yehohanan was crucified at the beginning of the first century A.D., possibly for participating in an anti-Roman rebellion. Buried in his family grave, his

> feet remained fixed to a portion of a wooden post by a single nail four and a half inches (11 cm) long through both heels. The nail had bent on entering the wood and apparently could not be pulled out without further damaging the body. Both legs were smashed, the left one by a single blow [which] hastened death by causing the victim's full weight to crush the lungs.[72]

The early followers of Jesus Christ, whose experience on the cross must have been like that of Yohohanan, found themselves in a peculiar—not to say, ambiguous—situation. Not only did their master suffer the agonies of Crucifixion, but he also ended his life as an outcast who was presumed guilty of a horrible crime. In one of his epistles to the Church at Corinth, the Apostle Paul attests that the cross became a stumbling block or a test for many non-believers: "The message of the cross is sheer folly to those on the way to destruction, but to us, who are on the way to salvation, it is the power of God." And later: "As God in his wisdom has ordained, the world failed to find him by its wisdom, and he chooses by the folly of the gospel to save those who have faith."[73]

Speaking about Christianity, we must distinguish between Jesus- and Christ-oriented Christian theology. Both are closely interwoven, but each emphasizes a specific aspect of the Christian worldview. Jesus-oriented Christianity focuses on

---

[72] J. R. Porter, *The Illustrated Guide to the Bible,* New York—Oxford: Oxford University Press, 1995, 204.
[73] 1 Cor. 1:18, 21.

what its founder taught his followers, while Christ-oriented Christianity is about who he was and how he lived his life. As far as the Apostle Paul was concerned, he focused his mission and thought on the power of the cross and thus transformed the nascent Christian faith into a world religion.

Here lies the uniqueness of the Christian religion and its cardinal distinction from such monotheistic faiths as Judaism and Islam. Jewish and Muslim traditions are based on the law, whether in its rabbinic or shariah versions. As members in good standing, the adherents of these religions should believe in their founders' prophetic mission and strictly follow the religious and legal obligations that originated from them. In the Christian faith, the situation is radically different.

To begin with, the teachings of Jesus have a purely moral and spiritual character. He did not deliver any new legal guidelines or regulations. The only explicit law of this kind in the Gospels is the prohibition of divorce. As Jesus famously stated in the Sermon on the Mount, "It has been said, 'Anyone who divorces his wife must give her a certificate of divorce.' But I tell you that anyone who divorces his wife, except for sexual immorality, makes her the victim of adultery, and anyone who marries a divorced woman commits adultery."[74] The Church has taken this instruction very seriously, but the legal precept *per se* was an exception rather than the rule in Jesus' teaching.

Even more so, let's imagine that the Jewish or Muslim Law was delivered not by Moses and Mohammad but by some other prophetic figures. The change of the messenger would not compromise the message or the divine law itself, and the practices of those religions would still be intact. If we apply the same thought experiment to Christianity, we will conclude that Christian institutions would immediately crumble without Christ. The Christian faith was based not only on the teachings of Jesus Christ, but also on his unique mediation be-

---

[74] Mat. 5:31–32.

tween God and humanity, the Son of God's sacrifice that was sealed by his Crucifixion and resurrection.

In the middle of the first century A.D., when Christianity was still in the cradle of its mother religion, the new faith leaders came to Jerusalem to discuss their relationship with Judaism. Until then, most converts, including the Apostles, were Jewish. As the Book of Acts attests, after the Apostle Peter baptized the first gentile, Cornelius the Centurion,[75] non-Jewish converts began to pour into the Christian fold. That created a problem—should the newly baptized Gentiles be circumcised? Should they study and obey Jewish law? In other words, is Christian identity an extension of Jewish identity, or is it something radically different? The Apostle Paul was among the Christian leaders who came to Jerusalem to discuss this issue.

Paul's original name was Saul, and he was a recent Jewish convert who suddenly changed his attitude from persecuting to promoting the new religious movement. The Book of Acts described Paul's dramatic experience when Jesus appeared to him on the road to Damascus: "Suddenly a light from heaven flashed around him. He fell to the ground and heard a voice [of Jesus] say to him, 'Saul, Saul, why do you persecute me?'"[76] Later, in another appearance—this time "to a disciple named Ananias"—Jesus announced about Paul: "This man is my chosen instrument to proclaim my name to the Gentiles and their kings and to the people of Israel."[77] So, after a series of miraculous visions and events, a devoted Pharisee, Saul of Tarsus, was baptized, changed his name, and became the Apostle Paul—perhaps, the most crucial figure in the Apostolic Age of Christianity.

At the Jerusalem council, St. Paul defended a position that would firmly separate Judaism from Christianity and affirm

---

[75] Acts 10.
[76] Acts 9:3–4.
[77] Acts 9:10, 15.

a unique Christian religious identity. He compared the new testament of Christ with the old covenant of Moses. Obedience to Jewish law was based on the proper functioning of the priesthood and, especially, the high priest. Once a year, on the Day of Atonement or Yom Kippur, the high priest would enter the Temple's inner sanctuary, the Holy of Holies, and offer an animal sacrifice to make amends before God for the sins of Israel. This sacrifice was repeated yearly since neither the high priest nor other Israelites were considered perfect. As Paul put it: "The law is only a shadow of the good things that are coming—not the realities themselves. For this reason, it can never, by the same sacrifices repeated endlessly year after year, make perfect those who draw near to worship."[78]

In the Christian religion, as he argued, Jesus became the high priest of the new covenant and the sacrifice to be offered to God. As the Son of God, he freely offered his own life for the salvation of humanity:

> But when Christ came as high priest of the good things that are now already here, he went through the greater and more perfect tabernacle that is not made with human hands, that is to say, is not a part of this creation. He did not enter by means of the blood of goats and calves; but he entered the Most Holy Place once for all by his own blood, thus obtaining eternal redemption.[79]

Hence, Paul continued, those who enter the covenant with Jesus are free from the bonds of Mosaic law and its requirements. Jesus' death and resurrection paved the way for the renewed relationship between God and humanity, a relationship in which redemption of sin is the direct consequence of the Crucifixion of Jesus, and salvation is offered to anyone

---

[78] Heb. 10:1.
[79] Heb. 9:11–12.

with faith in its mystery. He wrote, "Christ is the mediator of a new covenant, [so] that those who are called may receive the promised eternal inheritance—now that he has died as a ransom to set them free from the sins committed under the first covenant."[80] And, later: "Christ did not enter a sanctuary made with human hands ... he entered heaven itself ... he has appeared once for all at the culmination of the ages to do away with sin by the sacrifice of himself."[81]

Using such a sophisticated theological strategy, the Apostle Paul could reinterpret the Crucifixion's tragic events from the perspective of the biblical notion of sacrifice. And as a result, the Crucifixion of Jesus, which took place under the Roman imperial rule, was miraculously transformed from a type of capital punishment reserved for the worst criminals into a divine mystery of human redemption and salvation. Now, being the central event in Christian history, the Crucifixion became an endless source of inspiration for Christian artists in future millennia.

---

[80] Heb. 9:15.
[81] Heb. 9:24, 26.

Chapter One:

THE CRUCIFIXION IN TRADITIONAL CHRISTIAN ART

TO DISCUSS HOW AND BY WHAT means Christian artists depicted the Crucifixion of Jesus, let me introduce my theory of religious cycles to the reader. In the ninetieth and twentieth centuries Western scholars proposed various explanations of religion's origin and evolution. Often, they were inclined to reduce spiritual experiences to different forms of individual or social activity, which coincided with those scholars' specialization. Thus, French sociologist Emile Durkheim saw religion as an expression of communal social forces. The German economist and political theorist Karl Marx argued that religion is an instrument of economic oppression by one class of people over another. Austrian neurologist and the inventor of psychoanalysis, Sigmund Freud, claimed that organized religion reflects a collective human neurosis.

My theory of religious evolution does not aim to uncover the hidden origin of religion. It takes spiritual traditions at their face value and offers a phenomenological approach to world faiths by focusing on their empirical development's regularities.

It is well known that every historical religion (i.e., a religious system conceived after the invention of writing) is based on its scriptural texts and the sacred tradition of their interpretation. Those religions' scriptural texts form the foundation of the system because they exercise absolute authority over the community of believers. The sacred tradition may complement, clarify, add to, or interpret the scriptures, but it should never alter or contradict them, at least in theory. Those religious leaders who were entrusted by their community with legitimate rights to interpret the scriptures exercise this right and produce a body of interpretive texts, which later become invested with authority.

According to my theory, religion represents an organic system or organism that keeps evolving, based on different interrelationships between its sacred scriptures and sacred tradition. During its evolution, religion goes through various phases or stages of development. I distinguish six typical stages: formative, orthodox, classical, reformist, critical, and post-critical. Not every religion may evolve through all those phases. Similarly, not every human individual will live to experience adolescence, maturity, or old age. However, if a person had enjoyed a long-lasting life, (s)he would most certainly have gone through all those growth phases. It is the same with religion.

During its evolution, a religious system also undergoes two types of crises—structural and systemic. The questioning of a sacred tradition by its followers usually signals structural problems within the religious community. In most cases, the appearance of alternative practices of scriptural interpretations and the formation of new sects or denominations within a religious system successfully resolves the crisis.

In contrast to structural issues, a systemic problem arises when a religion's adherents begin doubting the sacred scriptures. Since the scriptures are fixed and cannot be changed or corrected, the resolution of systemic crises usually comes from the rise of alternative religious movements with their own sacred scriptures and sacred traditions. After giving birth to new religious systems, mother faiths are often rejuvenated and continue to flourish alongside their young competitors.

Here is what the entire cycle of religious evolution looks like in an abstract form:

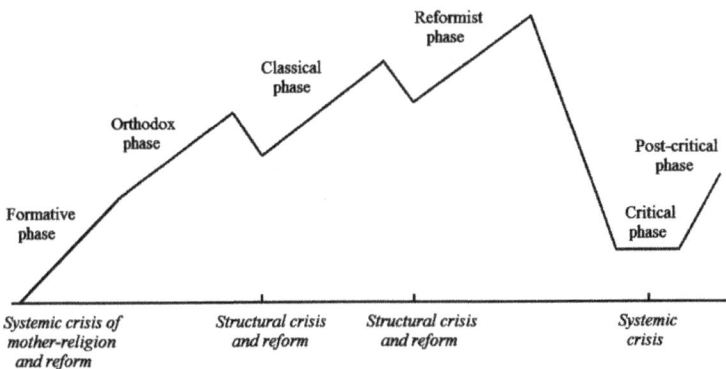

Diagram 1. Model of Religious Cycle

In my monograph *Theory of Religious Cycles*, I applied this abstract model to four world religions—Judaism, Buddhism, Christianity, and Islam.[82] For the present book, I will limit my discussion to Christianity and how the religious cycle model applies to its history and evolution.

Religious scholars divide the history of Christendom into three main periods—early, medieval, and modern. The early church period dates to the first four centuries and ends when the Christian faith becomes the state religion of the Roman Empire. The Middle Ages began with the barbarians' sack of Rome in the fifth century and lasted through the fifteenth century. In 1453 Ottoman Turks conquered the capital of the Byzantine Empire, Constantinople, and this last remnant of the ancient Roman Empire ceased to exist. Finally, the modern period of Christianity started during the fourteenth and fifteenth centuries. It encompasses such movements as the Renaissance, the Reformation, and the Enlightenment as expressions of cultural, religious, and scientific modernity.

My theory of religious cycles coincides with Christian historiography but only partially, since it focuses on changes in

---

82 Sergeev, Mikhail. *Theory of Religious Cycles: Tradition, Modernity, and the Bahá'í Faith*, Boston: Brill, 2015.

religious, not cultural, traditions. In my approach, Christianity's initial, formative phase is identical to the early church history of the first four centuries. During this time, Christians codified their scriptures, formed organizational structure, established everyday rituals, formulated the creed, and cemented the Church's support by political powers. All these are typical features of the formative stage of any successful religion. Let me discuss the formation of the biblical canon in more detail, since my theory emphasizes the interrelation between sacred scriptures and sacred tradition in the evolution of the Christian religious system.

The Bible, as we know it now, did not exist in the first several centuries of Christianity. In 70 A.D., the Roman army destroyed the Jewish Temple, and the Jews remained without a worship center. Sadducees or Jewish priests went out of business. In those dramatic historical circumstances, the Pharisees—who would lay the foundations for Rabbinic Judaism—compiled their version of the Hebrew scriptures. As for Christians, they used the translation of the Jewish sacred texts into the Koine Greek, known as the Septuagint (3rd-2nd B.C.), which eventually found its way to the Christian Bible in the form of the Old Testament.

Turning to the New Testament, the earliest materials included in the Bible were the Apostle Paul's letters and the four Gospels. Biblical scholars estimate that the Gospels were composed between the mid-sixties and the end of the first century. The rest of the books—Acts, Epistles, and Revelation—circulated in Christian churches for several centuries. Eventually, by the end of the fourth century, they were recognized as part of the biblical canon. In his thirty-ninth Festal Letter, written in 367 A.D., St. Athanasius, the bishop of Alexandria, listed all twenty-seven books of the New Testament, thus acknowledging their authority.[83]

---

[83] "Athanasius of Alexandria," The Development of the Canon of the New Testament, http://www.ntcanon.org/Athanasius.shtml.

From the fourth century onward, Christians also developed their sacred tradition. In any historical religion, religious tradition represents a cumulative outcome of legitimate interpretations of scriptural texts. In Christianity, the holy tradition resulted from the decisions of ecumenical councils—gatherings of the leaders of the Christian world, during which they discussed the most critical theological, administrative, and pastoral issues.

Orthodoxy and Catholicism recognize the Council of Nicaea as the first ecumenical Christian council. Emperor Constantine convened this gathering of Christian leaders in 325 A.D. to settle the controversial dispute about the relationship between Jesus Christ and God the Father. The council rejected Arianism, which taught that Jesus Christ was the Son of God but neither coeternal not consubstantial with the Father and, therefore, a subordinate being. Condemning this doctrine as heretical, the council sided with the bishop Athanasius who promoted a trinitarian view of the Godhead. According to Athanasius, the Son was of the same substance as the Father and, consequently, fully divine.[84]

The council adopted the Nicene creed—the only genuinely ecumenical Christian creed since "it is accepted as authoritative by the Roman Catholic, Eastern Orthodox, Anglican, and major Protestant churches."[85] The creed proclaimed Jesus Christ to be "the Son of God, begotten of the Father [the only-begotten; that is, of the essence of the Father, God of God,] Light of Light, very God of very God, begotten, not made, being of one substance with the Father."[86]

In the next four centuries, five more ecumenical councils convened in Constantinople, Ephesus, and Chalcedon to

---

84 "Arianism," Encyclopedia Britannica, **https://www.britannica.com/topic/Arianism**.
85 "Nicene Creed," Encyclopedia Britannica, **https://www.britannica.com/topic/Nicene-Creed**.
86 Ibid.

discuss the doctrinal issues of Christology. The bishops who participated in the councils agreed that Jesus Christ is fully man and God—having two wills, human and divine. They also concluded that, in the person of Jesus, "there are two distinct natures [which] are hypostatically united 'without confusion, change, division or separation.'"[87] The seventh ecumenical council held in Nicaea in 787 A.D. dealt with iconoclastic heresy and restored the veneration of icons.

Both Orthodox and Catholic Christianity accept the decisions of those seven ecumenical councils as authoritative and binding upon believers. Various Protestant denominations, however, "accept [their] teachings...but do not ascribe to the councils themselves the same authority as Roman Catholics and the Eastern Orthodox do." They contend that those councils "did not create new doctrines but merely elucidated doctrines already in Scripture that heretics had misinterpreted."[88]

In contrast to Orthodoxy, which is called the "Church of the Seven Councils," and which corresponds in my theory to the orthodox phase in the evolution of Christianity, Catholicism, which stands for its classical phase, accepts as authoritative later Christian councils that took place without representation from the Orthodox confession. The separation between these two major Christian branches dates to the fifth century, when barbarians sacked Rome and destroyed the Western part of the Roman Empire. The Eastern part survived for one thousand years more under the name of Byzantium.

Cultural and theological differences deepened the political division between East and West. The Western part of the Empire spoke Latin, and the Eastern cultivated its Greek heritage. The bishops of the Roman Church, later to be called Popes, argued for papal primacy over the whole Christian world.

---

[87] "Ecumenical Councils," Theopedia, https://www.theopedia.com/ecume-nical-councils.

[88] Ibid.

The Patriarch of Constantinople disagreed and, following ancient tradition, claimed that all heads of the five metropolitan Churches (Rome, Constantinople, Jerusalem, Alexandria, and Antioch) are equal in status.

Even the ecumenical creed was inadvertently affected by controversy over the infamous *filioque* clause that Orthodoxy refused to accept. Since the sixth century, the Catholic version of the Nicene-Constantinopolitan profession of faith (381 A.D.) proclaimed the belief in "the Holy Spirit, the Lord, the giver of life, who proceeds from the Father and the Son."[89] Orthodoxy always considered the insertion of the *filioque* ("and the Son" in Latin) an unacceptable theological mistake.

The mutual alienation between the Latin and Greek Churches grew until in the eleventh century—to be precise, in 1054 A.D.—Orthodoxy and Catholicism excommunicated each other. The schism was irrevocably sealed after the fourth Crusade when in 1204 A.D., the Crusader army sacked Constantinople and established Crusader states in the Byzantine Empire's territory. Since then, Catholicism has developed its unique sacred tradition. In addition to seven ecumenical councils, this included fourteen more Church assemblies—from the Fourth Council of Constantinople in 869 A.D. until the Second Vatican Council of the 1960s.

Protestantism represented the reform phase of the Christian religion when it branched off from Catholicism in the sixteenth century. Martin Luther started his Reformation movement in 1517 but did not intend to split from the Catholic Church and create his brand of Christianity. He strongly disagreed with some of the Church teachings and practices, most notably, indulgencies. Luther aimed to purify the community life of the Church and to make it compatible with the life of its founder, Jesus Christ.

---

[89] "Filioque clause," Theopedia, **https://www.theopedia.com/filioque-clause.**

The Church, however, mistook Martin Luther for another heretic and wanted to silence him by delivering the rebel to the Inquisition. It turned out that the authorities should have paid more attention to the potential of Luther's message. In 1521 he was excommunicated from the Catholic Church and summoned to the general assembly of the estates of the Holy Roman Empire.

Martin Luther arrived at the town of Worms the same year where he appeared before the Imperial Diet—prince-electors who were supposed to determine his fate. When asked to renounce his writing, Luther refused, unless he could be "convicted by Scripture and plain reason." He added: "I do not accept the authority of popes and councils, for they have contradicted each other—my conscience is captive to the Word of God. I cannot and will not recant anything, for to go against conscience is neither right nor safe."[90]

Since he was assured a safe passage to and from the city, the prince-electors did not hand Luther over to the inquisitors. But soon after he departed for his hometown of Wittenberg, the Holy Roman Emperor Charles V issued a decree declaring Martin Luther a heretic and an outlaw to be captured and delivered to state authorities. So, fearing for Luther's life, the prince-elector of Saxony, Frederick III, arranged for him to be secretly snatched by armed men and hidden in the Castle of Warburg. In Warburg Castle, where Luther spent several years, he started his seminal translation of the Bible from its original languages into his native German.

The key to Martin Luther's theology was the idea of *sola fide* or justification by faith alone. He rejected the Catholic theory of retribution, in which God justly punishes the sinners and

---

[90] "Diet of Worms," New World Encyclopedia, http://www.newworldencyclopedia.org/entry/Diet_of_Worms#cite_note-bainton-0. Quoted from Bainton, Roland H. *Here I Stand: A Life of Martin Luther*. New York: Penguin, 1995, 144.

rewards the righteous. In Luther's view, God grants salvation to whomever he wishes, even the most unworthy sinner. But what is the source of God's grace? For Martin Luther, as for every Christian, divine grace comes from Jesus Christ, God incarnate. Since the Bible is the only credible source of information about the life and teachings of Jesus, Martin Luther placed a particular emphasis on the accessibility of Holy Writings to every believer.

He embarked on the project of translating the Bible— a massive scholarly undertaking that he completed on his own. Luther rejected the authority of the Church councils and the Catholic Popes, who, in his view, were as fallible as other humans. He believed now that Christians must purge the Bible from mistranslations and misinterpretations accumulated over the centuries within the sacred tradition of the Church.

Because of his intense Bible study, Martin Luther rediscovered the scriptural roots of Christianity and set himself on a course to reform Christendom. He removed complicated Church hierarchy and numerous sacraments that find no support in biblical texts. He simplified Church services and introduced the sermon as its crucial element, so that the congregation may learn lessons from the Bible. Luther also abolished the priesthood and limited Christian rituals to baptism and the Eucharist since Christ himself had practiced them.

This doubt in the sacred tradition and the reaffirmation of holy scriptures constituted the heart of the Protestant Reformation. Such questioning is a characteristic feature of any structural crisis, which never affects the scriptures. Still, it leads to forming new branches within the existing religion— in our case, Protestant Christianity. The crucial difference between the structural and systemic crises is that the latter questions the sacred tradition and the holy scriptures. The European Enlightenment of the seventeenth and eighteenth centuries marked a systemic problem for the Christian religion.

Enlightenment thought was diverse and complex. In the area of religion, it included various intellectual trends—religious criticism, deism, and even atheism. What could a religionist who takes his faith critically, a believer in a distant God who rejects the idea of revelation, and a secular humanist who denies the concept of God and organized religion possibly share? The answer is quite simple: they all question the validity of the Holy Writings of Christianity.

Biblical critics challenge the authenticity of the Bible based on their various aims and perspectives. However, no matter the intention behind their criticism, questioning sacred scriptures inadvertently reveals the key symptom of the systemic crisis of religion, which initiates the critical phase in its evolution. According to my theory, only the appearance of new religious systems with their respective holy writings can overcome those situations. At that stage, which I call post-critical, the mother faith renews its foundation by adjusting to novel religious movements and eventually flourishing alongside them.

To reiterate, the European Enlightenment, which initiated the age of modernity in Western culture, signaled the coming of the systemic crisis of Christianity. The beginning of its post-critical phase dates to the nineteenth and twentieth centuries, which radically changed not only the political but also the religious map of the world. Hence, the entire spiritual cycle of Christianity would look as follows (*see next page*).

Let us now discuss the art of the Crucifixion as it correlates with the different phases of the Christian faith. We begin with the formative stage, or the period of the early Christian Church. The Church was largely persecuted in the first four centuries of its history. It grew and developed in the catacombs as an underground religious community of the Roman Empire where Pilate, who represented the Roman government, issued his order to crucify Jesus of Nazareth. In those circum-

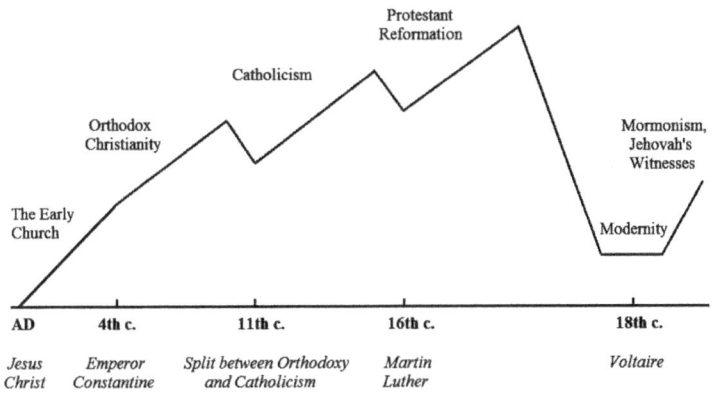

Diagram 2. The Cycle of Christianity

stances, Roman authorities could perceive any reminder of Jesus' Crucifixion in Christian thought or artistic creations as a challenge, even an assault on their political power.

Yet, from the middle of the first century onward, the Crucifixion became the focal point and critical belief for the developing Christian community. The Apostle Paul, in his theology, made the cross the very center of the Christian notion of salvation. In doing so, he disassociated the Crucifixion as a symbol of human cruelty and punishment from the cross as a sign of heavenly mercy and grace.

Paul understood the martyrdom of Christ as the ultimate—though paradoxical—expression of God's love toward all of humanity. As Paul wrote, love overcomes the power of evil and death itself: "Christ was innocent of sin, and yet for our sake, God made him one with human sinfulness, so that in him we might be made one with the righteousness of God."[91] Still, notwithstanding this theological ingenuity and sophistication, early Christian believers could not have changed or disregard-

---

[91] 2 Cor. 5:21.

ed the fact that the Roman soldiers had executed the founder of their religion in the way reserved for the worst criminals in the Roman Empire.

The complexity of this situation may have been one of the reasons why Crucifixion scenes, as far as we know, do not appear in Christian art in the first four centuries of Christianity. One of the earliest crosses known to us in the tradition of Christian art appears in the underground ceiling and wall paintings of the Catacomb of Saints Peter and Marcellinus in Rome, which dates to the early fourth century. On the top of this Catacomb, one sees "a large circle, akin to the Dome of Heaven, within which has been inscribed the symbol of the Christian faith, the cross."

A smaller circle in the center of the cross depicts a young Christ, the Good Shepherd, and the "loyal protector of the Christian flock." Christ was often portrayed as a youthful teacher in early Christian art, before Christianity became the Roman Empire's state religion. And it was after the fourth century, when Emperor Constantine legalized and supported the new religion, that the depiction of Jesus took on "such imperial attributes as the halo, the purple robe, and the throne, which denoted rulership, [with the later addition of] the beard of a mature adult."[92]

An ivory plaque Crucifixion in London is one of the oldest surviving figures of Christ. It was carved between 420 and 430 A.D. in North Italy, at the dawn of Imperial Christianity. The unknown artist still depicts Christ as young, muscular, beardless, and with his eyes wide open on this relief. He is hanging apparently with no pain on the cross, with only his hands nailed to it—symbolizing heavenly victory rather than human defeat, triumph instead of humiliation.

---

[92] Richard G. Tansey, Fred S. Kleiner, *Gardner's Art Through the Ages*, 10th ed., (1st ed. 1926), New York: Harcourt Brace College Publishers, 1996, 260.

Let us remember that the lack or rarity of early Christian depictions of the Crucifixion is not exceptional, and has precedents in other themes in Christian art as well. Take the Book of Revelation, for example. Here the absence of apocalyptic Christian art has a different set of reasons but a virtually identical result.

Revelation was one of the latest books accepted as part of the biblical canon. Christian leaders were reluctant to include Revelation because it portrayed Jesus Christ in a very different light from the Gospels. Evangelists depicted Jesus as being entirely peaceful and non-resistant to evil. The author of Revelation, on the contrary, showed him to be in full command of the Last Judgement, which is violent, cruel and involves massive amount of death and destruction. In the Gospels, Jesus conquers evil by his demise and sacrifice. In Revelation, he overcomes demonic creatures and beasts by destroying and throwing them into the lake of fire and sulfur.

Even after the fourth century, when Revelation became part of the scriptural canon, the book was not read as part of Church services. Only three centuries later, the council of Toledo (in modern Spain) decided to include Revelation in the Church liturgy. The book was still controversial, since the council declared that whoever disagreed with its decision would be excommunicated. After the council of Toledo, held in 776 A.D., at the monastery of Liébana in the province of Asturias in Spain, a monk named Beatus compiled various interpretations of the Book of Revelation as commentary on the Apocalypse. The illuminated copies of his work provide the first known instances of Christian apocalyptic art, dating back to the eighth century.[93]

At that moment in history, the art of the Crucifixion was already in a much stronger position. As mentioned earlier,

---

[93] Nancy Grubb, *Revelations: Art of the Apocalypse*, New York—London—Paris: Abbeville Press, 1997.

the first examples of crosses in Christian art date to the early church period in the fourth and fifth centuries. And during the Middle Ages, Crucifixion art was firmly established, from the sixth through the thirteenth centuries. Since the Eastern and Western parts of the Roman Empire were culturally and politically separated, Byzantine Orthodoxy and Roman Catholicism developed their own unique versions of the Crucifixion's artistic expression.

The Eastern part of the Roman Empire established the Byzantine style of the Crucifixion after Rome fell to the fifth century's barbarian invasions. Byzantium survived for a thousand years as the stronghold of Orthodox Christianity, with its capital in Constantinople and Greek as its citizens' common tongue. Moreover, Byzantine artists preserved the cultural heritage of antiquity and adapted it to their own tradition's needs.

Their religious art reflected the uninterrupted continuity of ancient pagan and Christian civilizations. Its model of the Crucifixion represented "the simplicity, dignity, and grace of Classicism fully assimilated by the Byzantine artist into a perfect synthesis with Byzantine piety and pathos." A mosaic in the monastery church at Daphne in Greece exemplifies the skilled blending of these two cultural paradigms. Dating back to the eleventh century, it depicts a Crucifixion scene and demonstrates "a masterful adaptation of Classical, statuesque qualities to the linear Byzantine style."[94]

The mosaic is more than a simple work of art; it manifests a devotional object's qualities. Its content is highly symbolic rather than historical. The artist portrayed Jesus Christ with a beard and a halo over his head, symbolizing his maturity and heavenly dominion. Although nailed to the cross, his body looks airy and light, displaying no signs of pain and suffering. His eyes are open, reinforcing the sense of divine glory and eternal life he brings to humanity. Overall, the pic-

---

[94] *Gardner's Art Through the Ages,* 309.

ture is an ideal representation of the "supernaturalism that determines the look of Byzantine figurative art—an art without solid bodies or cast shadows, with blank, golden spaces, with the perspective of Paradise, which is nowhere and everywhere."[95]

In contrast to the Byzantine model, the medieval Catholic Crucifixion gradually shifted its focus from the divine to a human Christ, from his glory to suffering, and from salvation to sin. The Byzantine *Christus Triumphans*, shown alive and emotionless on the cross and whose image displays both the Crucifixion and the resurrection, gives way to a new depiction of *Christus Patients*, "hanging dead on the cross, the head inclined, and the eyes closed."[96]

The Crucifixion image was relatively uncommon in the first ten Christian centuries. But in the second millennium its importance grew significantly as the central episode of the Passion cycle. Ultimately, it "gradually and increasingly became the principal theme of Christian art, continuing to reflect theological and religious trends up to the Reformation."[97] The Catholic Church established a doctrinal belief that Christ's death on the cross had a redemptive power and that the spilling of his blood had cleansed humanity of Original sin. This robust theology has led to a "progressive exaggeration of the degree of suffering shown in depictions of the Crucifixion [and to] excessive quantities of blood shown spurting from the wounds in the hands, feet, and side of Christ."[98]

The passion cycle, which "was a favorite subject of medieval and Renaissance artists and was considered the most am-

---

[95] Ibid, 298.

[96] Stephanie Brown, *Religious Painting: Christ's Passion and Crucifixion*, New York: Mayflower Books, 1979, 7.

[97] Gertrud Schiller, *Iconography of Christian Art*, vol. 2, *The Passion of Jesus Christ*, trans. Janet Seligman, Greenwich, Connecticut: New York Graphic Society, 1972, 99.

[98] *Religious Painting*, 7.

bitious of projects," described the last events in the life of Jesus, starting with his entry into Jerusalem, culminating in his Crucifixion, and ending with his entombment. The fourteen Stations of the Cross, an inalienable part of the Passion cycle, developed into a separate Crucifixion cycle in the High Middle Ages.[99] The Stations of the Cross or the Way of Sorrows refers to the last day in the Savior's life and a series of images depicting the events leading to his Crucifixion.

The concept of the stations "grew out of imitations of Via Dolorosa in Jerusalem, which is believed to be the actual path Jesus walked to Mount Calvary. The object of the stations [was] to help the Christians faithful to make a spiritual pilgrimage through contemplation of the Passion of Christ." Early depictions of the Crucifixion cycle included seven scenes:

Jesus accepts his cross.
Jesus falls for the first time.
Jesus meets his mother, Mary.
Veronica wipes the face of Jesus.
Jesus falls for the second time.
Jesus is nailed to the cross.
Jesus is placed in the tomb.

From the seventeenth century onward, more scenes were added, including, among others, the condemnation of Pilate, Jesus' death on the cross, and the deposition of his body. Today, out of fourteen traditional images or sculptures constituting a complete Crucifixion cycle, only eight have explicit scriptural references.

At the end of the twentieth century, the Catholic Church introduced the Scriptural Stations of the Cross as an alternative

---

[99] "Passion Cycle," The Free Dictionary, https://encyclopedia2.thefree-dictionary.com/Passion+cycle.

to the traditional stations and based on those celebrated by Pope John Paul II on Good Friday in 1991:

"First Station: Jesus in the Garden of Gethsemane
Second Station: Jesus, Betrayed by Judas, is Arrested
Third Station: Jesus is Condemned by the Sanhedrin
Fourth Station: Jesus is Denied by Peter
Fifth Station: Jesus is Judged by Pilate
Sixth Station: Jesus is Scourged and Crowned with Thorns
Seventh Station: Jesus Bears His Cross
Eighth Station: Simon the Cyrenian Helps Jesus Carry His Cross
Ninth Station: Jesus Meets the Women of Jerusalem
Tenth Station: Jesus is Crucified
Eleventh Station: Jesus Promises His Kingdom to the Good Thief
Twelfth Station: Jesus Speaks to His Mother and the Disciple
Thirteenth Station: Jesus Dies on the Cross
Fourteenth Station: Jesus is Placed in the Tomb."[100]

Still, no matter what version of the Stations of the Cross we take—medieval or modern, pictorial or scriptural—the Crucifixion retains its essential and dominant position in the whole cycle.

Art historians distinguish three main phases in depicting Crucifixion in Christian art. These phases parallel the Christian religion's chronological development from the Byzantine period through the Middle Ages and up to the Renaissance. There is a direct continuity between medieval and Renaissance

---

[100] Louise Merrie, "Praying The Stations of the Cross," *Catholic Exchange*, https://catholicexchange.com/praying-the-stations-of-the-cross/.

depictions of the cross. The newfound interest in the humanity of the Savior and his vulnerability in medieval Crucifixions has resulted in a growing trend to portray the Crucifixion as an actual historical event rather than a spiritualized symbol, a trait that will eventually become one of the most characteristic features of Renaissance art.

To be sure, the traditional symbolism of medieval Crucifixions did not entirely disappear during the Renaissance. The Crucifixion picture remains a sacred image depicting an act of divine redemption and the hope of resurrection for the faithful. Renaissance painters inherited the symbolic code developed and used by the Christian artists of the first millennium. According to its symbolism, the sun and the moon denote Christ's sovereignty; the Lamb refers to Christ and his sacrificial death. The lion and eagle suggest his resurrection and ascension. The images of Ecclesia and Synagogue evoque the continuity between the Old and New Testaments; the serpent stands for God's adversary, while the Tree of Life represents salvation; the hand of God, the throne, and the dove are a visual metaphor for the Trinity, and so on.

In Renaissance Crucifixion paintings, one can still see the witnesses to this event who are mentioned in the Gospels— Mary, Jesus' mother, John the Apostle, the Centurion, and the Pharisees. The novel element in Renaissance art is its attention to historical details and the accuracy of pictorial representation, known as illusionistic perspective. Renaissance artists aimed to faithfully reflect and even imitate the external world of appearances in its historical and natural dimensions. Art scholars point out that the *Holy Trinity*, a fifteenth-century canvas by Masaccio, "at the very beginning of the history of Renaissance painting, embodies [these] two principal Renaissance interests: realism based on observation and the application of mathematics to the pictorial organization in the new science of perspective." "In the *Holy Trinity*," we read further, "Masaccio gives a brilliant demonstration of the organizing value of [Renaissance] perspective. [He] places the vanishing point at the center of the masonry altar. With this point at eye level, the spectator looks up at the Trinity and down at the tomb,"[101] which reinforces the religious message of the painting.

In Western cultural history, the Renaissance marks the beginning of early modern times. However, from the perspective of religious history, the Reformation of the Christian Church and the subsequent Age of Enlightenment play a much more significant role in establishing the reign of modernity. The Protestant Reformation signaled the coming of religious modernization, and the Enlightenment ushered in the era of modern science. According to my theory of religious evolution, Reformation and Enlightenment corresponded to the reformist and critical phases of Christianity. How did the art of Crucifixion change in the wake of those transformations?

The second commandment that Moses delivered from God to his people prohibited idolatry and was directly related to the art of sculpture and painting. It said:

> You shall not make for yourself an image in the form of anything in heaven above or on the earth beneath or in the waters below. You shall not bow down to them or worship them; for I, the Lord your God, am a jealous God, punishing the children for the sin of the parents to the third and fourth generation of those who hate me, but showing love to a thousand generations of those who love me and keep my commandments.[102]

In the history of monotheistic religions, this commandment was taken very seriously by Jews and Muslims. For them, it meant the prohibition of depicting human beings, especially

---

[101] *Gardner's Art Through the Ages*, 697–698.
[102] Exodus 20:4–6.

prophets, because, according to the Scriptures, humans were created in God's image and likeness, and creating the likeness of God was strictly forbidden.

Honoring the commandment, traditional Jews preferred music and theater to visual arts. Classical Islam cultivated the practice of calligraphy and abstract painting with floral and geometrical patterns. On the contrary, since the formative years of the church, Christianity has disregarded the prohibition and promoted religious images of various kinds, including the depiction of the Savior and his Crucifixion. Why would Christians do that?

Religious art historians' standard explanation is that peasants who formed most Christian communities in the Middle Ages were unschooled and may have had difficulties absorbing Christian doctrines from the scriptures. Hence, Church leadership used visual art as a teaching strategy and icons, statues, and frescoes as educational tools. Church art played the role of life-size cartoons that helped believers get accustomed to biblical stories and teachings. Once a week, they would come to a Church service and see inside the images of Jesus and Mary, of Christian saints and teachers, and the depiction of various scenes from the Gospels and the New Testament.

However, when the Reformation spread all over Europe, Protestants rejected many Catholic doctrines and practices as incompatible with biblical texts. Protestant theology emphasized a direct communication between God and the worshipper, free from mediation by the Catholic Popes and religious hierarchy. It also reinterpreted the meaning of the central Christian sacrament of the Eucharist. Catholic doctrine insisted on the literal transubstantiation of Christ's body and blood into the bread and wine of communion. Most Protestants, in turn, tended to view the Eucharist as a symbolic gesture, a remembrance ritual, and a reminder of God's grace and salvation.

In practical terms, as far as biblical art was concerned, the Reformed Churches terminated their sponsorship of "grandiose images of Jesus or the Virgin Mary; big set-piece scenes from the Bible (like the Passion of Christ); images of the Saints; and, in particular, depictions of the Popes and other senior clergy." Although the "reaction of churchmen, congregations and secular leaders varied considerably from country to country, and from region to region,"– reads an article on Protestant art, —"in general, the Protestant Reformation triggered a wave of iconoclastic destruction of Christian imagery." Some of the radical reformers—Calvinists, for instance—"banned all figurative altarpiece art and considered most religious images to be idolatrous."[103]

To the Protestant removal of sacred art "from their churches and urban spaces, preferring instead to champion their faith via small-scale, humble Biblical images in various printed formats, including illustrated bibles," the Catholic Counter-Reformation responded by continuing to promote "its own brand of 'sacred art,' which illustrated important issues of Catholic dogma, or celebrated Catholic traditions, notably the liturgy, the sacraments, and the saints."[104] Such was the Christian art world situation when the Enlightenment movement came to the forefront of European culture in the eighteenth century and radically changed traditional approaches to religious art and Crucifixion paintings, yet again. The next chapter will discuss those profound changes and their theological and social implications.

---

[103] "Protestant Reformation Art," Encyclopedia of Art History, http://www.visual-arts-cork.com/history-of-art/protestant.htm.
[104] Ibid.

Chapter Two

THE CRUCIFIXION
AND THE RISE OF MODERNITY

IN THE EIGHTEENTH CENTURY, WESTERN CIVILIZA-
TION enters another historical epoch known as the Enlightenment, which establishes a new cultural and artistic paradigm of modernity. Enlightenment ideology questioned the
traditional authority of religion and asserted the independence and self-sufficiency of human reason. For the first time
in Christian history, it developed an all-encompassing worldview that stemmed from rational inquiry and analysis rather
than scriptural authority. The concepts of human reason, nature, liberty, and progress, along with their profound reinterpretation, played a crucial role in forming the ideological canon of modernity.

Humans acquire knowledge in five primary ways through:
sense perception, reason, intuition, tradition, and revelation.
Throughout history, various thinkers especially valued three
of them—human rationality, traditional practices, and divine
providence. The dominance of one of them over the others de-
pended upon the particularities of the cultural environment.
In the classical Greece of Socrates, Plato, and Aristotle, human
rationality prevailed over tradition and the gods' will. In Con-
fucianist China, ancestral customs were in the highest esteem
since Confucius believed they were in tune with Heaven's
mandate. In Hindu or Buddhist India, the scriptural authority
of the Vedas or the Buddhist sutras took precedence, and the

purpose of human reason was to support the truth inscribed in those sacred texts.

In medieval Christian societies, rationality was subservient to revelation and philosophy, as the ultimate product of reasoning, was considered the servant of theology as the science of scriptural interpretation. Since the fourteenth century, however, Christian intellectuals have separated the domains of philosophy and theology. Theology dealt with God's heavenly realities, the angelic world, and the afterlife, while the sphere of philosophy was limited to the natural and human realms. The Enlightenment thinkers brought this tendency to its logical conclusion. They claimed the absolute supremacy of reason as the instrument of human cognition, which can discover the mysteries of the universe without the help of revelation.

Perhaps the first thinker to formulate this new approach was the seventeenth-century French philosopher and mathematician René Descartes (1596–1650). For medieval Christian intellectuals, philosophy begins with faith, while Descartes starts with doubt. He wants philosophy to become an exact science like mathematics or physics and is searching for a self-evident truth that no one could ever question. His intellectual journey leads Descartes to establish doubt *per se* as the only thing he could never question. "I suspect; therefore, I think," — he continues this train of thought. — "And mental activities indicate that I exist; otherwise, who else is thinking?" The famous Cartesian motto *"Cogito ergo sum"* — I think; therefore, I am — becomes the slogan of modern rationalism, the inalienable imprint of its philosophical brand.

But Descartes does not end there. He moves on to prove the existence of God from an initial position of universal skepticism. The process of thinking, he argues, presupposes the absence of understanding. And any deficiency, including the lack of knowledge, means that the thinker is imperfect since the fullness of being characterizes perfection. Thus, the idea of shortage is measured only as related to abundance. And since there are inferior creatures like humans, there must also exist a perfect creator called God. God is omnipotent, omniscient, and omnibenevolent, by definition. He could not betray his creatures by tricking them into believing that the world of experience is real while it is only an illusion. Hence, Descartes concludes that the world is a reality, and we, as rational beings, can get to know and understand it.

What is then the nature of the created world and human beings? Traditional Christian thought answered that the world is essentially different from God, who ultimately controls what is happening in the realm of creation. God could suspend the laws of nature, perform miracles, and bring the dead back to life. As for human nature, it was created perfectly but, due to Adam and Eve's disobedience and fall from grace in the Garden of Eden, all humans were born with traces of Original Sin. Their nature is corrupted; only baptism can cleanse it and make salvation possible.

Both approaches to the nature of creation were challenged by those Enlightenment thinkers who aimed to expand human powers in physical and social domains. If God could intervene in human affairs at any moment and suspend or even change natural laws, scientific endeavors would be useless and never provide absolute and universal knowledge. If human nature, in its turn, is so fragile and wicked, everyone should cultivate obedience and quit any attempts to reform society for the better. In both cases, humanity would remain like a child in constant need of a strong and caring Father, represented by divine power and human authorities. In contrast, the Enlightenment intended to make humans more independent and mature—like rational adults who could care for themselves without outside help.

Enlightenment thinkers needed to make considerable adjustments to the classical Christian worldview. Those who preferred moderation leaned toward deism, which taught that God created the universe and its laws, withdrew from further direct interventions, and observed the evolution of his creatures from a distance. Deists retained their faith in God and religious viewpoints but rejected the notion of revelation and cleared the way for science as a reliable and universal form of knowledge. More radical intellectuals, along with scriptures and religious faith, denied the existence of God altogether. However, the rise and popularity of atheistic beliefs had the same implications for human rationality and the development of science and technology.

Whether on the deist or atheist side, Enlightenment thinkers also reinterpreted the concept of human nature. The founding father of modern liberalism, John Locke (1632–1704), formulated its most enduring secular notion. According to Locke, humans are born with a *tabula rasa* (blank slate) and acquire knowledge from personal experience. Two essential consequences came from his hypothesis. First, since human nature is neither good nor evil at birth, the aristocracy's social status is not innate but acquired. Locke's theory ideally fits democratic political ideology, presupposing peoples' equality. Second, in the nature vs. nurture debate Locke decisively affirmed the primacy of the latter. He asserted that individual and social progress, mainly, if not solely, depends on family values, the educational system, and social practices. According to Locke, we must reform our social structures, including economics, politics, and education, to better our society.

Hence, the idea of liberty, which is Enlightenment's third crucial notion. In traditional Christian societies, kings' might symbolized the power of the Almighty over his creatures. In seventeenth-century Europe, absolute monarchy was a commonly accepted and respected political institution. However, Enlightenment thinkers challenged the legitimacy of the *status quo*, on various fronts. To begin with, they proposed political reforms that aimed to limit state control. After all, power tends to corrupt, as Lord Acton famously remarked a couple of centuries later, and absolute power corrupts absolutely. Civil society must provide safeguards through checks and balances against the possible abuses of governmental officials. Local, state, and federal elections, the division into executive, legislative, and judicial branches of government, and the separation of church and state were designed to serve that purpose. Next, the Enlightenment thinker and the "Father of Capitalism," Adam Smith (1723–1790), introduced the idea of liberty into economics by laying the foundation for free-market economic theory. Finally, other theorists proposed educational reforms and the establishment of public schools, which offered free compulsory learning for children.

The Enlightenment intellectuals believed that political, economic, and educational innovations would eventually lead to humanity's infinite progress, where everyone would live happily ever after. Here, as elsewhere, they seemed to have challenged the biblical narrative. Christian theologians prioritized revelation over reason, preached Original Sin instead of human goodness, preferred obedience to the monarch over republican liberties, and believed in the biblical revelation about the end of history.

The Bible portrays the universe's evolution from the creation *ex nihilo* proceeding inevitably to the Apocalypse. In those last days of God's Judgment, the sun will darken, the moon will stop giving light, and the stars will fall from the sky. Graves will open, and resurrected creatures will rush to the throne of the Judge, who will examine their deeds. Heaven or hell will await them as the ultimate reward or punishment for what they have done in their lives.

Twentieth-century history confirmed those apocalyptic predictions more than the naïve enthusiasm of Enlightenment dreamers. The immediate, practical results of Enlightenment thought were revolutions. The American Revolution for national independence came first, in 1776. It reverberated through the nineteenth and twentieth centuries, in numerous insurrections in Latin America and Africa, which ended the Western colonial system.

Soon after the American uprising, the French Revolution of 1789 shook the European continent. It was much bloodier and pursued the goal of societal transformation rather than national liberation. The social and political upheaval in France was echoed in similar outbursts of revolt and violent restorations worldwide and, most importantly, in the Russian communist overthrow of the Tsarist government in 1917, which led to the establishment of the Soviet Union as the only atheist empire in human history.

Several centuries after the launch of the Enlightenment, we find ourselves living in the middle of it while observing a wholly transformed, global socio-political, economic, and cultural map. The founding of the United States of America marked the birth of the first Enlightenment-type political state based on the progressivist ideas of reason, liberty, and human brotherhood. European countries followed suit, which neither the First nor the Second World War could stop or undo. The alternative communist vision of the Soviet Union did not stand the test of time and, by the end of the twentieth century, collapsed along with the Soviet Empire and its Eastern European satellites. By the beginning of the twenty-first century, most countries of the American continent had already established multi-party democratic state systems.

The radical impact of the Enlightenment, which initiated modern times, is readily observed in political, social, and economic areas. But how did modernity transform the theory and practice of the arts? One of the most ardent defenders of the "incomplete project of modernity," Jürgen Habermas, noted that "in its Latin form 'modernus' was used for the first time in the late fifth century to distinguish the present, which had become officially Christian, from the Roman and pagan past."[105]

---

[105] Jürgen Habermas, "Modernity—An Incomplete Project," in *The Anti-Aesthetic: Essays on Post-Modern Culture*, edited by Foster, H., Port Townsend, Washington, 1983, 3.

According to Habermas, this separation from Greek and Roman cultural heritage is reintroduced each time "the consciousness of a new epoch formed itself through a renewed relationship to the ancients—whenever, moreover, antiquity was considered a model to be recovered through some kind of imitation."[106]

This observation is especially accurate regarding the first modern art movement, which historians labeled Neoclassicism. It was a revival of classical antiquity, this time connected with the Enlightenment program. In the second half of the eighteenth-century artistic scene, the appeal to reason and nature often meant the rejection of the ornate and aristocratic Baroque and Rococo styles in favor of the rational dignity of the classics. In his book *Thoughts and Imitation of Greek Works in Painting and Sculpture*, published in 1755, the German theorist, Johann Joachim Winckelmann popularized a memorable slogan for that approach—"noble simplicity and calm grandeur." The archeological excavations at Herculaneum and Pompeii in the mid-eighteenth century, which for the first time uncovered evidence of the daily life and diverse arts and crafts of the ancients, increased even further the fascination of Europeans with antiquity.

The leading Neoclassical painter of the time, Jacques-Louis David (1748–1825), followed the French Baroque painter Nicolas Poussin (1594–1665) in his style, favoring clarity and order and preferring line over color. David's accomplishments served as the foundation for our understanding of the movement. In his masterpiece, *The Death of Marat* (1793), David immortalized a historical figure as a secular hero and revolutionary martyr. In another famous painting, *The Death of Socrates* (1787), David turns to the champion of the "religion of reason," a Christ-like image of a worldly saint, Socrates, whom he portrays right before his suicide by poison. Here the classical approach to art is merged with devotional imagery and historical narrative.

---

[106] Ibid., 4.

In sculpture, Neoclassicism was explored by Jean-Antoine Houdon (1741–1828), who specialized in portraiture. His *Voltaire Seated* (1781) displayed all the features of Neoclassicism and was rightly acclaimed as a "modern classic." The neoclassical elements of the sculpture include Voltaire's Roman toga and classical headband. At the same time, Houdon portrays his personage as a modern man and an Enlightenment philosopher who is unheroic, skeptical, and in the middle of an intimate conversation.

In architecture, England was the birthplace of the Neoclassical style. The spirit of Neoclassicism manifested in the first half of the eighteenth century in the so-called "Palladian revival." An Italian Renaissance architect, Andrea Palladio (1508–1580), believed architecture must follow the principles of reason and specific rules embodied by the ancients' constructions and edifices. Initiated by Lord Burlington (1694–1753) in Great Britain, Palladianism spread abroad to the American colonies, branded as the Georgian style. Thomas Jefferson's House in Monticello, Charlottesville, Virginia (1784) represents a magnificent example of the Neoclassical style in the United States.

In the nineteenth century, European culture produced three new modern art movements—Romanticism, Realism, and Symbolism. While Romanticism dominated the first half of the century, Realism and Symbolism flourished in its second half.

The philosophical outlook of Romanticism represented a reaction, almost a revolt, against the hyper-rationalism of the Enlightenment and Neoclassicism. Romantic theorists and artists stressed the importance of feelings and emotions over dry human intellect. They idealized personal freedom and intuitive subjectivity, which they valued more than the dictates of politics and society. The Romantics rediscovered nature in its pristine beauty and hidden divinity. They advocated running from polluted cities and their vain, busy lifestyle to the rustic but authentic life of peasant villages. They praised the natural state of undomesticated animals, uneducated children, and "noble savages" in tribal cultures as superior to modern civilized men. And they glorified artistic geniuses who never obey ordinary rules but follow their instincts, are rejected, and misunderstood by the masses, and spend their lives searching for truth in the infinite variety of creation.

In visual arts, painting became the most striking achievement of Romanticism. In nineteenth-century European societies, the professional and commercial classes rose to prominence and eventually replaced aristocratic sponsorship and state commissions as the most significant source of income for artists. And painting was less expensive and dependent on public approval than sculpture or architecture.

Much in demand, Romantic artists rediscovered and thoroughly explored the richness of landscape painting as a distinctive genre of modern art. Focusing on emotional intensity and colorful palettes, Romantics also loved to portray people in extreme circumstances—revolutionary wars, mass executions, massacres, miraculous rescues, and so on. *The Raft of the "Medusa"* (1819) by Théodore Géricault (1791–1824) and *Liberty Leading the People* (1830) by Eugène Delacroix (1798–1863) readily come to mind. Overall, Romanticism generated a whole pleiad of European masters, including a Spaniard, Francisco Goya (1746–1828), a British painter Joseph Mallord William Turner (1775–1851), and the German landscape artist Caspar David Friedrich (1774–1840).

By the middle of the nineteenth century, continental Europe's economic and social conditions have drastically changed. The Industrial Revolution that had begun in England in the preceding century had expanded over the Continent and tremendously impacted European living standards. The development of railroads and steamships, the establishment of factories and the following rapid urbanization, innovations in medicine, and improvements in hygiene have led to the increase and spread of wealth and prosperity, plus unprecedented population growth. Socially, the power of the aristocracy weakened, and industrial laborers, while suffering from many hardships, including poor living conditions and wages, began to utilize their political strength.

The intellectual atmosphere in Europe was also rapidly shifting at that time. Novel approaches in science and philosophy transformed the sphere of scholarly interests and public discourse. With his *Course on Positive Philosophy* (1842), the founder of positivism Auguste Comte (1798–1857), laid the foundation for sociology as the new queen of the sciences. Comte insisted that social knowledge, which results from study and experimentation, should aim to improve society.

Another scientific breakthrough occurred in biology in 1859, when Charles Darwin (1809–1882) published his seminal work *On the Origin of Species*. Darwin's theory of natural selection identified heredity and environment as the main determining factors of human evolution. One had to control either the first or the second in order to predict and regulate human behavior. While nascent genetics studied and experimented with heredity, most thinkers and social scientists pursued various projects intended to transform society. In their *Manifesto of the Communist Party* (1847), Karl Marx (1818–1883) and Friedrich Engels (1820–1895), offered their vision of social and economic transformation that would radically change the political landscape of the planet in the twentieth century.

As a new movement in art and literature, Realism also rose to prominence in those cultural circumstances. Great Realist writers—Honoré de Balzac (1799–1850) in France, Charles Dickens (1812–1870) in England, Henrik Ibsen (1828–1906) in Norway, and Leo Tolstoy (1828–1910) in Russia—rejected the conventions of Romanticism, along with its escapist aesthetic focusing on the supernatural, idealized, or idyllic. Instead, those novelists and playwrights turned their attention to the reality and truth of contemporary societies. They described the sufferings of ordinary men and women with compassion and objectivity without bypassing life's low, distressing, and evil facets. Realist authors hoped that uncovering existing social ills, injustices, and conflicts in their literary works would help heal and improve the social environment.

The Realist movement was not confined to literature and theater but also involved visual arts, primarily painting. French painter Gustave Courbet (1819–1877), made it his artistic goal to depict the "heroism of modern life" (Baudelaire), by relying on direct experiences. In 1849 Courbet exhibited his first programmatic canvas, *The Stone Breakers*, a life-sized picture, which portrayed two men working on a road. Politically, Courbet sympathized with Socialism, and his artwork came to be viewed as a Socialist manifesto in visual form. Two other French artists, Jean-François Millet (1814–1875) and Honoré Daumier (1808–1879), also dedicated their art to the movement of social realism. The first depicted the life of the peasants, while the second became known for his political cartoons and satirical drawings.

In the last quarter of the nineteenth century, European art connoisseurs observed the flourishing of another cultural and artistic movement: Symbolism. Having rejected the social criticism of Realist artworks, the Symbolist writers and artists turned their attention to the inner world of humanity with its evil passions and forbidden desires. Symbolism offered its proponents a coherent mindset, which allowed for various styles as long as they embodied its peculiar vision.

The French *poètes maudits* or "accursed poets," as the critics dubbed them—such as Charles Baudelaire (1821–1867) and Arthur Rimbaud (1854–1891)—explored the "cemetery of the soul" with no mercy or self-forgiveness. In 1857, Baudelaire published his infamous collection of poetry, *Flowers of Evil,* which contained supplications to Satan and was banned as obscene. Decadence, rejection of conventional morality, the spirit of absolute non-conformity and eternal restlessness, the use of drugs and alcohol to upset all the senses and liberate artists from mundane rationality by experiencing altered states of consciousness—those were the characteristic features of the symbolist aesthetics and poetic practices.

In painting, the Belgian James Ensor (1860–1949) and the Norwegian Edvard Munch (1863–1944) were among the most distinctive representatives of the Symbolist approach to art and society. Ensor's works display an intensely pessimistic view of human nature by portraying crowds of people who cover their true faces with carnival masks. Munch's paintings—for example, his famous *The Scream* (1893)—visualize the feelings of anxiety and fear that escape rationalization and, as such, acquire a terrifying and nightmarish character.

The twentieth century brought even more diversity and depth to the Western art scene. In so many ways, that century became unique in human history. The era of space flight and world wars, the age of penicillin and the nuclear bomb, the time of Einstein and Hitler. In the field of art, it produced an unprecedented array of movements and creative originality. Today, looking back at the cultural baggage of that century, experts naturally strive for a comprehensive appraisal of its heritage. They pay attention, not to various styles and techniques, but to the main trends in modernist art.[107]

In a period of incredible progress in science and technology, the twentieth century also witnessed an unprecedented crisis of spirituality and religious consciousness. Contemporary artists reflected the drama of the situation with poignancy as people realized they were powerless before the fruits of their own inventions. The little man, unable to defend his dignity and turned into one of the cogs of a giant machine, became one of the typical characters in the artistic palette. He is tormented by the meaninglessness of life, haunted by hopelessness and despair. The novels of Gabriel García Márquez

---

[107] In this part of the chapter, I use my article "Modern Art: Main Trends in the Twentieth Century," which was published in Russian in the almanac *The Coast*, Philadelphia, 2000, 223–229.

and the plays of Samuel Beckett, the short stories of Franz Kafka and the operas of Alban Berg, the films of Charlie Chaplin, and the poems of T. S. Eliot vividly reflect the breakdown of traditional values and the decline of morality.

However, the enormous scope of the cultural crisis made an even more profound impact on the modern artistic landscape. The noted twentieth-century Russian thinker Nicholas Berdyaev once remarked: "Art has experienced many crises in its history, but what is happening to art in our epoch cannot be called one of the crises among others. We are witnessing a profound upheaval in the thousands of years of its foundations."[108] German philosopher Jürgen Habermas narrowed things down to the following matter: "The Enlightenment project formulated by the Enlightenment thinkers in the eighteenth century consisted in their desire to create an objective science, a universal morality and law, and an autonomous art based on their internal logic of development."[109]

In pursuit of this proclaimed ideal of total autonomy, twentieth-century artists revised the three most essential principles of art. The masters of modernism reinterpreted a traditional relationship between the means of representation and the object of art. They developed a new understanding of the role of the author in creating an artwork. And, finally, they changed their view of the relationship between art and life. In my opinion, those three features comprise the substantive evolution of twentieth-century modern art. Let us consider each of them in more detail.

The revision of the traditional relationship between the means of representation and the object of art in European cul-

---

[108] Nicholas Berdyaev, "Krizis iskusstva" [The Crisis of Art], *Filosofiya tvorchestva, kul'tury i iskusstva* [Philosophy of Creativity, Culture, and Art], Moscow: "Iskusstvo," 1994, Vol. 2, 399. All translations from Russian are made by the author.

[109] Habermas, "Modernity—An Incomplete Project," 9.

ture began at the end of the nineteenth century. Impressionism, which became popular with the European public, radically changed views on painting and led to a rejection of the artistic standards introduced during the Renaissance. This change was embodied in the late canvases by the "Father of Modernism," Édouard Manet (1832–1883), which depicted not so much the external world as their author's subjective perception and experiences.

According to the Renaissance tradition, the pictorial canvas served the viewer as a window into three-dimensional reality. Therefore, it had to copy its properties as they appeared to the human eye. The invention of photography in the nineteenth century confirmed the correctness of perspective as discovered and mastered by Renaissance artists. At the same time, the spread of photography challenged painting as an art form and forced painters to find other bases for their art. As a result, they gradually abandoned the blind imitation of the physical world and turned instead to exploring the two-dimensional nature of the pictorial canvas.

In Fauvism and Expressionism, two movements that emerged at the dawn of the twentieth century, painters emphasized the inner side of human existence even more. Trying to embody the spiritual world of man, representatives of these two groups broke radically with traditional forms of artistic expression. The colors in their paintings looked unrealistic, and the objects were distorted and disproportionate. The color schemes and compositional structures of such artworks reveal, first and foremost, the outlooks of their authors. The French artist Henri Matisse (1869–1954), leader of the Fauvists, expressed the credo of the new art as follows: "Composition is the art of decorating the various elements at the disposal of the artist and serving to express his feelings."[110]

---

[110] Henri Matisse, "Notes of a Painter," 1908, in Herschel Chipp, *Theories of Modern Art: A Source Book by Artists and Critics*, Berkeley: The University of California Press, 1968, 132.

Cubism and Futurism took the next step toward rejecting the mirror image of the world in works of art. These two movements, which also experienced their heyday at the dawn of the twentieth century, just before World War I, showed how one could visually embody a reality that was neither material nor subjective, but conceptual. The technique of color separation and the decomposition of forms, favored by the Futurists and Cubists, aimed to penetrate beyond psychophysical appearances and express the ultimate essence of being. For the Futurists, this foundation of existence was the *élan vital* or "life impulse" of the French philosopher Henri Bergson (1859–1941), the inexhaustible source of evolution. The Futurists conveyed the power of this universal force, its engulfing whirlwind blurring the clear outlines of objects and erasing the boundaries between people, flowing one into another in their paintings. Cubist art was more analytical and static than dynamic, intuitive Futurist paintings. However, in their pictorial experiments the Cubists, too, dissecting objects and bodies into geometric figures, were absorbed by the desire, as Berdyaev wrote, "to get to the skeleton of things, to the solid forms hidden behind softened coverings."[111]

The culmination of such experiments was the birth of abstraction, no longer constrained by anything—neither objective, subjective nor even conceptual limits. Abstraction in all the arts renounced the very idea of representation. In their search for pure spirituality, abstract artists completely dissolved the object of art into the pictorial means characteristic of individual artistic activities. Painting focused entirely on color and form, dancers—on storyless body movements, literary authors—on writing styles and compositional techniques, and so on. Each of these artists acquired uniqueness by focusing on a manner of expression exclusive to them. That is why

---

[111] Nicholas Berdyaev, "Picasso," *Filosofiya tvorchestva,* Moscow: "Iskusstvo," 1994, Vol. 2, 420.

abstraction became known in contemporary culture as "art for art's sake," and was recognized as "High Modernism" in the second half of the century.

Another novel understanding of the creative act emerged in early twentieth-century France. Following the innovations of abstraction, the adherents of modern art proposed reconsidering the artist's role in creating artworks. In 1907, one of the founders of modernism, Pablo Picasso (1881–1973), completed his famous painting *Ladies of Avignon*, now recognized as one of the masterpieces of the modernist style. In this painting, Picasso depicted five women whose bodies are unnaturally large and angular and whose faces look like African or Iberian masks.

Later, in interviews with journalists, Picasso acknowledged the influence of aboriginal art on his work. He admired African 'primitivism' but not because of its formal techniques. He appreciated the spiritualist function it fulfilled in archaic societies. Picasso said, about his visit to the Trocadero Museum in Paris (now the Musée de l'Homme), where a collection of African masks was on display:

> They [these masks] were weapons. They were tools. Tools to free people from spiritual slavery; to gain independence. By giving physical form to spirits, we liberate ourselves from them and gain independence. The spirits, the unconscious [and] emotions, it all has the same meaning. Now I understood why I had become an artist. Perhaps it was at that moment that the Ladies of Avignon were summoned to life... It was my first exorcist painting.[112]

Such a confession from the great Spaniard is precious, since it reveals one of the characteristic features of twentieth-century art. For Picasso, the role of the artist was not one of

---

[112] Paul Crowther, *The Language of Twentieth Century Art: A Conceptual History*, New Haven: Yale University Press, 1997, 33.

self-expression but, on the contrary, that of self-erasure. Artists should strive, not to convey their spiritual experiences, but to ensure that their individuality does not interfere with releasing emotions accumulated in the subconscious. The idea of the artist's personality disappearing from his creations, foreseen by Picasso, fell on fertile ground. It rang particularly true of the Surrealists, whose activity later took center stage.

Surrealism was founded in the mid-nineteen-twenties by André Breton (1896–1966), precisely to liberate the subconscious by various techniques designed to limit or completely exclude human rationality from the creative process. The practice of this school in art and literature, which became fashionable in Europe between the world wars, grew out of the psychoanalytic concepts of Sigmund Freud (1856–1939), with which Breton, a physician by training, was well acquainted. The Surrealists translated subconscious impulses into works of art using a specially developed technique: automatism, which they opposed to conscious creativity. By applying automatism, the writers or artists aimed, as did the shamans in tribal religions, to purify their consciousness and get out from under the control of the mind. They were called upon to accommodate the paradoxical and terrifying world of unconscious impulses. It was no longer solely a question of artistic talent, but also psychological training.

Depriving the artist-creator of the halo of chosenness bequeathed by the Romantics found an enthusiastic response in the modernist art of the second half of the twentieth century. Inspired by the experience of the Surrealists, the Abstract Expressionists in post-war America began to blaze new trails leading to the labyrinth of the unconscious. Some of the techniques they used were only indirectly related to traditional art. One of the idols of Abstract Expressionism or, as it was called, "action painting," was Jackson Pollock (1912–1956). Adopting Surrealist methods, he favored the creative process more than the final artwork, and instead of painting in the old-fashioned way, he preferred to splash paint—in a seemingly random fashion—on the canvas.

Another movement in post-war America, Pop Art, rejected the role of human individuality in art, based on other considerations and using different techniques. Pop Art emerged in the West in the nineteen-sixties as a reaction to the prevailing abstract art of the previous two decades. It challenged abstraction and the opposition between "low" and "high," the vulgar and the refined, the popular and the elitist. Pop Art practitioners made art familiar and understandable to ordinary people. They were not squeamish about everyday life and boldly introduced elements of commercial culture into their works. Pop artists craved to depersonalize their artworks to blend in with the world of mass production and consumer society.

They achieved this goal through specially developed methods. One of them was the principle of seriality, exploited, for instance, by the American artist and pop icon Andy Warhol (1928–1987). Much of Warhol's painting consisted of identical, monotonously repetitive subjects like cans of Campbell soup or postage stamps. Often, they were portraits of pop and movie stars, whose images Warhol copied from photographs and then replicated with the help of silkscreen technique.

Twentieth-century Minimalists went even further along the path of depersonalizing artworks. Minimalism, like Pop Art, emerged in the sixties as a reaction to Abstract Expressionism. However, unlike Pop Art, Minimalism rebelled not against abstract elitism but against expressionist subjectivity. Minimalists believed that art should finally get rid of its mania for self-expression. True creativity, they argued, resists authorial arbitrariness, and reveals its pristine literalness, simplicity, and conceptual clarity to the public. The structures of Dan Flavin (1933–1996) and Donald Judd (1928–1994), which usually represent a set of identical modules—cubes, tubes, and so on—are suitable examples of Minimalist artistic strategies. When formulated conceptually, some Minimalist compositions may not even seem to require professional skills and may look like a set of objects produced in a factory.

While abstraction completely dissolved the subject of art in the visual medium, Minimalism led to the final disappearance of the artist's personality from his works. Freed from the dictate of the object and the subject of the creative act, art finally achieved full autonomy. As a result, its borders became blurred and virtually indistinguishable from life itself.

The disembodiment of art and its atomization in the flow of life constitutes the third general tendency of twentieth-century modernism. The long-held dream of the Romanticists, of a theurgic creation uniting art and life in a single impulse and becoming an extension of divine creation has come true. Sharing this noble vision, Nicholas Berdyaev remarked: "Never before has there been such a thirst to move from the creation of works of art to the creation of life itself, of new life."[113] However, the similarities here are only superficial.

In their theurgic ideal, the Romantics aimed at uniting the various arts and enriching life with their synthesis. Furthermore, in theurgy, life would dissolve in the art to become one of the voices in the multivocal chorus of universal creativity. In modernism, on the contrary, the idea of the fusion of art and life is imbued not with the spirit of unity but of separation, division, or, to use a now-fashionable term, deconstruction. Tearing off one of its shells after another, art gradually dissolves into life and merges with it, since nothing is left to distinguish one from the other.

This tendency was already apparent in an artistic movement called Dadaism, at the beginning of the century. Dada emerged during the First World War in neutral Zurich, Switzerland, and after the end of the war it became widespread in Europe. Dada activities reflected a spontaneous European reaction to the immorality and horrors of war. Its participants

---

[113] Nicholas Berdyaev, "The Crisis of Art," 400.

expressed their contempt for the established institutions of European culture, which they saw as responsible for senseless slaughter. They couched their protest in mockery, parody, and an absurdist posture intended to debunk the traditional values they hated.

Dadaism was not so much an art group as an anti-art movement. As one of its adherents, Hans Richter (1888–1976), wrote: "Dada hates art, but Dada renews art through a movement in art that is against art."[114] And the future founder of Surrealism, André Breton, added that Dada is more than art or anti-art; it is "a state of mind."[115] The emergence of Dadaism marked the onset of a Western counter-culture that opposed the establishment and made itself known with anti-war marches and youth demonstrations in the second half of the century.

Behind the façade of the Dadaist artistic rebellion, however, was a deeper and more serious intention. It was about rethinking the very nature of the creative act and giving the status of works of art to the objects of everyday life. One of the idols of Dadaism, the French artist Marcel Duchamp (1887–1968), who strongly influenced twentieth-century modernism, discovered "found objects," that later became infamous. Those objects, or ready-mades, consisted of ordinary things like a toilet bowl or a hat rack, removed from common usage and offered as works of art at exhibitions.

The Frenchman's extravagant antics have found grateful followers in the century's later half. The emergence and epidemic spread in the nineteen-sixties and seventies of Conceptualism crowned Duchamp's efforts to surrender art to

---

[114] *Dada Artifacts*, Iowa City: The University of Iowa Museum of Art, 1978, 24.

[115] Andre Breton, "Dada Manifesto," Litterature May 1920, no. 13. Quoted in Dawn Ades, "Dada and Surrealism," *Concepts of Modern Art: From Fauvism to Postmodernism*, ed. Nikos Stangos, 3rd ed., London: Thames and Hudson, 1997, 111.

life. Following their master, the Conceptualists believed that the true essence of creativity is not artistic skill or technique but ideas or concepts, alone. If it plays any role, their material embodiment is somewhat secondary. Therefore, the activity of Conceptualists was highly diverse and full of unexpected experimentations. It ranged from transmitting telepathic messages to photographing invisible gases in the atmosphere. Technically, any action, even frankly meaningless, could have been elevated to the rank of art if its organizer proclaimed it as such. Thus, by the end of the century, much of modern art achieved complete autonomy from the standards that had recently seemed inviolable and wholly dissolved into the whirlpool of life. But did contemporary art become more spiritual as a result? And what happened to the genre of Crucifixion paintings in the nineteenth and especially in the twentieth century?

To answer, I will remind the readers about the secularization of life in the West since the inception of modernity. The church separated itself from the state, and religion became a private matter rather than a crucial part of the social or public sphere. As a result, both Church and state sponsorship of religious art has significantly decreased. In its stead, individual patronage and professional institutionalization have led to the commercialization and secularization of artworks. Free market and consumer demand now dictated what artists should paint, if they desired success and decent sales.

To be sure, Christianity remained the most prominent religion, globally, with more than two billion adherents. Traditional religious art, including Crucifixion paintings, also endured, and persisted through the rise and spread of modernity. One might even say that the genre of Crucifixion flourished as part of the new styles and movements. But in the nineteenth and, primarily, the twentieth century, painters formed a distinctive and novel type of Crucifixion painting that we appropriately call modern.

In twentieth-century art, the Crucifixion narrative acquired a new and broader meaning, not confined to Christian theological doctrines. In contrast to the Byzantine, Medieval, and Renaissance models, the modern image of the crucified Christ transcended the boundaries of the Christian faith. It became a universal symbol of redemption through righteous suffering, a cultural instrument by which artists measured their contemporary society.

The Byzantine glorification of Christ, the Catholic emphasis on suffering, and the Renaissance historicizing of Crucifixion fail to do justice to the various approaches that emerged on the twentieth-century artistic scene. Modern Crucifixion paintings escape the usual definitions, extend customary borders, expand historical frameworks, and transcend religious traditions.

Twentieth-century artists experimented with various genres, styles, and viewpoints reflecting their artistic individuality and worldviews—Christian, non-Christian, agnostic, or atheist. They were attracted to the Crucifixion, not necessarily for its sacred origin or salvific value. The Crucifixion sparked their interest by its ability to reflect the painter's perspective on cultural and historical occurrences of the day. This modern-day Crucifixion art was developed and perfected within the framework of the critical twentieth-century movements of Expressionism, Cubism, Surrealism, Abstraction, and Postmodernism. I will now discuss those movements in more detail, while focusing on the metamorphosis and potential of modern Crucifixion paintings.

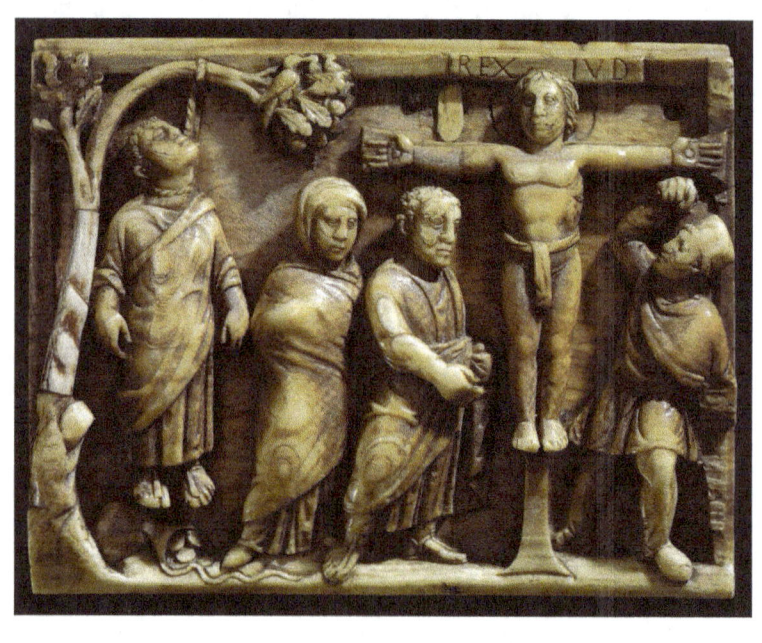

Ivory relief, c. 420–30. North Italy. Casket. Crucifixion, Death of Judas.
London, Great Britain.

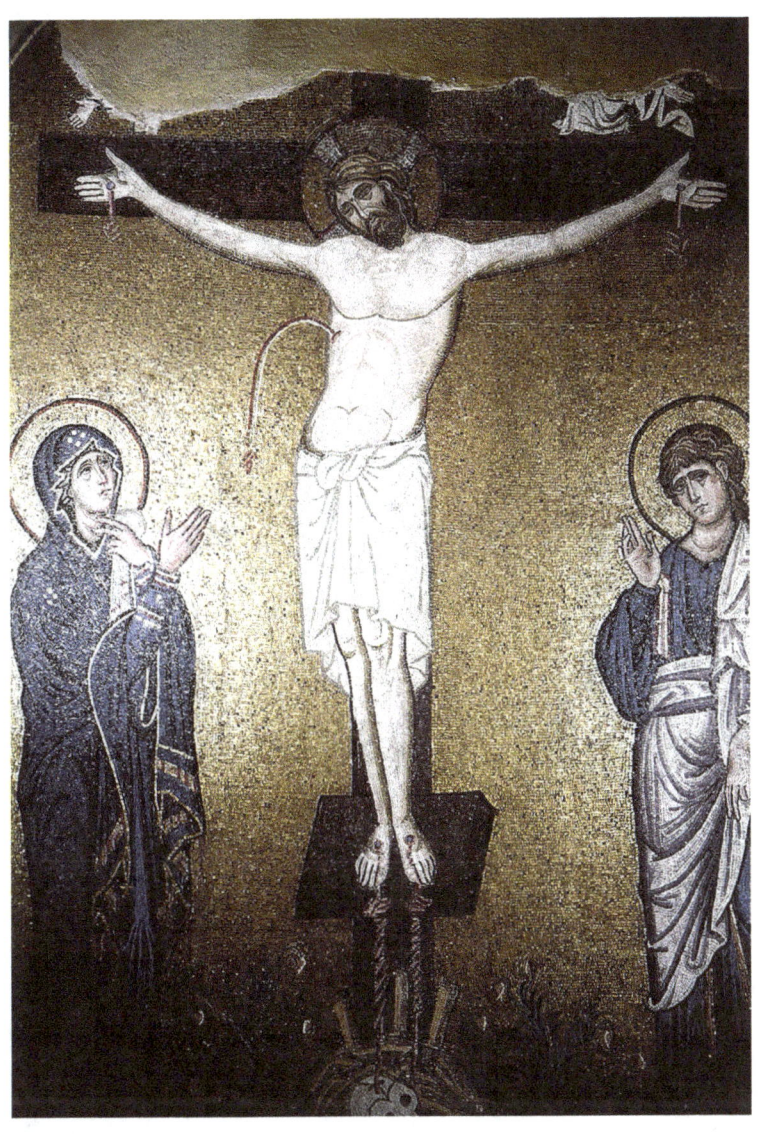

The Crucifixion, mosaic in the monastery church in Daphne, Greece,
1090–1100.

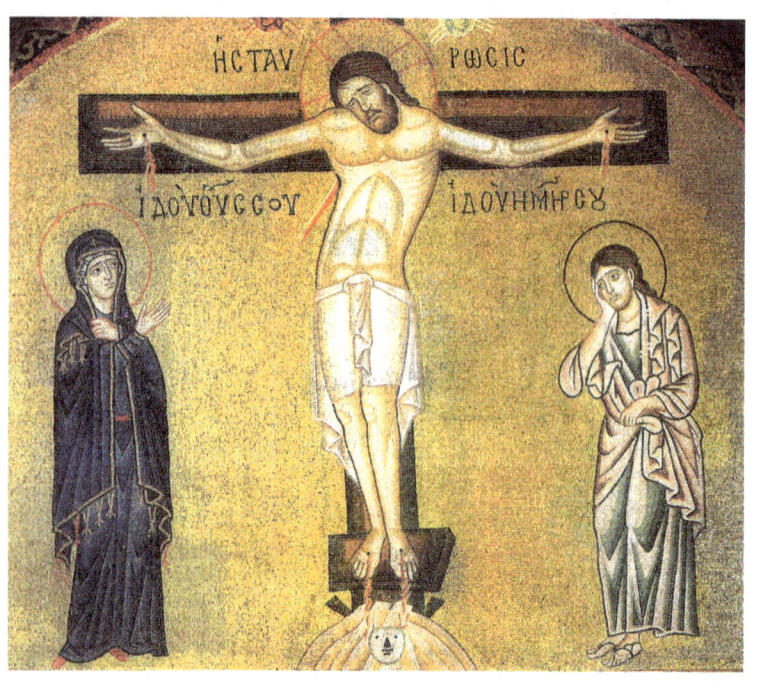

Byzantine Mosaics, *Crucifixion*, 1025,
the Monastery of Hosios Loukas, Greece.

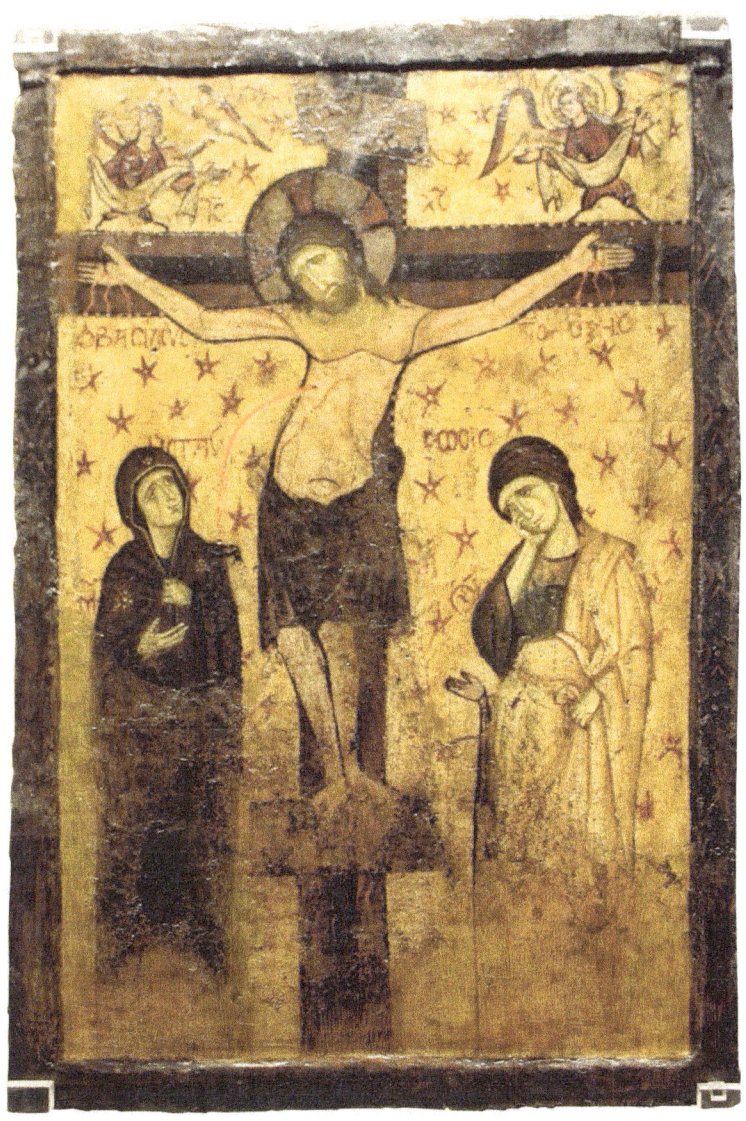

Crucifixion, Orthodox Icons, 1200–1300,
Byzantine and Christian Museum, Athens, Greece.

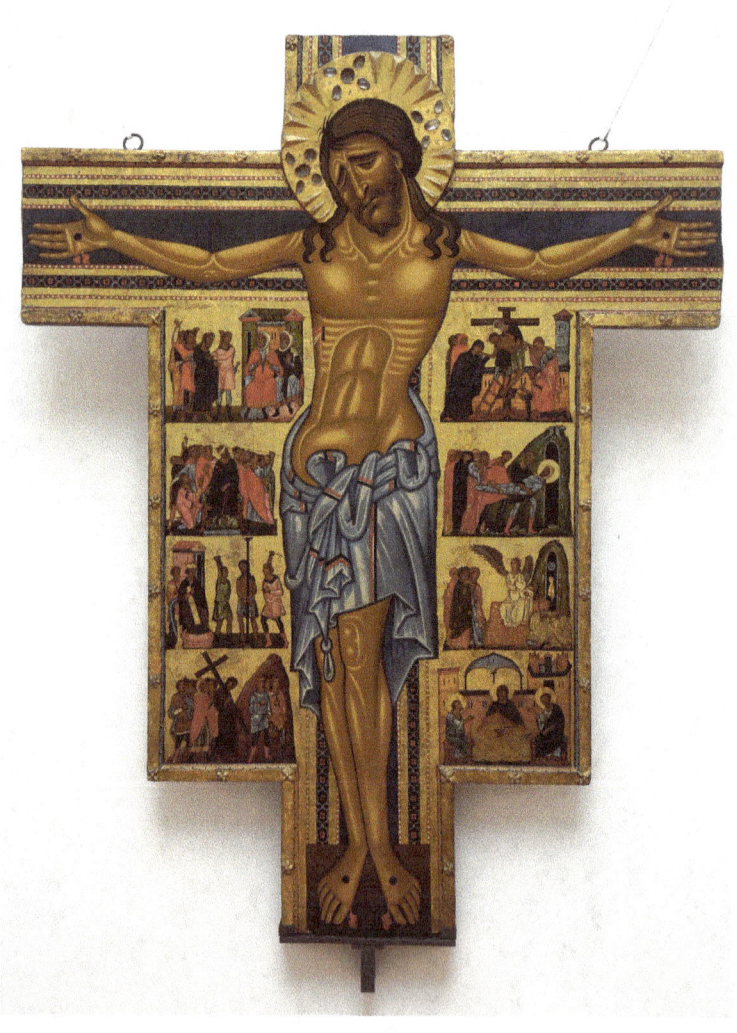

School of Pisa: *Crucifix with Episodes from the Passion*,
the second half of the 13th century, Uffizi, Florence, Italy.

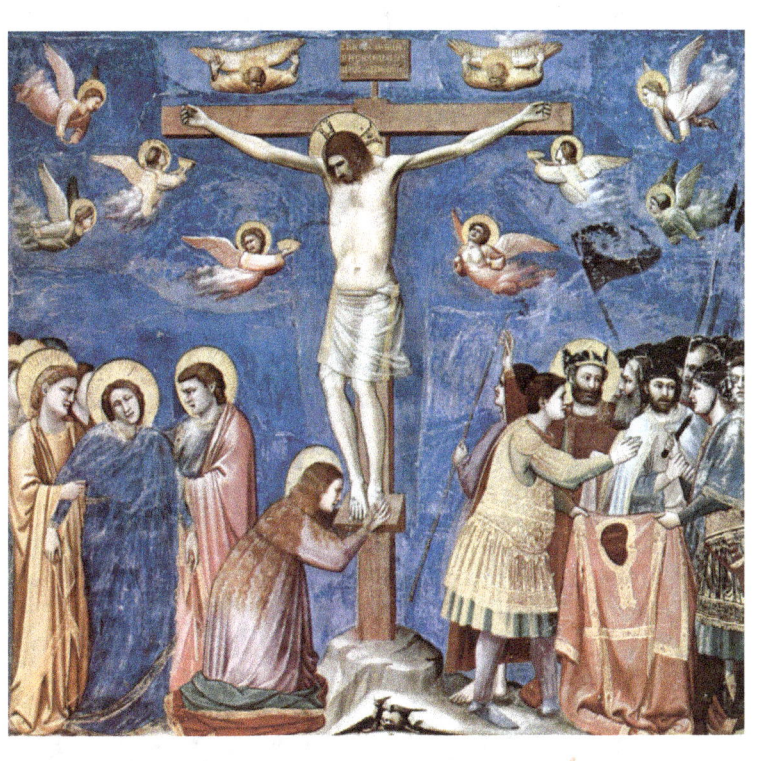

Giotto di Bondone (c. 1267–1337), *Crucifixion*, c. 1300,
Scrovegni Chapel, Padua, Italy.

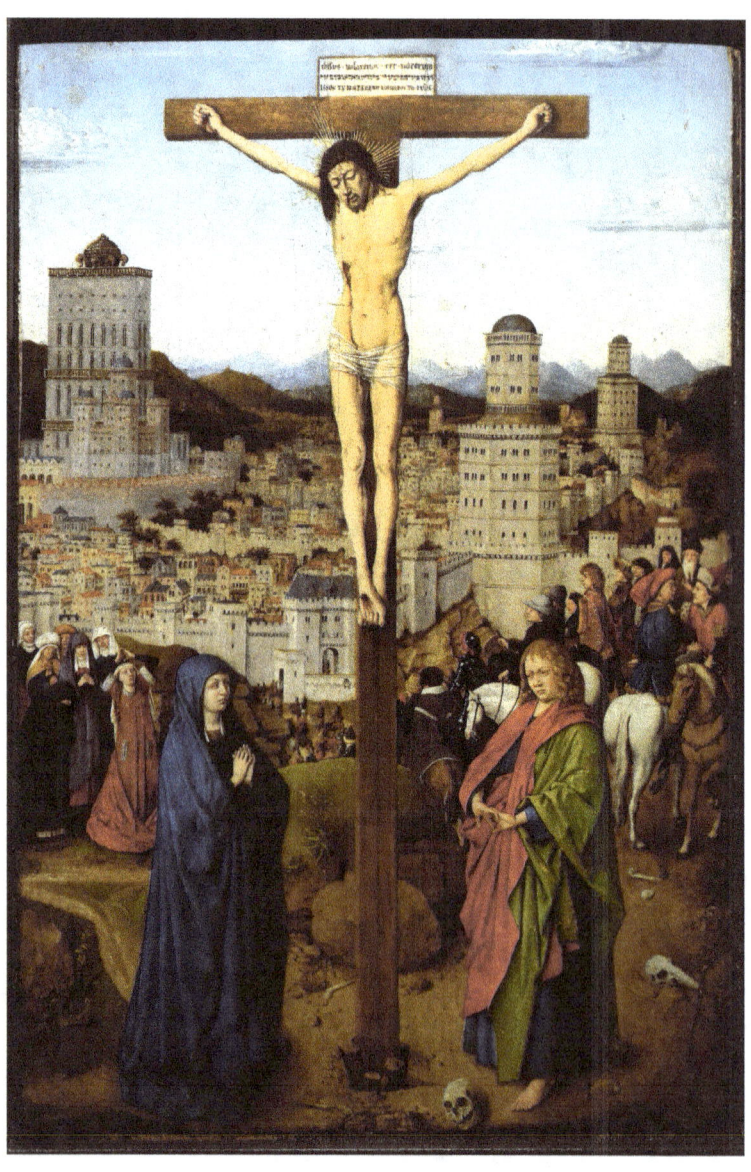

Hubert Van Eyck (c. 1390–1426), The *Crucifixion*,
Galleria Franchetti alla Ca' d'Oro, Venice, Italy.

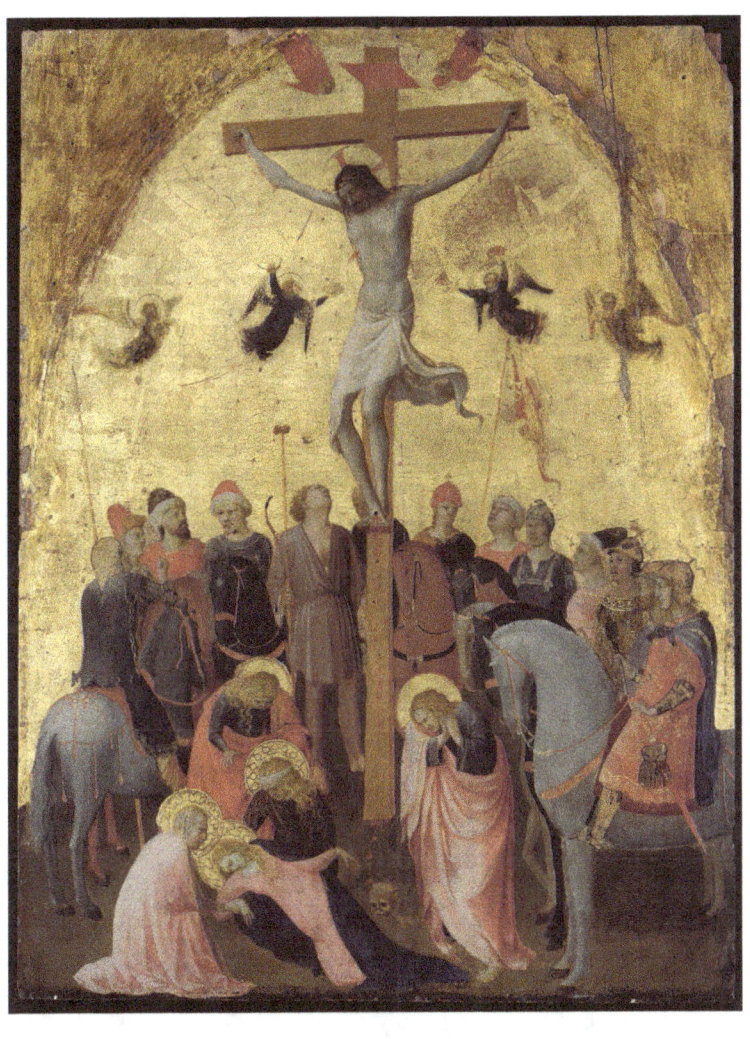

Fra Angelico, (Guido di Pietro; c. 1395–1455), *Crucifixion*, c. 1420–23, the Metropolitan Museum of Art, New York, NY, USA.

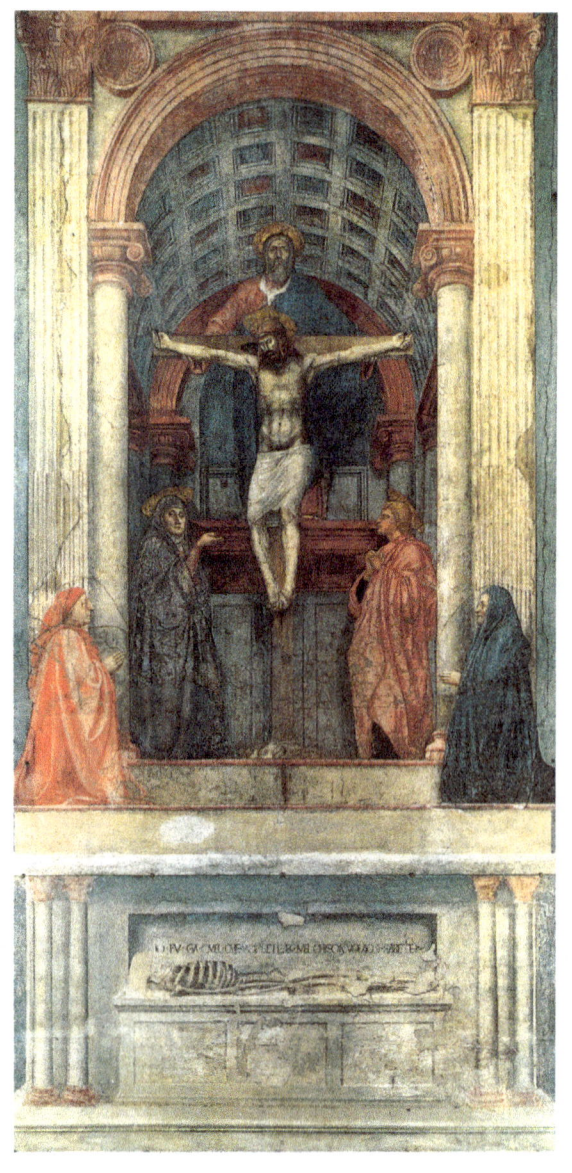

Masaccio (1401–1428), *Holy Trinity*, c. 1428,
Santa Maria Novella, Florence, Italy.

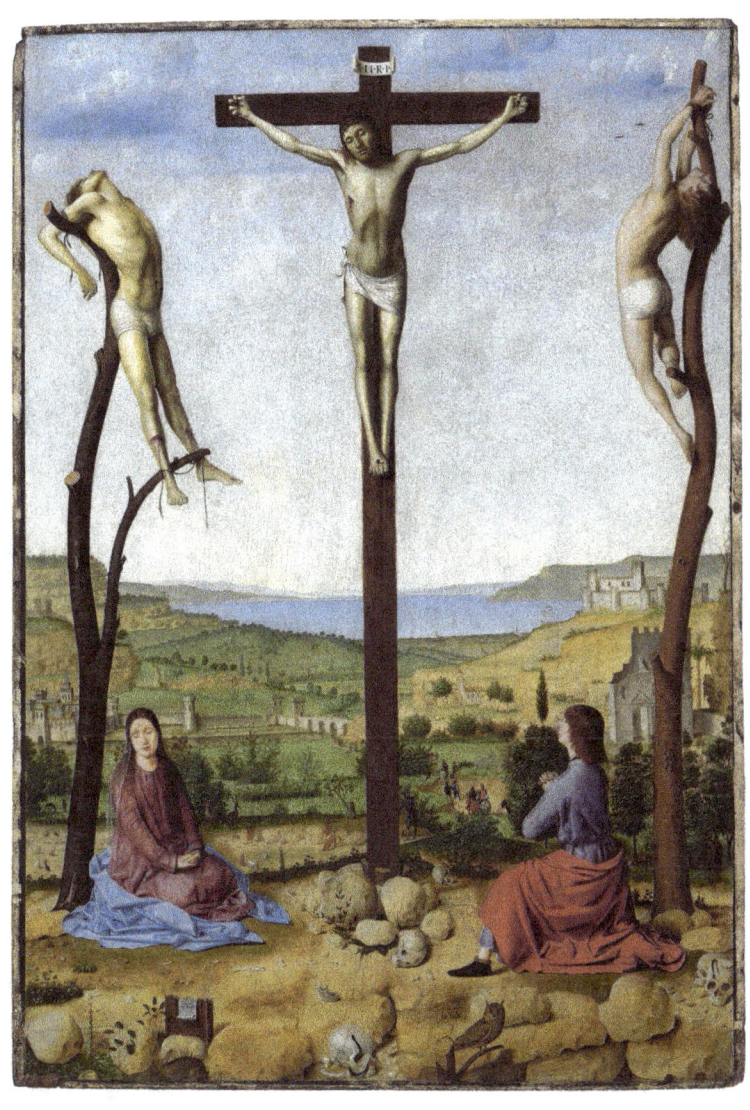

Antonello da Messina (c. 1425/30–1479), *The Antwerp Crucifixion*, 1475,
Royal Museum of Fine Arts of Antwerp, Antwerp, Belgium.

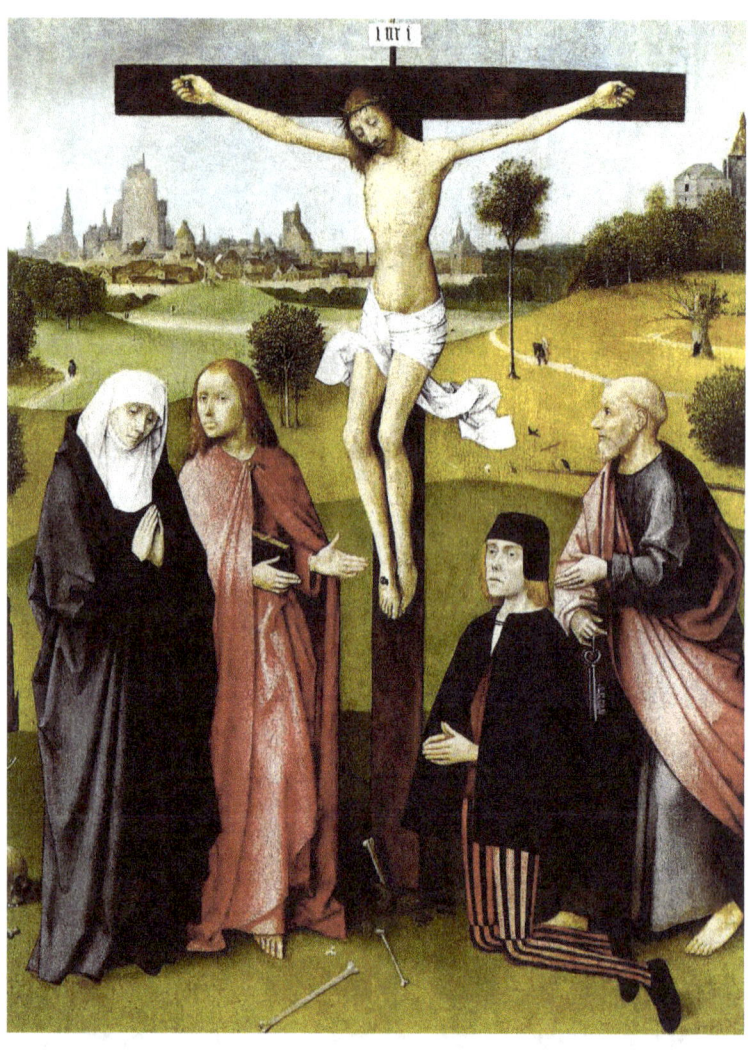

Hieronymus Bosch (c. 1450–1516), *Calvary with Donor*, c. 1490,
Musées Royal des Beaux-Arts, Brussels, Belgium.

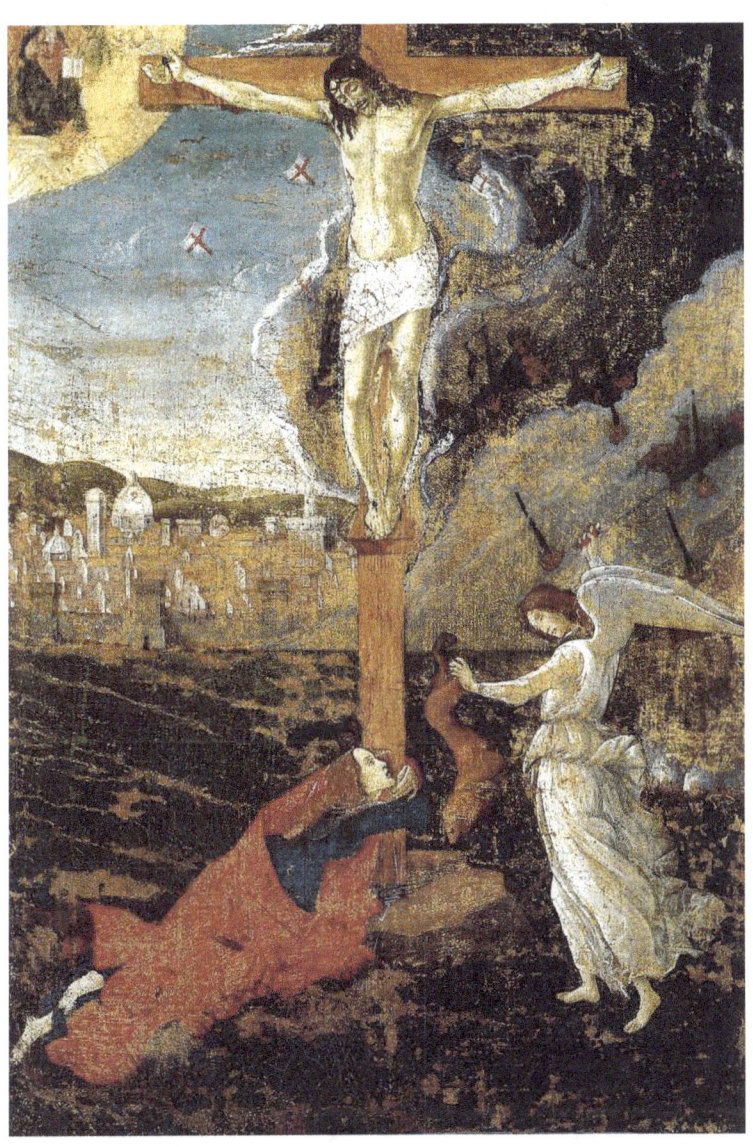

Sandro Botticelli (c. 1445–1510), *Crucifixion*, c. 1497,
Harvard Art Museums, Cambridge, MA, USA.

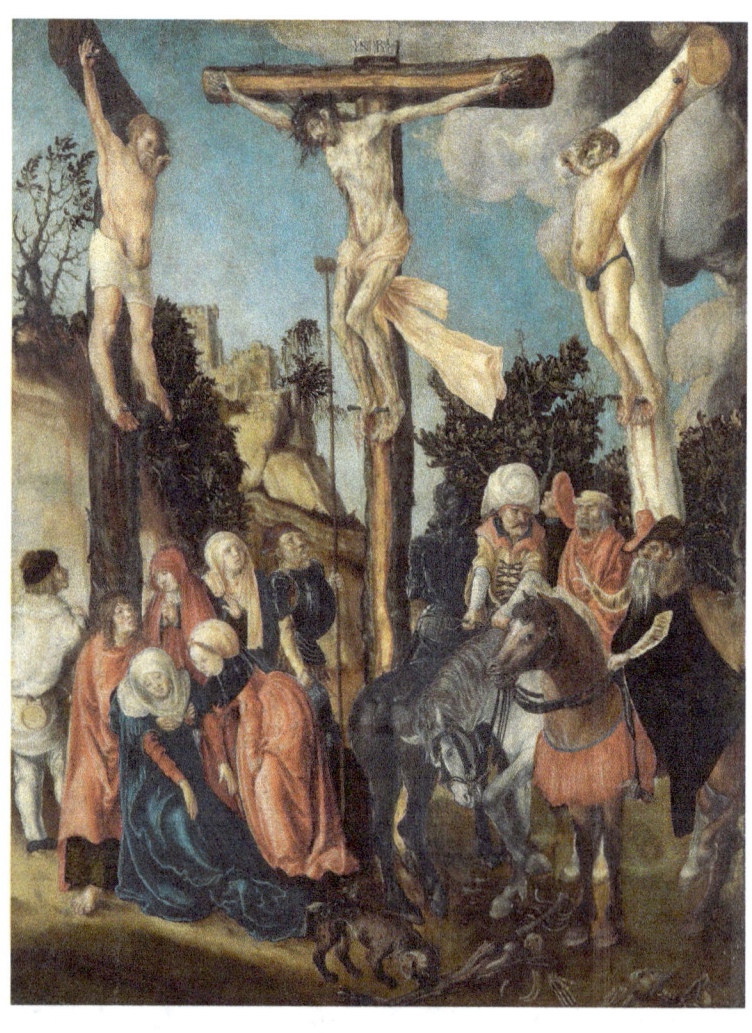

Lucas Cranach the Elder (c. 1472–1553), *Crucifixion*, c. 1500–1501,
Lucas Cranach d. Ä., Kunsthistorisches Museum Wien, Vienna, Austria.

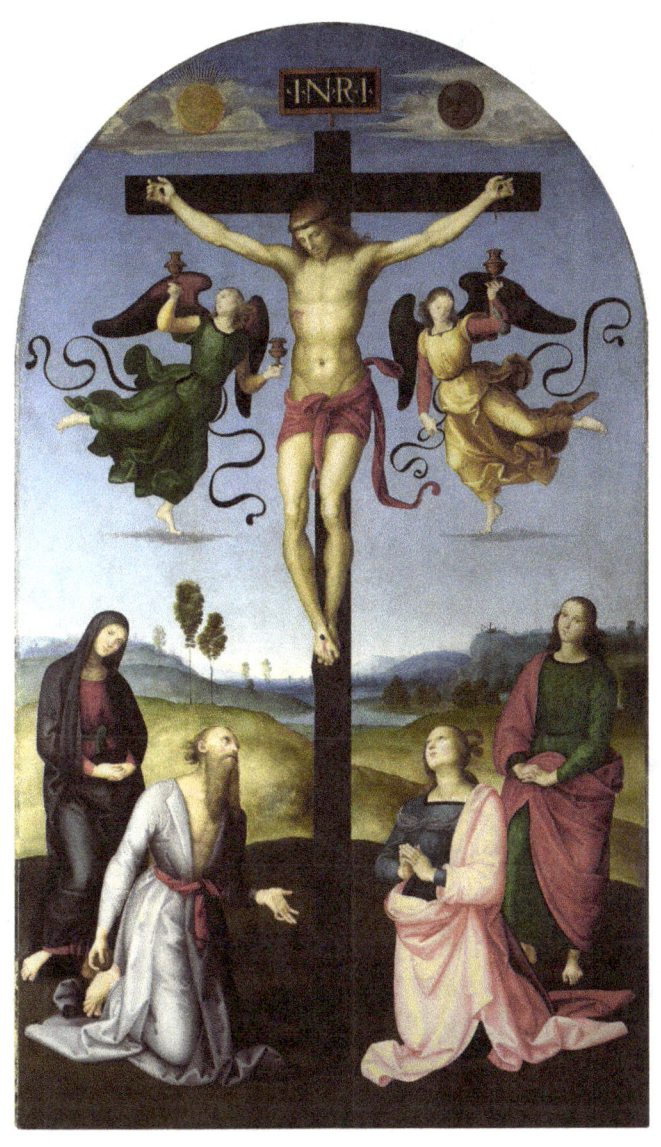

Rafael (1483–1520), *Crucifixion*, 1503,
National Gallery, London, Great Britain.

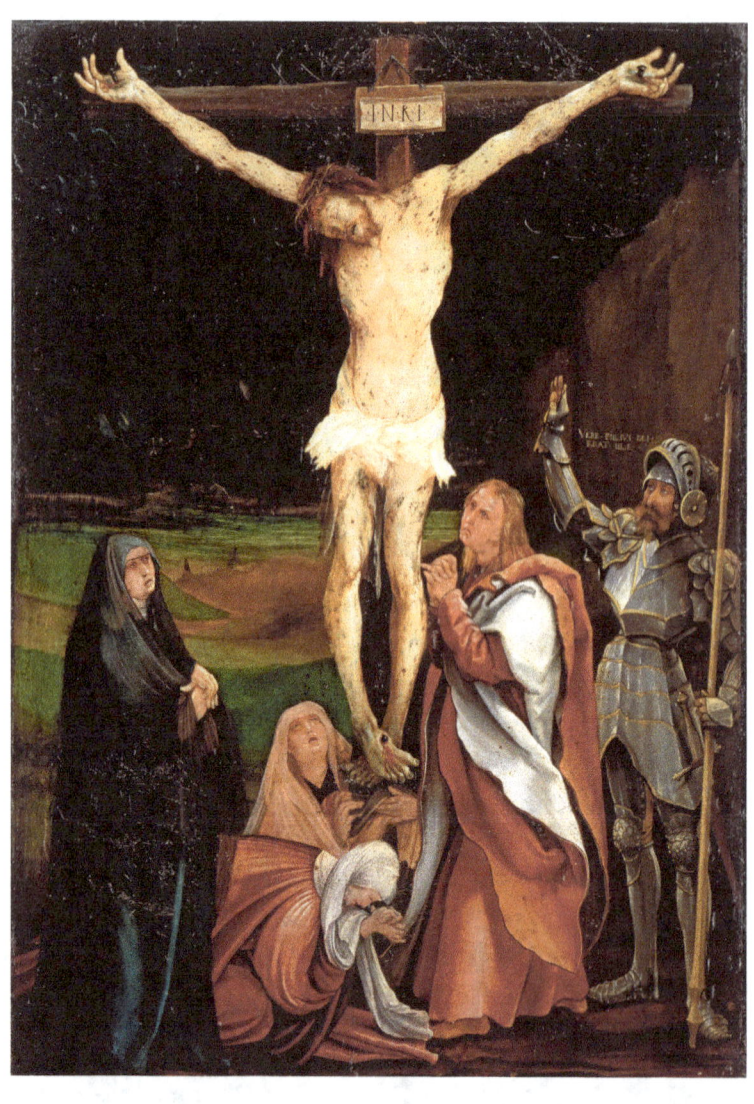

Matthias Grünewald (c. 1470–1528), *Crucifixion*, c. 1510,
Öffentliche Kunstsammlung, Basel, Switzerland.

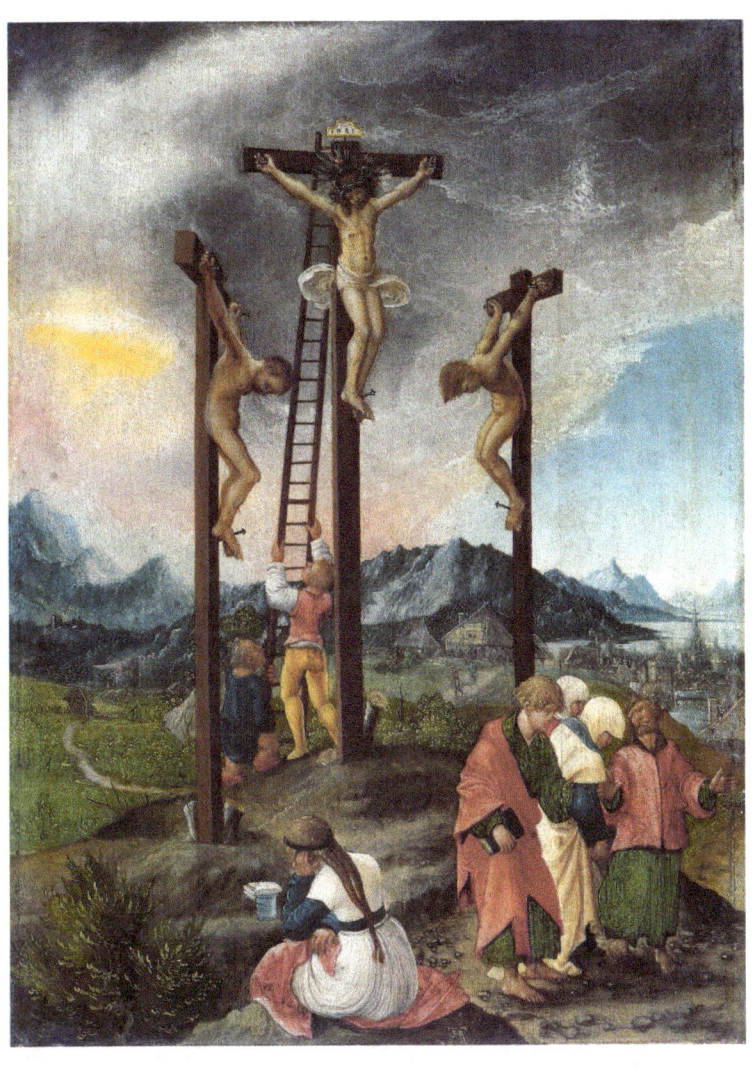

Albrecht Altdorfer (c. 1480—1538), *Crucifixion*, c. 1526,
Gemäldegalerie, Staatliche Museen, Berlin, Germany.

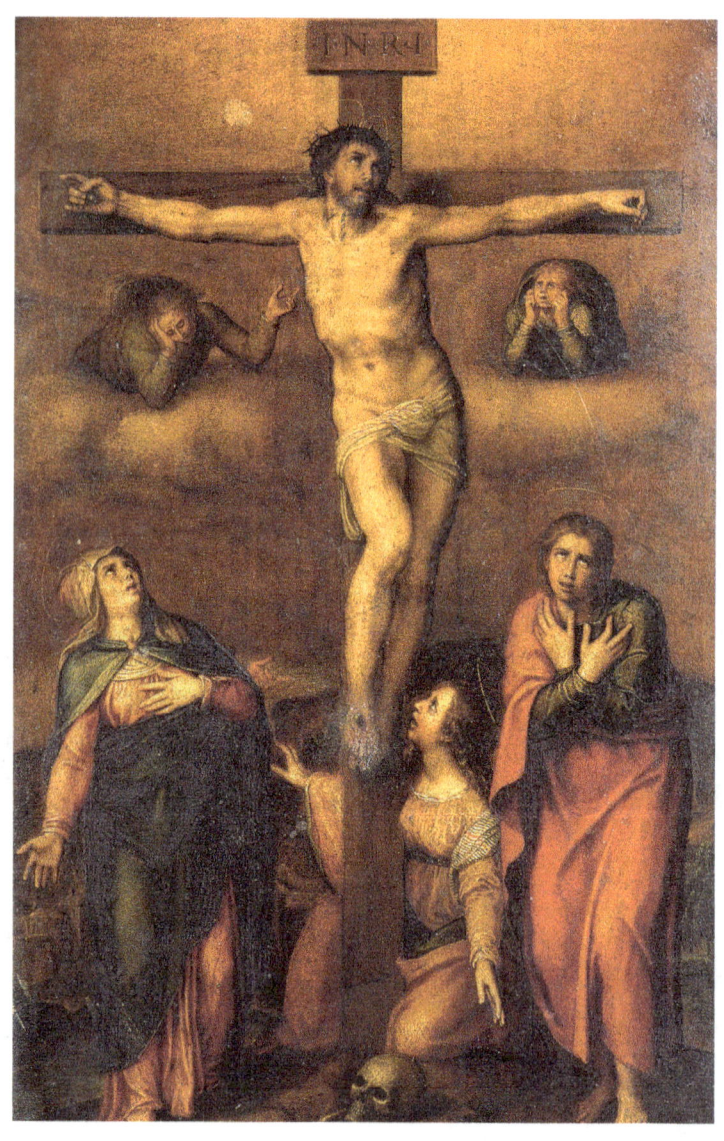

Michelangelo (1475–1564), *Crucifixion*, ca. 1540,
Concatedral de Santa Maria de la Redonda, Logrono, Spain.

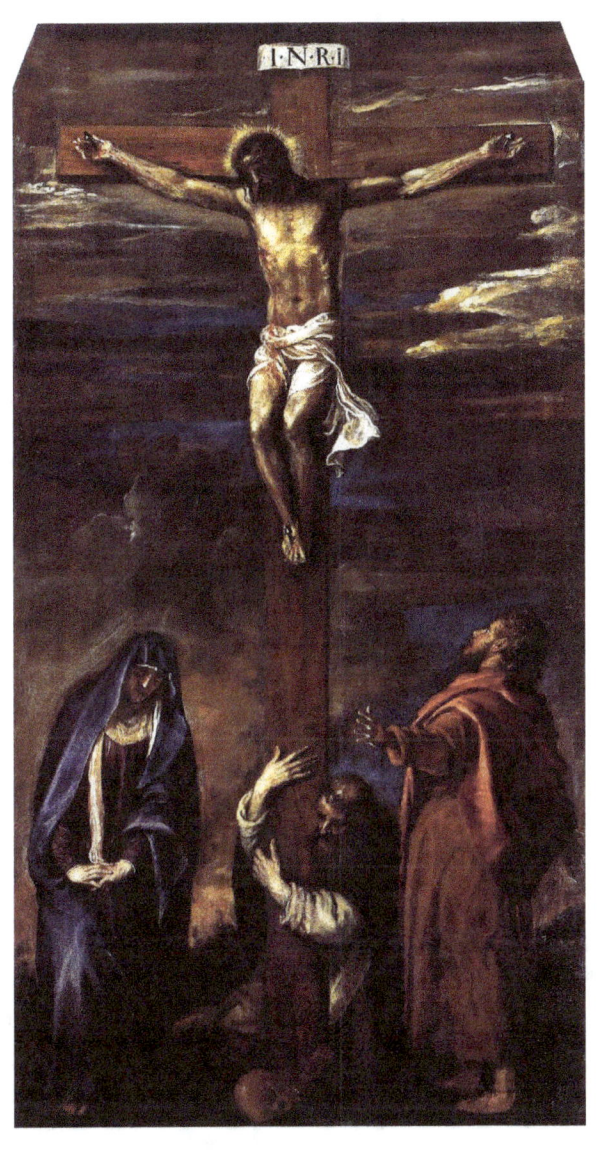

Titian (Tiziano Vecellio; c. 1488/90–1576), *Crucifixion*, 1558,
San Domenico, Ancona, Italy.

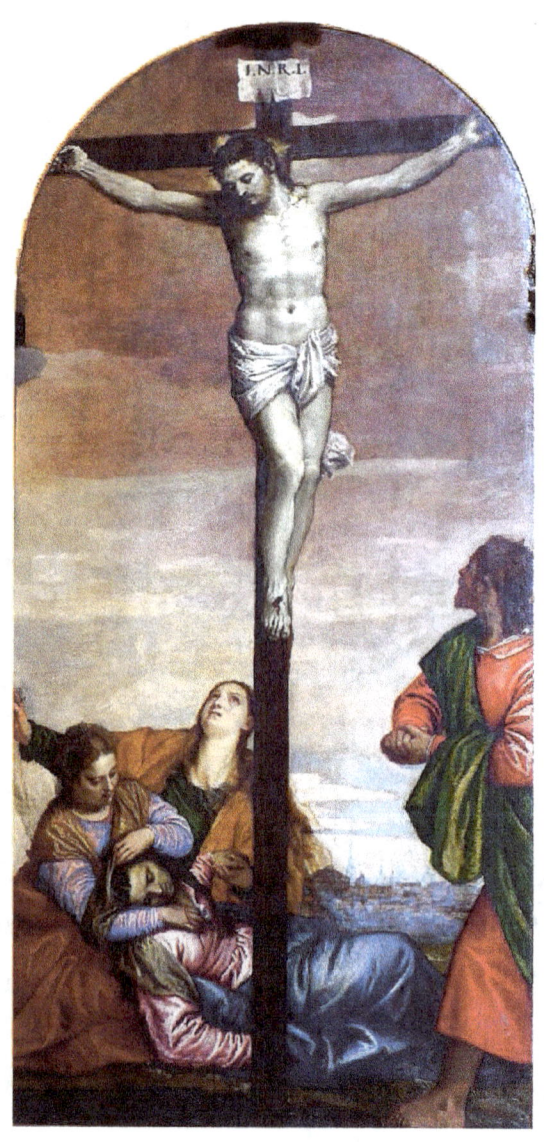

Paolo Veronese (1528–1588), *Christ on the Cross, the three Marys and St. John the Baptist*, ca. 1570, S. Sebastiano, Venice, Italy.

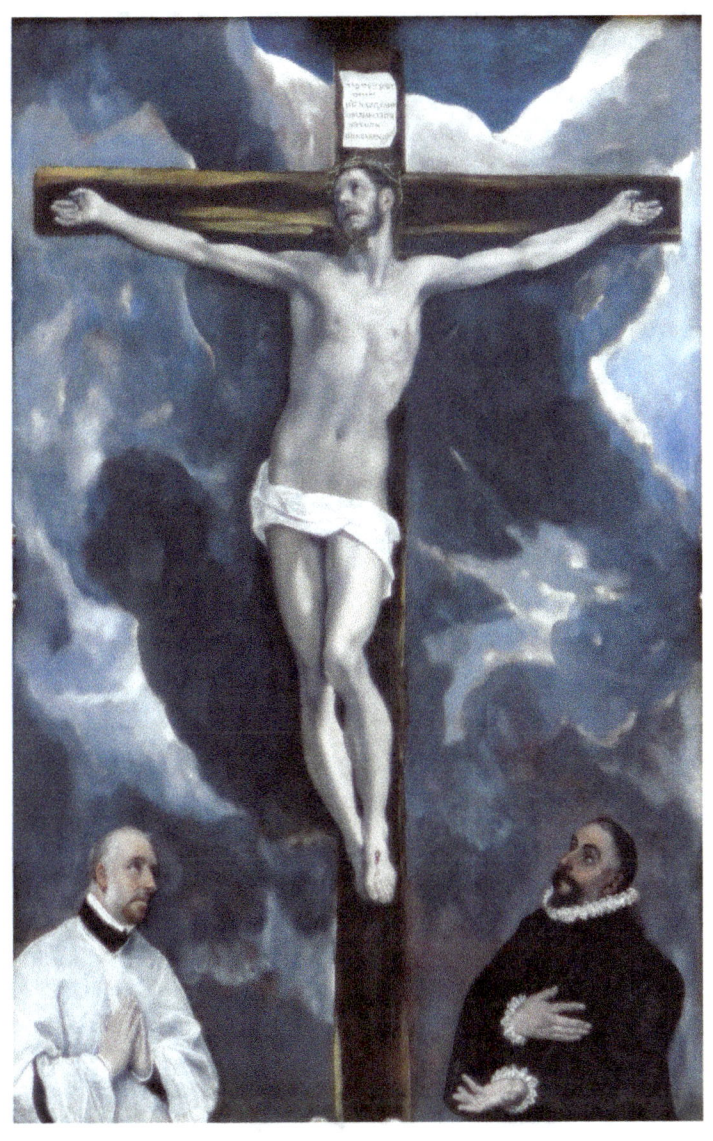

El Greco (1541–1614), *Christ on the Cross*, c. 1580,
Louvre, Paris, France.

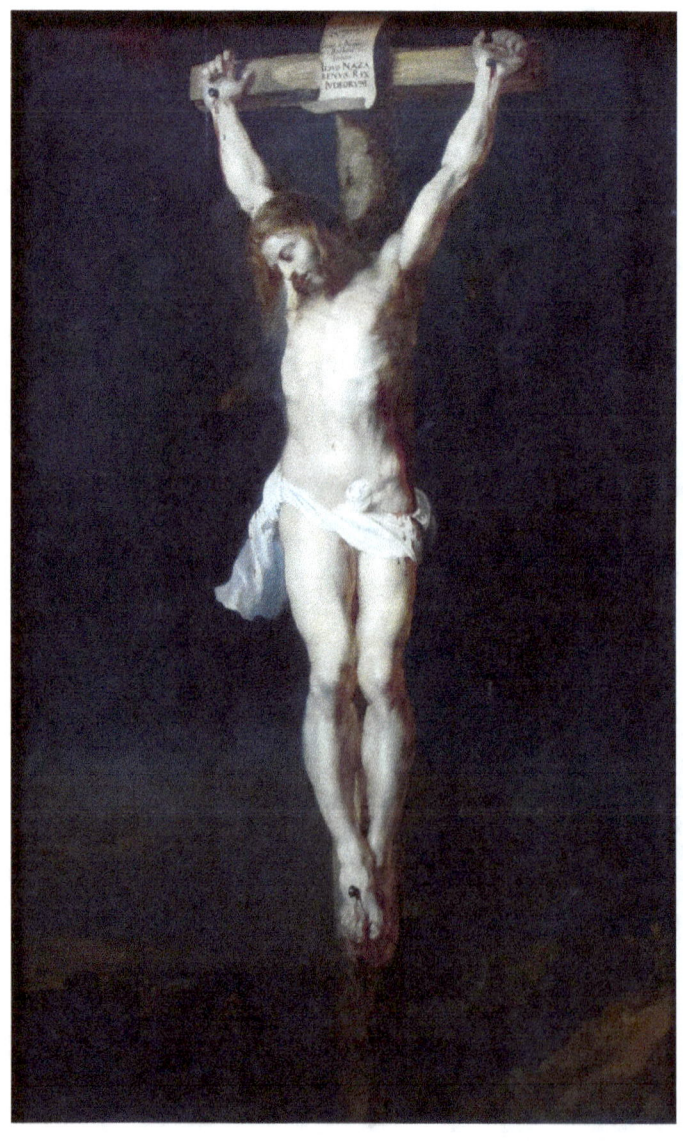

Peter Paul Rubens (1577–1640), *Christ on the Cross*, 1615–16,
Alte Pinakothek, Bayerische Staatsgemäldesammlungen, Munich, Germany.

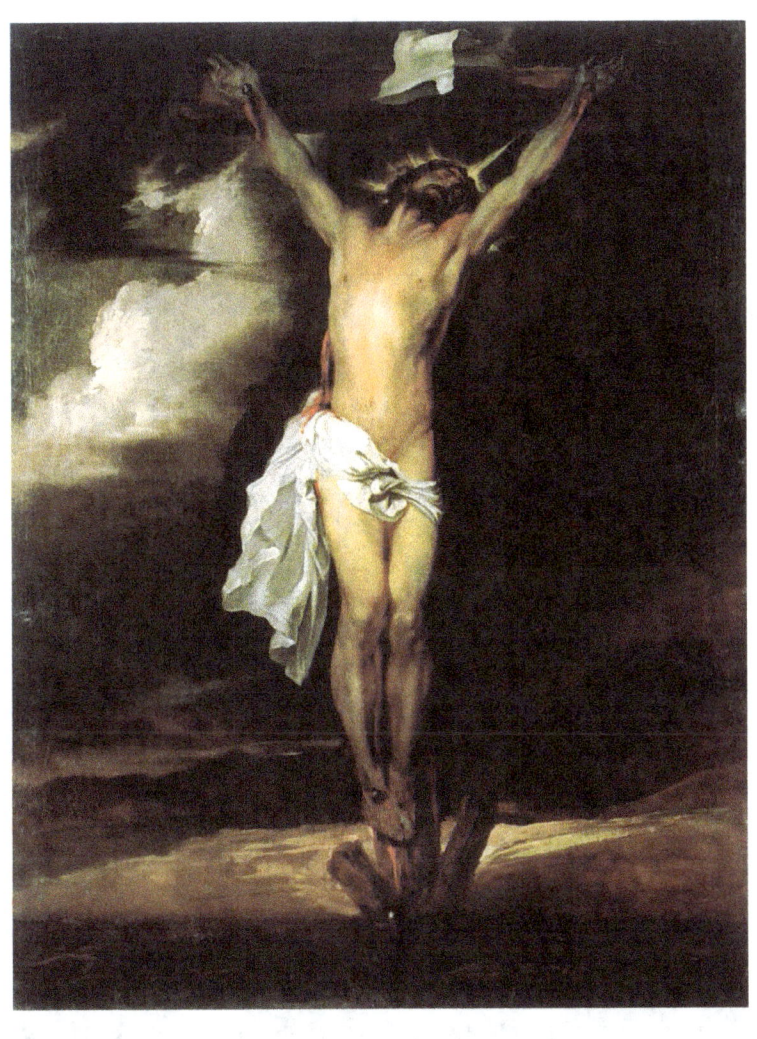

Anthony van Dyck (1599–1641), *Crucifixion*, 1622,
Museo Nazionale di Capodimonte, Naples, Italy.

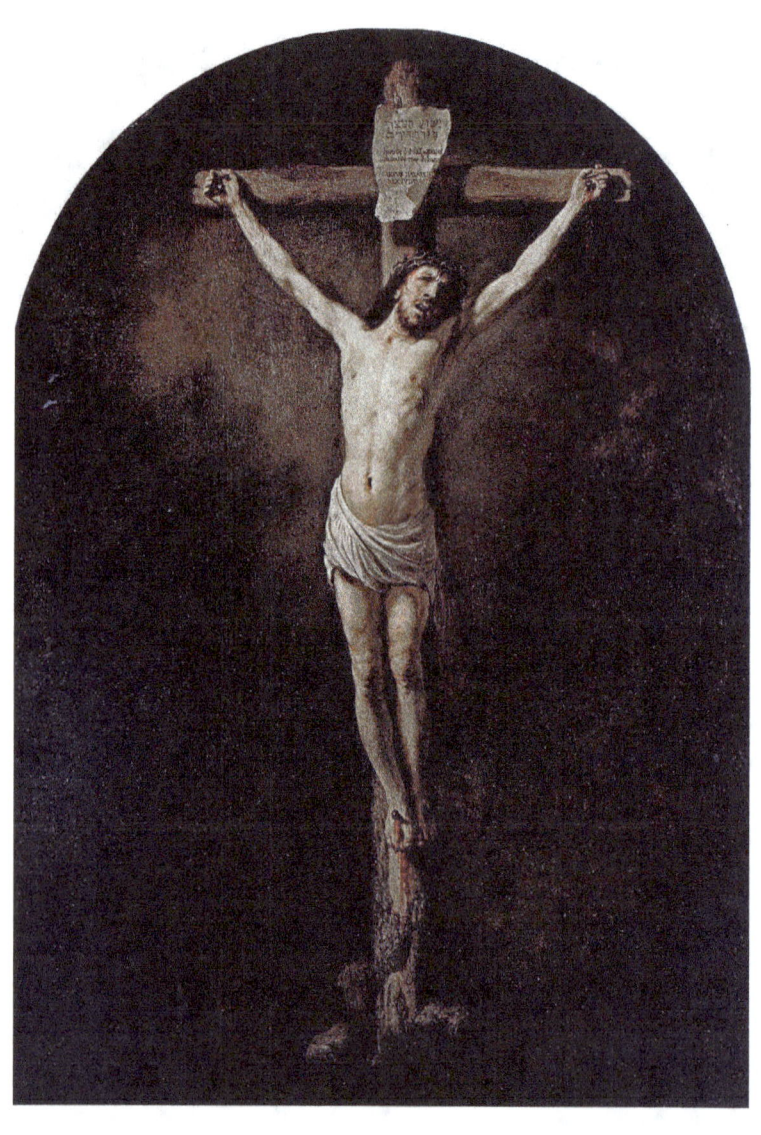

Rembrandt (1606–1669), *Crucifixion of Jesus*, 1631,
Church of St. Vincent, Lot-et-Garonne, France.

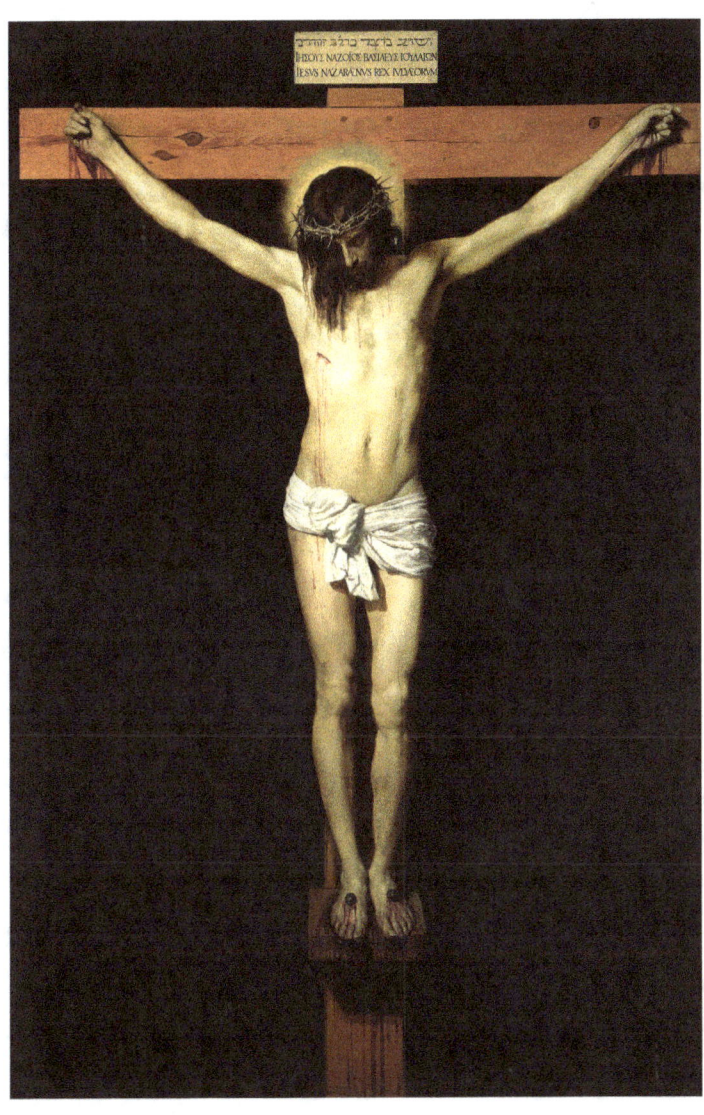

Diego Rodriguez Velazquez (1599–1660), *Christ Crucified*, ca. 1632,
Museo del Prado, Madrid, Spain.

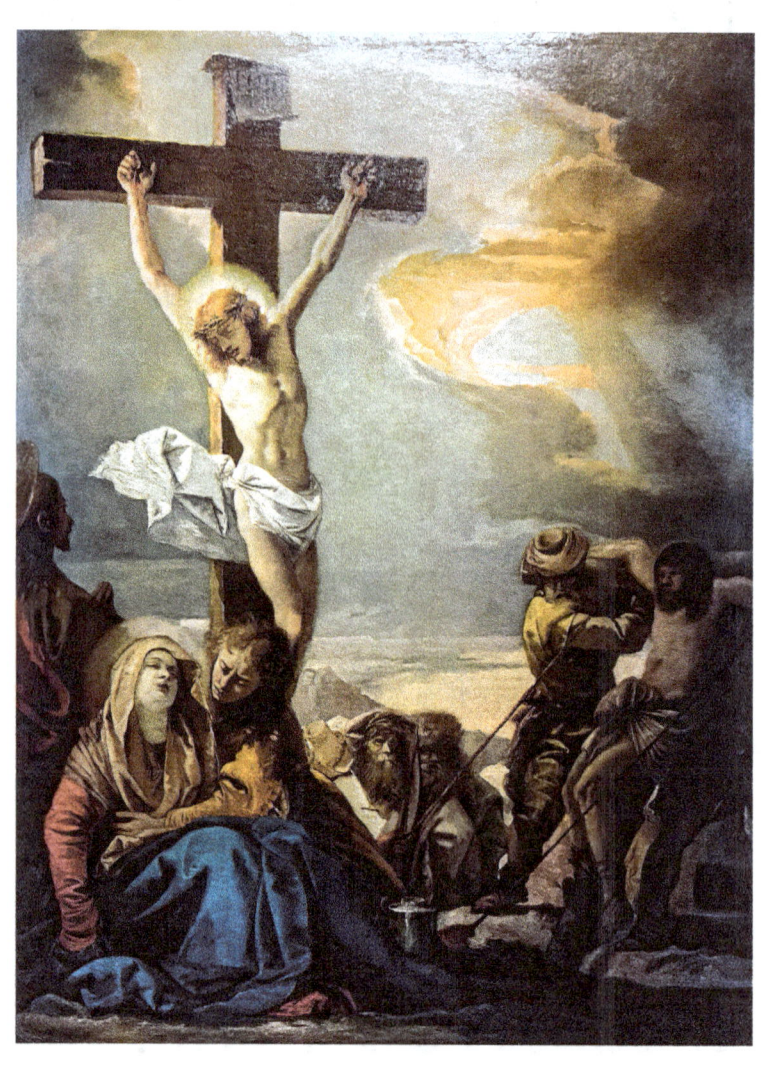

Giovanni Domenico Tiepolo (1727–1804),
Christ's Death on the Cross, 1749, S. Polo, Venice, Italy.

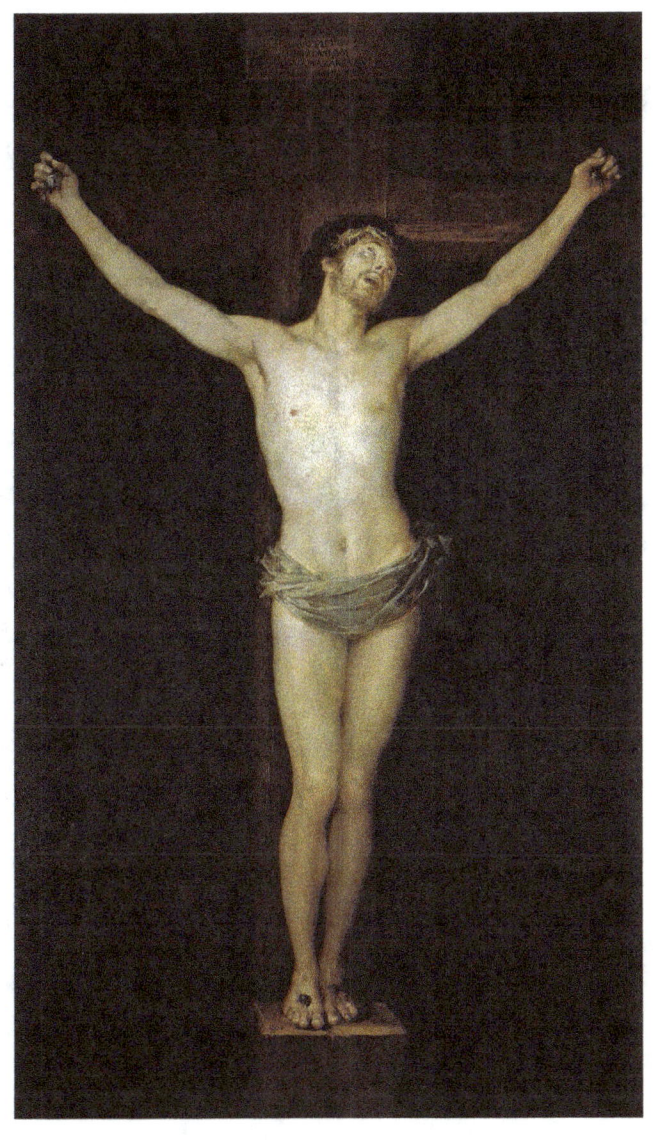

Francisco De Goya Y Lucientes (1746–1828), *Christ Crucified*, 1780,
Museo del Prado, Madrid, Spain.

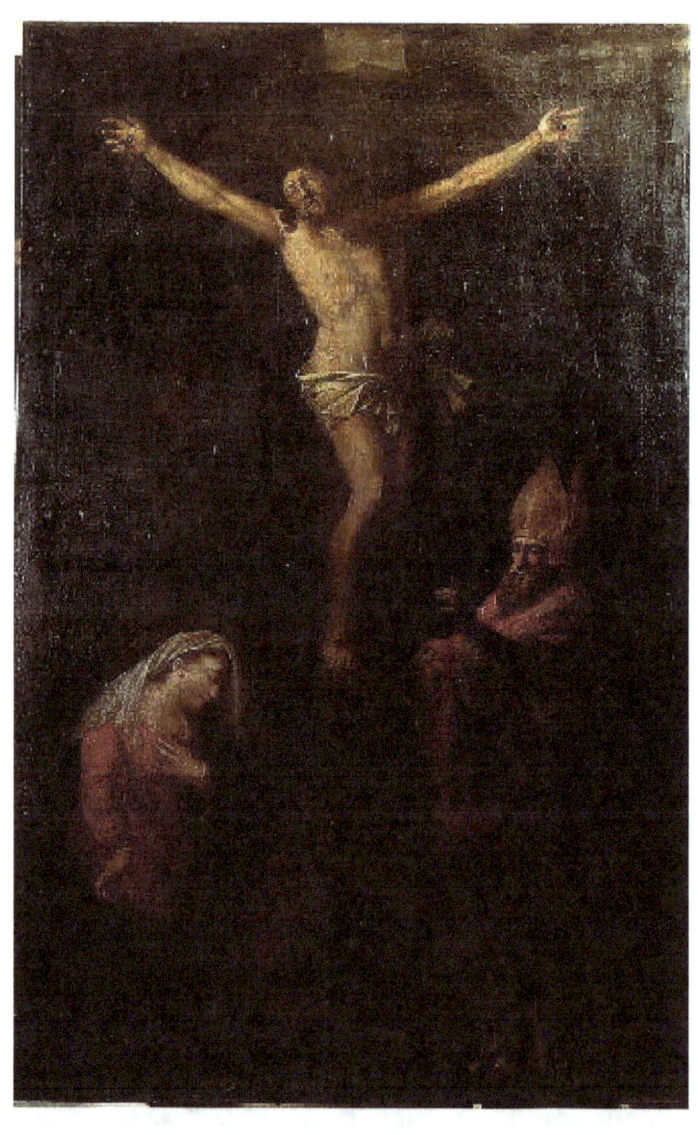

Jean Auguste Dominique Ingres (1780–1867), *The Crucifixion*, 1809, Musée Ingres, Montauban, France.

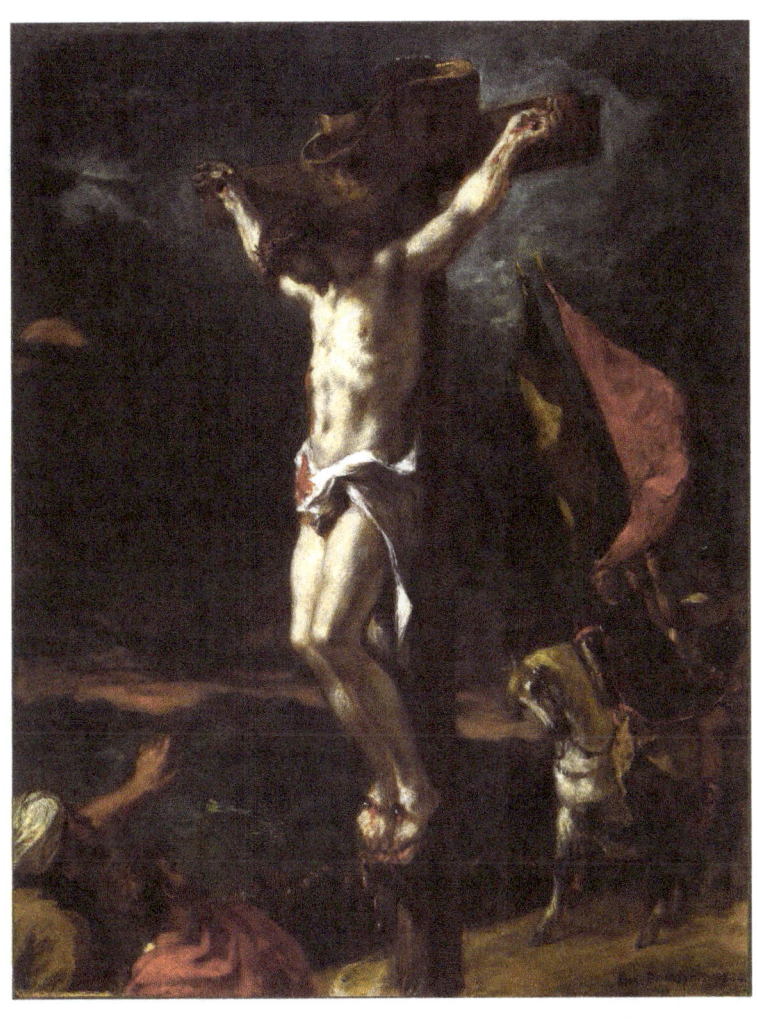

Eugene Delacroix (1798–1863), *Crucifixion*, 1848,
Museum Boijmans Van Beuningen, Rotterdam, Netherlands.

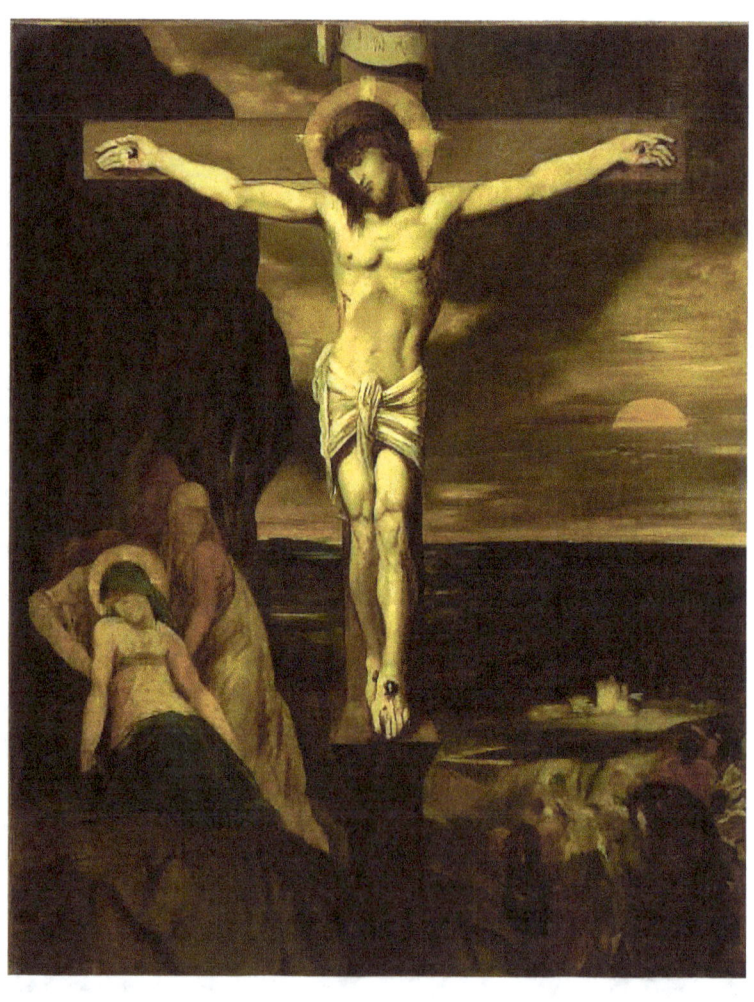

Gustave Moreau (1826–1898), The Stations of the Cross,
12th station: *Christ Dying on the Cross*, 1862,
Eglise Notre Dame de Decazeville, Place Wilson, Decazeville, France.

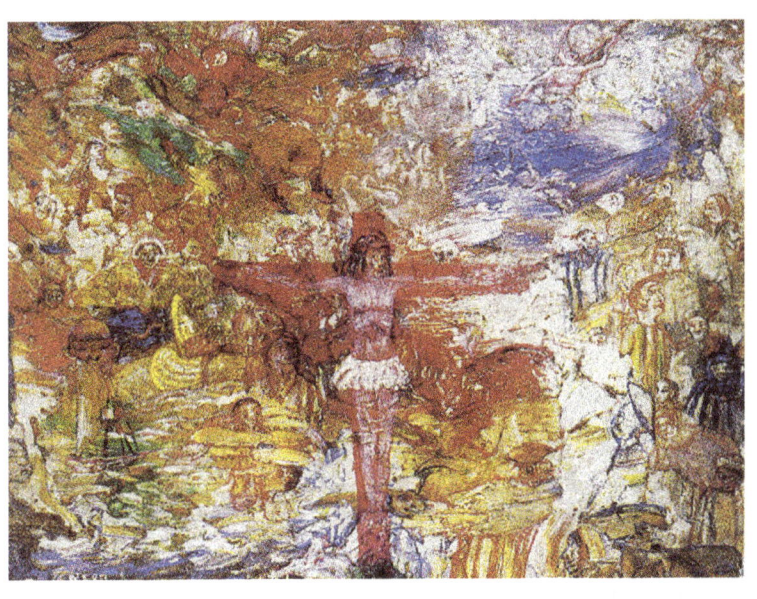

James Ensor (1860–1949), *Christ in Agony*, 1888,
Galerie Bellier, Paris, France.

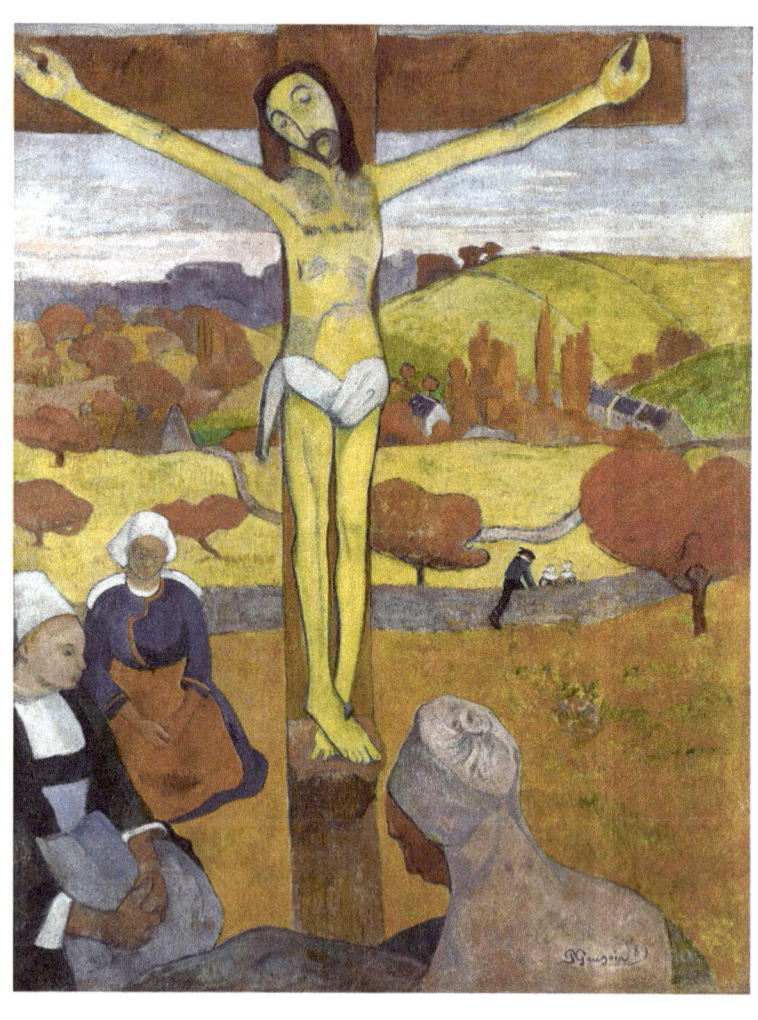

Paul Gauguin (1848–1903), *Yellow Christ*, 1889,
Albright–Knox Art Gallery, Buffalo, N.Y., USA.

Chapter Three

THE CRUCIFIXION IN EXPRESSIONISM

EXPRESSIONISM WAS THE FIRST ART MOVEMENT to explore the new possibilities of the traditional Christian narrative. Expressionist tendencies existed in art long before the twentieth century. In a certain way, modern art was always about expression—the expression of the artist's individuality and style, personal feelings, and emotions. Twentieth-century Expressionism turned this facet of art into its primary focus and ultimate creed. Art's essence and significance in the new movement would consist of self-expression, and such a preoccupation would dominate over all other artistic needs and concerns. The first group of painters to proclaim this approach was the Fauvists.

Fauvism was a short-lived movement that flourished in France at the beginning of the century between 1904 and 1907. Its French name *Les Fauves* meant "wild beasts" and suggested the shocking freedom with which these artists broke the creative boundaries and conventions of the day. French painters Henry Matisse (1869–1954), André Derain (1880–1954), and Maurice Vlaminck (1876–1958) were the prominent representatives of the movement that reached its peak in 1906 when Matisse exhibited at the Salon des Indépendants his programmatic painting *Joie de Vivre* (Joy of Life).

The painting, which depicts nude women joyfully playing and dancing in the forest near the beach, faithfully reflects the central tenets of Fauvist experimentation. Pure and vi-

125

brant colors, distortions in drawing and perspective provide freedom of pictorial expression. As H. W. Janson points out in *A History of Art*: "What makes the picture so revolutionary is its radical simplicity, its 'genius of omission': everything that possibly can be, has been left out or stated by implication only, yet the scene retains the essentials of plastic form and spatial depth."[116] In his "Notes of a Painter," Matisse himself remarks about his art: "What I am after, above all, is expression... the purpose of a painter must not be considered as separate from his pictorial means, and these pictorial means must be the more complete..., the deeper is his thought."[117] The main content of Matisse's art was this very *joie de vivre*, which he was translating into his canvases. He remarks in another passage: "What interests me most is neither still life nor landscape but the human figure. It is through it that I best succeed in expressing the nearly religious feeling that I have towards life."[118]

Although the Fauvists succeeded in putting the idea of self-expression on the century's art map, their vision was quite far from what one usually thinks of twentieth-century Expressionism. Fauvism cultivated joy, pleasure, and happiness—in a word, positive attitudes, which would be lacking in later versions of the movement. The development of twentieth-century Expressionism is traditionally associated with the opposite negative feelings and emotions—fear, anxiety, sadness, and sorrow. That makes it closer and a true successor to nineteenth-century Symbolism, preoccupied with the themes of decadence and growing moral decay of the *fin-de-ciècle* European society.

---

[116] H. W. Janson, with Dora Jane Janson, *A History of Art: A Survey of the Visual Arts from the Dawn of History to the Present Day*, 3rd ed., (1st ed. 1962), London: Thames and Hudson, 1981, 632.

[117] Chipp, *Theories of Modern Art*, 1968, 131–32.

[118] Ibid, 135.

In this sense, the real beginning of Expressionism took place in Germany in 1905 with the forming of the Dresden group of artists who called themselves *Die Brücke* or The Bridge. Unsurprisingly, Germany became the birthplace and the movement's home. Unlike most nations of Europe, Germans had achieved political unification relatively late, in 1871, due to the Franco-Prussian War of 1870–71. The "Iron Chancellor," Otto von Bismark, defeated Napoleon III. After his victory, at the meeting at Versailles, he joined the States of Southern Germany in the North German Confederation. By the turn of the century, Germany became one of Europe's "troubled" nations, eager to compete with its neighbors and challenge the new democratic order spreading over Europe. Ahead of Germany was the defeat in two World Wars and the terrible atrocities of the Nazi regime. At the dawn of the century, the most discerning German-speaking artists had an intuitive foreboding of the looming national disasters. They reflected in their artworks the nightmarish atmosphere of despair and disillusionment.

In addition to the historical circumstances, German artists were more inclined toward a pessimistic type of Expressionism because of their cultural and artistic heritage. For them, "expressionism" meant "anti-naturalistic subjectivism," a tendency commonly characteristic of German culture and art at moments of stress. One is reminded, for example, of the "art of Dürer, Altdorfer, Bosch, and others on the eve of the Reformation [which] is marked by expressionistic qualities and particularly by an apocalyptic anxiety that appeals strongly to our century." Furthermore, "[t]heir contemporary Grünewald, painter of the famous Isenheim altarpiece of about 1515, has [also] inspired admiration and direct imitation"[119] on the part of modern German Expressionists.

---

[119] *Concepts of Modern Art,* 31.

The Bridge, the first modern twentieth-century group of German Expressionist painters, survived for eight years—from 1905 to 1913 when it was dissolved. One of the Dresden group founders was a young artist Ernst Ludwig Kirchner (1880–1938), who wrote in his Manifesto of Expressionism in 1906: "Everyone belongs with us who, directly and without dissimulation, expresses that which drives him to create."[120]

In the words of one scholar, the Dresden Expressionists were attracted to the concept of art "as original creativity, not as technique; their goal was something that they believed could not be taught... their goal was the essence of art, above all form and color."[121] As for painterly practice, they brought to their canvases what had already been explored by the Fauvists and was characteristic of Expressionism in general—namely, compositional and figurative distortion as a way to transmit emotionally charged messages.

Another group of German Expressionists was the artists in Munich who associated with the art magazine *Der Blaue Reiter* (The Blue Rider). Wassily Kandinsky (1866–1944) and Franc Marc (1880–1916) were the two editors of this almanac, the only issue of which was published in print in 1912. They also organized a couple of exhibitions in Munich in the same years of 1911–12. Along with their fellow painter friends, they formed the group's backbone.

The founders of the Munich school—Kandinsky and Marc—gave it its distinctive flavor. One of the significant innovations of twentieth-century Expressionism "was the discovery that abstract compositions could serve... as effectively as subject pictures" and that the "expressive power of colors

---

[120] Ibid, 36.

[121] Wolf-Dieter Dube, *The Expressionists*, trans. from German Mary Whittall, (original printing 1972), London: Thames and Hudson, 1985, 25.

and shapes, of brushstrokes and texture, of size and scale [can] be sufficient"[122] in conveying emotions. Kandinsky laid the ground for this discovery by producing the first abstract composition in 1910. The work of Franc Marc moved in the same direction—from object-oriented painting to an art of abstract expression.

German Expressionism flourished in painting during the years before World War I. It experienced a relative decline in the postwar world when confronted by the New Objectivity movement, which sought to revive the natural and eradicate the subjective, especially in its abstract-expressionist version. Still, expressionist tendencies entered German post-World War I literature, cinema, theatre, and architecture. In 1919, the art and design school named Bauhaus opened in Weimar. It pioneered the theory and practice of modern industrial art and architectural design, and Kandinsky, along with another Blue Rider member, Paul Klee, was among its prominent teachers.

Because of its intense emotionality, twentieth-century Expressionism seemed the ideal medium for religious art, especially depicting the Passion of Christ. It seems natural that many Expressionist artists painted their version of the Crucifixion. It also comes as no surprise that Expressionist Crucifixions often dwell on the physical pain and suffering of Christ—following the tradition of the sixteenth-century German painter Matthias Grünewald. Grünewald's *Basel Crucifixion* (1510), according to one scholar, "is feverish, convulsive and saturated in suffering" while displaying the qualities of an "almost hysterical mysticism."[123] *The Crucifixion* by Emil Nolde (1867–1956), made in 1911–12, represents, perhaps, the best-known example of this approach as applied to the new artistic practices of the twentieth century.

---

[122] *Concepts of Modern Art*, 30.
[123] *Religious Painting*, 45, 47.

EMIL NOLDE (1867–1956)

A work becomes a work of art when one re-evaluates the values of nature and adds one's own spirituality.

Emil Nolde

EMIL NOLDE (BORN EMIL HANSEN) WAS an Expressionist painter who created, in the words of one art critic, a "unique pictorial language [–] a language which endowed the mystical spirit of the North and a turbulent personal fantasy with a command of color, unprecedented in power."[124] Nolde made his first oil painting late in life—when he was already thirty years old. In his thirties, he studied art in Munich, Paris, and Italy, and in 1906 he joined the Expressionist group *Die Brücke*. Nolde was a member of the Dresden group for a short period, but he is considered one of its most potent representatives. In 1907, he resigned from the group and remained a solitary painter with a highly individual style pursuing pictorial excellence for the rest of his life.

Nolde had his first solo exhibition in 1905 in Dresden, and by the 1920s, he became a renowned artist. He held an honorary doctorate from the University of Kiel and had one-person shows and retrospective exhibitions all over Germany. In the art world, Nolde was known for his "persistent anti-intellectualism," "admiration for the primitive and the primeval,"[125] and his attachment to the German art of 'blood and soil.' When Hitler rose to power in Germany, Nolde didn't leave the coun-

---

[124] Peter Selz, *Emil Nolde*, New York: The Museum of Modern Art, 1968, 72.

[125] Ibid, 9, 10.

try, hoping to find common ground with the new regime. Fortunately for him, this didn't happen. The Nazis labeled Nolde a 'degenerate artist.' They removed his works from German museums and forbade him to exhibit, sell or paint. After the end of World War II and the Nazi persecution, fame and recognition came back to Nolde, never to leave him again.

From an early age in his life, Nolde was attracted to religion. He "frequently seems to have experienced deep religious feelings and mystic identifications with Christ's Passion."[126] Religion and spirituality occupy an important place also in his artistic endeavors. Nolde's intense religiosity contributed to the formation of his Expressionist painting style. Like many other Expressionists, he searched for some spiritual dimension in his art. In his own words, the "techniques of Impressionism suggested to me only a means, but no satisfactory end... A work becomes a work of art when one re-evaluates the values of nature and adds one's own spirituality."[127] In his autobiography, Nolde also said: "Knowledge and science are inadequate when it comes to the simplest questions about time and eternity, about God, about heaven and Satan. Faith alone has no limitations."[128]

During his career, Nolde produced numerous paintings, etchings, and woodcuts devoted to religious themes. The period between 1909 and 1912 became the most prolific in this respect. In three years, he completed a series of religious paintings, including *The Last Supper, The Pentecost, The Derision of Christ,* and *The Crucifixion.* "Without much intention, knowledge," confesses Nolde, "I had followed an irresistible desire to represent profound spirituality, religion, and tenderness."[129] Later, he also wrote about this time: "The concepts of the small

---

[126] Ibid, 9.
[127] Emil Nolde, from *Jahre der Kämpfe,* in *Theories of Modern Art,* 146.
[128] Ibid, 148.
[129] Ibid, 146.

boy, who during the long winter months used to spend all his evenings earnestly reading the Bible, were reawakened. They were pictures of the richest Oriental fantasy. They kept rising in my imagination until the adult man and artist could paint them in dreamlike inspiration."[130] Nolde got so immersed in his work on the first of these canvases, *The Last Supper*, that he developed almost an obsession with the process of painting it: "I painted and painted, hardly knowing whether it was night or day, whether I was a human being or only a painter. I saw the painting when I went to bed, it confronted me during the night, it faced me when I woke up. I painted happily."[131]

Even more characteristic was that Nolde's intense painterly enthusiasm was coupled with his utterly non-canonical view on the climax of the Christian narrative. He completed his most ambitious project of the series—a sizeable nine-part cycle, *The Life of Christ* with a *Crucifixion* as its central panel—in 1912. Along with Nolde's other compositions on biblical events and characters, such as, for example, *Dance Around the Golden Calf* (1910) or *Mary of Egypt: The Conversion* (1912), the cycle reveals "devotional images to powerful and authentic statements about life, and its ultimate values [and it stands as a] myth-making representation of violence and tragedy."[132]

In defense of his approach to Crucifixion, Nolde argued that as a necessary condition for depicting those tragic events in the life of Christ truthfully, he should not have been restricted by Christian indoctrination of any kind. As he put it himself:

> I doubt that I could have painted with so much power the *Last Supper* and the *Pentecost*, both so deeply fraught with feeling, had I been bound by a rigid dogma and the letter of the Bible.

---

[130] Nolde, *Jahre der Kämpfe*, Berlin: Rembrandt Verlag, 1934, p. 189. Quoted in Selz, *Emil Nolde*, 24.

[131] Emil Nolde, from *Jahre der Kämpfe*, in *Theories of Modern Art*, 147.

[132] Selz, *Emil Nolde*, 27.

I had to be artistically free, not confronted by a God hard as steel like an Assyrian king, but with God inside of me, glowing and holy like the love of Christ. *The Last Supper* and *The Pentecost* marked the change from optical, external stimuli to values of inner conviction. They became milestones—in all likelihood, not only for my own work.[133]

Indeed, such a vision became the landmark of twentieth-century artistic development. It assigned intensely personal and universally spiritual significance to the event—a value transcending traditional boundaries of historical and dogmatic Christianity. The depiction of the crucified Christ acquired a new, highly individualized, and non-canonical dimension. It is of no surprise, therefore, that although Nolde may be considered one of the most significant twentieth-century religious painters, he "never found acceptance for his work among ecclesiastical authorities... none of his religious paintings was ever commissioned, or even [with rare exceptions] permanently installed in a church."[134]

---

[133] Emil Nolde, from *Jahre der Kämpfe*, in *Theories of Modern Art*, 149.
[134] Selz, *Emil Nolde*, 26–27.

GEORGES ROUAULT (1871–1958)

My art is not based on exaggeration...
I agree that the grotesque and the tragic
exist cheek by jowl in my works, but surely,
they are as closely jointed in life.

Georges Rouault

A FRENCH PRIMITIVIST, GEORGES ROUALT, WAS AN-
OTHER influential twentieth-century artist who freed "the
image of the Crucifixion, the 'capital sign of Christianity'...
from that academicism to which it seemed condemned for
two centuries, even in the works of great painters."[135] Georges
Henri Rouault was born to a family of a cabinetmaker. In his
youth, he worked as an apprentice to a stained-glass painter
and attended classes at the École des Arts Décoratifs in Paris.
Later, when Rouault decided to become a painter, he studied art at the École des Beaux-Arts in the studio of Gustave
Moreau, who considered him his favorite pupil.

Rouault belonged to the "generation of the Fauves." In the
early 1900s, he exhibited his works at the Salon d'Automne
with Matisse and other fellow artists. The common subjects in
his drawings and watercolors of that period were the workers
and peasants, clowns, acrobats, and prostitutes. Pierre Courthion points out: "Rouault always considered himself as above
all a manual worker...a descendent of those...who in earlier
times had built the cathedrals [and he] concentrated in his
paintings on...the lot of the simple people, the poor, the op-

---

[135] Jacques Maritain cites an opinion of Maurice Morel in Jacques
Maritain, *Georges Rouault*, New York: Harry N. Abrams Publishers,
1952, 20.

pressed, and the disinherited... "[136] Rouault also developed his unique artistic style in those years, which may be characterized as metaphysical primitivism. "Like it or not," he would write later, "I am just a poor primitive afloat on the bottomless sea of painting."[137] And, "like a true primitive, [Rouault] opened the eyes of that generation to the barbarous and the spontaneous."[138]

Rouault's art gained recognition slowly. In 1910 he had his first one-person show in his native Paris. In 1930 he had the first two exhibitions outside France—in London, New York, and Chicago. In the 1950s, his retrospective exhibitions were already held on the three continents of Europe, Asia, and America. Rouault's critique of contemporary bourgeois society and his compassion for the suffering of the ordinary people joined in his art with the depiction of religious subjects and, especially, the Passion of Christ—this acme of human cruelty and evil in the face of divine love and mercy. By the end of his life, Rouault was honored as a master artist. And, a French philosopher and Rouault's friend Jacques Maritain said that he was "now recognized as the greatest religious painter of our time, one of the greatest religious painters of the ages."[139]

As Maritain suggests further, one "cannot overemphasize the importance of the renewal that religious painting owes to Rouault."[140] Maritain defines Rouault's art style as "transfigurative realism." Art scholar Pierre Courthion uses a different expression—the "realism transcended."[141] Both, however, suggest the same kind of artistic expression that "is in no way

---

[136] Pierre Courthion, *Georges Rouault*, New York: Harry N. Abrams Publishers, 1977, 20.

[137] Ibid, 32.

[138] Ibid, 17.

[139] Jacques Maritain, *Georges Rouault*, 18.

[140] Maritain, *Georges Rouault*, 20.

[141] Courthion, *Rouault*, 17.

realism of material appearances [but] of the spiritual significance of what exists (and moves, and suffers, and loves, and
kills); it is realism permeated with the signs and dreams that
are commingled with the being of things."[142]

The two central themes in Rouault's paintings are the
spiritual focus of human existence—humanity's suffering and salvation. Moreover, these two motives merge into
his art with each other. On the one hand, Rouault revolts
"against the baseness and hypocrisy of a loveless world."[143]
He portrays the passion of humanity, its evil, and cruelty, but
"in the disinherited people that he depicts for us, there can
be seen glimmering the persistent light of redemption."[144] So,
on the other hand, when Rouault paints his religious subjects
and, mainly, the Passion of Christ, he expresses this symbolic
gesture of bringing salvation through divine suffering. It is
this "moving correspondence between a biblical psalm and
some aspect of contemporary life[, the] synthesis of the eternal and the transitory" that sustains Rouault's art and turns
it into "an outpouring of the heart, the unfolding of a secret
launched into space and time, a form of prayer."[145]

As Jacques Maritain attests, biblical paintings were, for
Rouault, "a lifelong effort which has never been interrupt-
ed."[146] Rouault's first experiments in this direction date back
to the very dawn of his artistic career—to 1891–92 when as
a young disciple of Moreau, he produced "a series of religious
subjects in a Rembrandtesque style."[147] In 1918, Rouault began his work on Christ's Passion, including the *Crucifixion*—
"a theme that Rouault frequently treated, especially from 1918

---

142 Maritain, *Georges Rouault*, 12.
143 Ibid, 14.
144 Courthion, *Rouault*, 17.
145 Ibid, 25, 23.
146 Maritain, *Georges Rouault*, 18.
147 Courthion, *Rouault*, 59.

to 1950." As Courthion explains, he "shows us the drama of the Cross on two levels: that of the historical event, a reminder of Christ's death in the presence of the Virgin and St. John; and that of Christ on the Cross, who seems to travel toward us, across space and time."[148] In one particular *Crucifixion*, finished around 1939, Rouault uses the arms of Christ as a metaphor for heavenly love and compassion. Christ's hands are cut off by the edge of the painting, suggesting that the hands of God are limitless and embrace the whole world with the fire of mercy, redemption, and sacrifice.

Rouault's artistic achievements are monumental because they are never in the mainstream; they never follow "the fluctuations of external events." As Courthion points out, the "people in his paintings do not wear the costumes of a particular period; their dress is timeless, their expression is the universal expression of [hu]mankind."[149] However, the monumentality and greatness of Rouault's paintings are most of all revealed in their inner grace and the artist's "faith [that is] marked by a respectful modesty, a disinclination to inscribe very patch of canvas with the image of that Divine Being who was always his ultimate model."[150]

---

148 Ibid, 120.
149 Courthion, *Rouault*, 34.
150 Ibid, 22.

OSKAR KOKOSCHKA (1886–1980)

> *I cannot paint everybody. It is only people*
> *who are on my antennae… certain people*
> *whom I discovered an affinity with—with*
> *one facet of my own being.*
>
> Oscar Kokoschka

ONE MORE EXAMPLE OF THE AVANT-GARDE pictorial treatment of the Crucifixion comes from the art of Oscar Kokoschka. An Austrian-born painter, poet, and playwright, Oskar Kokoschka is often called an Expressionist *par excellence.* He studied art at the *Kunstgewerbeschule* of the Austrian Museum for Art and Industry and had his first solo exhibition in 1910 at the Folkwang Museum in Hagen. Kokoschka maintained contact with the members of the *Blaue Reiter* group and friendly relations with many other Expressionist writers and actors. In 1937 the Nazis confiscated hundreds of Kokoschka's paintings from German museums and counted him among the so-called 'degenerate artists.'

Oskar Kokoschka lived a very long life and created numerous paintings devoted to various subjects. Well-traveled, he produced many landscapes and cityscapes. He made commissioned portraits of state officials, for example, of the Czech President Thomas G. Masaryk. Having been active in the anti-Nazi émigré movement during the Second World War, Kokoschka created a series of anti-war paintings. He also dealt in his art with literary, mythological, and religious subjects. The exhibitions of Kokoschka's paintings occurred worldwide, including in Germany, Italy, France, Austria, Switzerland, England, and Japan.

"As an artist [he] was an individualist, combining elements of Expressionism and Symbolism," says Richard Calvocoressi in his book about Kokoschka, "with a sense of space and movement inherited from the Baroque, to create images of tremendous vitality and strength."[151] In the history of the Expressionist movement, Kokoschka is best known for his portraits in which "he concentrated less on giving a literal record of his sitters than on portraying their psychological traits. Factual likeness, though not to be ignored, was subservient to capturing the emotional mood or feel of his subjects." "In this respect,"—Calvocoressi suggests,—"Kokoschka differs substantially from his German Expressionist contemporaries—in whose work the portrait plays a relatively minor role."[152]

Critics praised Kokoschka for his so-called "X-ray eyes" and his gift of capturing the souls of his models on canvases. They often compared the distortions, deformities, and exaggerations seen in his portraits to the art of caricature. However, Kokoschka's contribution to contemporary portraiture goes much deeper. He "can lay claim to have painted the first existential image of alienated modern man, in which the individual is stripped of mask and pretense—or, to use his own word, 'opened.'"[153] Late in his life and following his artistic philosophy Kokoschka "emerged as a public figure—to some a prophet—who spoke out against the dehumanizing effect of mass society whenever he detected it, in art as much as in politics."[154]

---

[151] Richard Calvocoressi, *Kokoschka: Paintings*, New York: Rizzoli International Publications, 1992, 7.

[152] Ibid, 7, 9.

[153] Ibid, 11.

[154] Ibid, 24.

Among the old masters whose art influenced Kokoschka was the Spanish painter El Greco, whom he considered a fellow Expressionist. The inspiration for El Greco's style is discernible in Kokoschka's portraits "with their frontality, austerity and, not least, dark, almost black backgrounds," as well as in his religious paintings, including *Crucifixion*. As Calvocoressi puts it: "The figures in Kokoschka's small religious pictures probably derive from El Greco, their pale, drawn faces, elongated bodies, and stylized hand gestures evoking a mystical dimension in keeping with the subject matter."[155]

Kokoschka's *Crucifixion*, made in 1911, displays a gloomy, almost nightmarish vision of the tragedy reflecting the artist's spiritual mood and emotional dispositions. In his essay "On the Nature of Visions," written a year later in 1912, Kokoschka describes the nature of his religious art in words that evoke Nolde's attitude toward the subject. He says, "...we must harken closely to our inner voice... 'The Word became flesh and dwelt among us.' And then the inner core breaks free—now feebly and now violently—from the words within which it dwells like a charm. 'It happened to me according to the Word.'"[156]

---

[155] Ibid, 11.

[156] Oscar Kokoschka, "On the Nature of Visions," in *Theories of Modern Art*, 172. The last sentence of the quotation alludes to Mary's reply to the angel at the Annunciation: "Let it be done to me according to your word" (Luke 1:37–38).

OTTO DIX (1890-1969)

We don't have to discuss my pictures—we can see them.—I base everything on the visible.—What I most like to do is to see the fundamental themes of humankind with my own eyes in a new light.

Otto Dix

OTTO DIX WAS AN EXPRESSIONIST PAINTER whose artistic creed reflected the very essence of the aesthetic program of the movement. He wrote once about art: "What is important in the picture is not the objects, but the personal message of the artist. In other words, not the *what*, but the *how*." He continued: "The first thing that the artist demands from the observer is not loud discussion but modest silence. For there is little in an artwork that can be explained, its substance can't be explained; it can only be contemplated."[157]

Otto Dix produced his first drawings and paintings in 1908, and he then studied art at the Dresden Commercial Art College between 1909 and 1914. In 1920 he participated in the first Dada Fair in Berlin and the "German Expressionists" exhibitions in Darmstadt and Berlin. His first solo exhibition was shown in 1926 in Berlin and Munich. In his long and productive career as a painter, Otto Dix created hundreds of artworks, participated in numerous national and international exhibitions, and received various honors, prizes, and awards.

Although not formally religious (he left his Protestant faith), Otto Dix had a deep appreciation and thorough knowledge of the Bible, the book he admired for its cultural and historical legacy. Late in his life, Dix told his friends that "the

---

[157] Quoted in Eva Karcher, *Otto Dix, 1891–1969*, London—New York: Taschen, 2002, (original ed. 1989), 198.

141

Bible is a wonderful history book. There is a great truth...in all of its realism, including the Old Testament...it is the book of books...in terms of cultural history, social history, a magnificent book in every respect, simply magnificent!"[158]

After World War II, Otto Dix devoted much of his creative energy to work on religious subjects. From 1946 to 1960, he produced paintings, pastels, lithographs, and stained-glass windows that deal with various religious themes, including three stained-glass windows for St. Peter's church at Kattenhorn, am Untersee, which depict some key episodes from the life of St Peter. However, he focused his artistic efforts on the Passion of Christ, with the Crucifixion as its main event. In 1946 Dix made a series of paintings and drawings of the Crucifixion and other scenes in the Passion of Christ, including *Gethsemane*, *Ecce Homo I and II*, a *Flagellation of Christ*, the *Mocking of Christ*, *Veronica's Veil*, and *Great Crucifixion*.

As an art critic, Eva Karcher pointed out, "...what apparently fascinated Dix above all else [in the Passion of Christ] was the physical aspect of this suffering and death." As Otto Dix explained it himself, "...when you read a detailed description of a crucifixion...that is so horrible, awful. How the limbs swell up...How the person can't breathe. How the face changes color. How he dies a horrible, utterly horrible death." Then, despite such an unspeakable tragedy, Christ is depicted in classical Crucifixion paintings "as a wonderfully beautiful youth. Well," Dix exclaimed, "that's all fraud... That is what I really reject." He continued: "I see it totally realistically...It was worse than the way it was in the war. He was completely alone. Nobody helped him. Nobody was with him. Everyone abandoned him. A magnificent description of the human being who is alone... Of the brilliant human being who is alone. And who understands that."[159]

---

[158] Ibid, 202.
[159] Ibid, 203–204.

Chapter Four

THE CRUCIFIXION IN CUBISM

CUBISM IS ONE OF THE MOST radical innovations in twentieth-century art. Launched in 1906–07 in Paris by Pablo Picasso (1881–1973) and Georges Braque (1882–1963), it challenged five hundred years of the Renaissance tradition of naturalistic representation in Western European painting. In its stead, the movement's founders evolved an entirely new and original form of pictorial reality based on anti-naturalistic figuration. Picasso and Braque developed a pioneering and unique artistic approach, which is still significant now "for they originated attitudes and ideas that spread rapidly to other areas of culture and that to an important degree underlie artistic thought even today."[160]

Since its beginnings, Cubism has been a movement primarily in painting. However, Cubist painters sought the truth in visual experience by portraying the reality of conception, not vision. One of the art critics of the day wrote: "*The ruling preoccupation of the [new] artists is with cutting into the essential TRUTH of the thing they wish to represent, and not merely the external and passing aspect* of this truth... One must seek the truth and stop making sacrifices to the banal illusions of optics."[161]

---

[160] Edward F. Fry, *Cubism*, London: Thames and Hudson, 1978, (1ˢᵗ ed. 1966), 9.

[161] Oliver-Houcade, "The Tendency of Contemporary Painting," 1912, in *Cubism*, 74.

The search for conceptual truth in painting at the price of sacrificing the visual imitation of the external world was started already by post-Impressionists in the last quarter of the nineteenth century. Painters such as Vincent Van Gogh (1853–1890) and Paul Cézanne (1839–1906) wished to penetrate appearances and arrive at a deeper, conceptual understanding of the subject matter. Paul Cézanne, for instance, whose artistic innovations critics consider one of the significant sources of Cubism, deconstructed the Renaissance illusionism through a 'passage'—the connecting on canvas of several planes that are otherwise separate in real space—a technique that would later become the hallmark of the new movement.

'Primitive,' mainly African art, served as the second most important source of Cubism. Unlike the classical Western tradition of realism, African art aimed at non-naturalistic rather than imitational representation of reality and thus created a hyper-phenomenal world of images. However, the influence of African art on Cubism was not limited to its stylistic features but extended to the very understanding of art and its purpose. In Chapter Two, I cited how Cubism's founding father, Pablo Picasso, described the impact of African masks on him at the Trocadero Museum in Paris: "They were [instruments] to free people from being the slaves of the spirits...If we turn the spirits into material forms, we [re]gain our independence. [Then] I understood why I was a painter."[162]

Pablo Picasso created his soon-to-become-famous *Demoiselles d'Avignon* by the end of 1906, thus ushering in the movement of Cubism, which was about to last for some twenty years. During its evolution, Cubism went through two major phases known as analytic and synthetic. Analytical Cubism started with a representational image and presented it in a se-

---

[162] Paul Gowther, *The Language of Twentiesth-Century Art: A Conceptual History*, New Haven and London: Yale University Press, 1997, 33

ries of abstract, geometric forms and shapes. On the other hand, synthetic Cubism worked from abstraction to figuration, a technique described by its leading representative and theorist, the Spanish painter Juan Gris as 'deductive' or 'synthetic.' As Juan Gris said, "Cézanne turns a bottle into a cylinder... I make a bottle, a particular bottle out of a cylinder."[163]

No matter what technique Cubist painters used, the movement seemed always to rely on and be about art *per se*. Pablo Picasso wrote in 1923: "Cubism is not either a seed or a fetus, but an art dealing primarily with forms, and when a form is realized, it is there to live its own life... Cubism has kept within the limits and limitations of painting, never pretending to go beyond it."[164] In 1935, he added: "When we invented Cubism, we had no intention of inventing Cubism. We wanted simply to express what was in us."[165]

Art critics in the West usually follow Picasso's understanding of the movement. Many of them agree that it was a purely stylistic phenomenon—highly original and innovative but hardly applicable to the realities of life. In contrast to these views, Russian philosopher Nicholas Berdyaev argued that Cubist experimentation revealed a deep crisis in art and an unprecedented and overwhelming breakdown of culture and life. Artists like Picasso have demonstrated dissatisfaction with traditional beauty standards and artistic imagery. Similarly, the early twentieth-century European elites were generally disillusioned by social and cultural formations that served them for centuries. As an innovative artist profoundly influenced by the spiritual and cultural atmosphere of the turn-of-the-century Europe, Picasso uniquely expressed the spirit of those times.

---

[163] Notes in *L'Esprit nouveau*, no. 5, Paris, 1921, p. 531. Quoted in John Golding, "Cubism," *Concepts of Modern Art*, 72.

[164] Pablo Picasso, "Statement, 1923," in *Theories of Modern Art*, 265.

[165] Pablo Picasso, "Conversation, 1935," ibid, 271.

In his article on the Spanish master, Berdyaev wrote: "Picasso is a marvelous painter, deeply moving, but he lacks the achievements of beauty. He is all in transition, all in crisis."[166] In his insatiable thirst for new artistic forms, Picasso dematerializes his subject matter and thus seemingly dehumanizes his models. Berdyaev notes: "There is no human being anymore in Picasso's art. That which he discovers and unfolds is no longer human at all; he gives away the human being to the will of the dispersing wind."[167]

The results of Picasso's deconstructive efforts, as Berdyaev repeatedly points out, are not the new foundations of culture but the ultimate devastation of both the material and spiritual dimensions of life. He writes: "Picasso is a genius of expressing the decay, the sprawling, the dissipation of the physical, fleshy, embodied world... The painter's insight does not reveal the substantiality of the material world—this world turns out to lack substance." As a result, Cubism itself turns into a warning symptom of the decline of modern civilization, and Picasso expresses its spirit by becoming "a merciless unmasker of the illusions of the embodied, material, synthesized beauty [who] sees the horror of decay and dissipation...the demonic grimaces of the chained spirits of nature."[168]

---

[166] Nicholas Berdyaev, "Picasso," in *Philosophy of Creativity*, vol. 2, 424.
[167] Ibid, 424.
[168] Ibid, 420–21.

PABLO RUIZ PICASSO (1881–1973)

> *We all know that art is not truth. Art is*
> *a lie that makes us realize the truth, at*
> *least the truth that is given us to under-*
> *stand. The artist must know the manner*
> *whereby to convince others of the truthful-*
> *ness of his lies.*

Pablo Picasso

PABLO PICASSO IS PERHAPS THE MOST celebrated painter of the twentieth century. He made his first painting when he was seven years old. He had his academic training at La Lonja, Barcelona's School of fine arts. He also attended the Academy of San Fernando in Madrid.

Picasso went through many periods in his long artistic career, experimenting with various styles and participating in different movements. Art critics distinguish his "Blue period" (1901–04), which was followed by the "Rose period" (1904–07) and culminated with the discovery of Cubism in 1907. After the Cubist and Classical years (1907–14 and 1917–24), Picasso was profoundly influenced by Surrealism, whose motifs resurface in many of his paintings of the late twenties and thirties. After World War II, Picasso's paintings, sculptures, and ceramic pieces flourished in various directions.

The retrospective exhibitions of his paintings were held all over the world, including the Tate Gallery in London, England; the Grand-Palais and Petit-Palais in Paris, France; UCLA Art Gallery in Los Angeles; and the Museum of Modern Art in New York, USA, the National Museum of Modern Art of Tokyo, Japan, as well as in Toronto and Montreal, Canada. The Soviet government twice awarded Picasso the Lenin Prize for

Peace, and in 1963 the Picasso Museum in his native Barcelona opened its doors to the public. The Spanish master died at the age of ninety-two—widely recognized and praised as the most innovative artistic genius of his time.

In his private life, Pablo Picasso was an atheist and a communist. Although he did not allow his religious or political views to interfere directly with his art, his paintings reveal a deep spiritual frustration sharply noticed by Berdyaev. Those metaphysical levels in Picasso's paintings escape formal definitions, transcend the boundaries of any ideology, either confessional or secular, and suggest a grandiose, almost apocalyptic transformation that unfolds in the depths of the human soul. Picasso penetrates the appearances of the material world and discovers the demons of suffering humanity, which he desperately wishes to exorcise through his art. In this complex and sometimes ambiguous context, one should understand and approach Picasso's involvement with one of Western art's most traditional religious themes—the Crucifixion.

Picasso made drawings of Christ on the cross many times. Perhaps, one of the earliest known drawings dates to 1918 when "in the style of Ingres, Picasso used... a nervous, more sophisticated line for a picture of ... Christ on the cross."[169] In 1932, he revisited the theme of the Crucifixion, and from September 17 to October 21 at Boisgeloup, France produced "thirteen drawings [which are] based on Grünewald's *Crucifixion*." As Christian Heck points out in his article about Grünewald's *Crucifixions* and twentieth-century art, the so-called Boisgeloup series of drawings is "a product of both Picasso's own research and the twentieth-century tradition of mining the art of Grünewald."[170] These works, as the critic sums up, "repre-

[169] Brigitte Léal, Christine Piot, Marie-Laure Bernadac, *The Ultimate Picasso*, New York: Harry N. Abrams, 2000, 194.

[170] Christian Heck, "Between Myth and Model: Grünewald's *Crucifixions* and Twentieth Century Art," *The Body on the Cross: Picasso,*

sent, above all, reflections on death and sufferings, and thus embody the triple thematic of the Minotaur, the Crucifixion, and tauromachy"[171] that attracted the Spanish master in those years.

In the early 1930s, when Picasso became interested in Surrealism, he was "asked to do the cover for the review Minotaure, which was edited by [the founder of the movement] André Breton."[172] Picasso's main *Crucifixion*, also painted in 1930, is marked by the new Surrealist influences and the Cubist technique. After all, the drive toward violence and death constitutes one of the primordial human impulses, according to the founder of psychoanalysis, Sigmund Freud, and his faithful Surrealist admirers. In tune with "Picasso's interest in using the Crucifixion as a focus for investigating sadism and brutality, amongst other aspects of irrational behavior,"[173] one may also find in the painting allusions to sexual desire—another dominant human urge, according to Freudian psychoanalysis. It is expressed in "the overt sexuality of the contorted Magdalene-type figure immediately below Christ, whose facial features are confounded with her genitalia."[174]

As one art critic, Christine Piot, suggests, Picasso's masterpiece "brings together a number of themes specific to Picasso, combining, in very different proportions, women's profiles, religious allusions, and even bullfighting (with a rider who resembles a picador carrying a lance)."[175] At the center of the canvas, the viewer sees "the figures of Christ on the cross and a veiled woman are highlighted in white against a black

Bacon, Dix, De Kooning, Guttuso, Sutherland, Saura, a catalogue, Paris: Réunion des musées nationaux, 1992, 84.

[171] Ibid, 106.

[172] Josep Palau I Fabre, *Picasso*, New York: Rizzoli, 1981, 17.

[173] Kaufmann, Ruth, "Picasso's *Crucifixion* of 1930," in *The Body on the Cross*, 79.

[174] Ibid, 77.

[175] *The Ultimate Picasso*, 255.

background. At their feet lie the two thieves who have been removed from their crosses, and to the right, two centurions throw dice on a drum for Christ's tunic." As Christine Piot continues: "As enormous yellow-and-red head with its hair standing on end is at the side of Marie-Thérèse's transparent profile, while to the left a massive character climbs the steps to the cross with difficulty, his mouth open." Overall, as she points out, the "scene is painted in great detail and in bright colors that can be found in the most expressive paintings of those years: the red and yellow dominate in sulfurous tones, which are broken up with areas of green and blue."[176]

Art critics usually agree that this complex and violent picture "must have had some special significance for Picasso [although for him] its meaning has little to do with traditional religious attitudes."[177] They also notice that the *Crucifixion* started a series of Picasso's works that would culminate in his monumental *Guernica*, painted in 1937 as a painter's reaction to the bombardment of the Basque city of Gernika in his native Spain. Both paintings share plenty of motifs in common. They are vivid testimonies of Picasso's reaction to the inhumanity and horrors of the Spanish Civil War, which in some ways were more devastating than the soon-to-be-fought World War II. In both canvases, Picasso "transmits the intensity of his feelings through the broken, disfigured, distorted form, through the screaming colors... through chaos and dissonance,"[178] which reflected the outbursts of human violence and cruelty on the European continent.

Indeed, there are many commonalities between *Guernica* and the *Crucifixion*. As Ruth Kaufmann writes in her article

---

[176] Ibid, 255.

[177] Kaufmann, Ruth, "Picasso's *Crucifixion* of 1930," ibid, 74.

[178] Irina Iazykova, "'Se chelovek'. Iisus Khristos v izobrazitel'nom iskusstve XX veka" ['*Ecce Homo*'. Jesus Christ in Twentieth-Century Visual Art], *Mir Biblii* [*Bible's World*], an illustrated almanac of St. Andrew's Biblical-Theological College, 10(2004), 53.

on *Crucifixion*: "The screaming, wounded horse in the center of the *Guernica* bears a visual and conceptual resemblance to the wounded Christ and screaming woman in the center of the *Crucifixion*." Furthermore, she notes, "both pictures have bull-fight imagery—the centurion who recalls the picador in the earlier work, and the bull and the horse in the later one." Also, the "two works have open beaked, earthbound birds and degraded images of the sun—the sun with the electric light bulb of the Guernica and the sun of Mithraism"[179] in the *Crucifixion*.

The striking similarities between *Guernica* and the *Crucifixion* do not stop there. As Kaufmann continues:

> Both have the upraised arms of the female figure at the right and the bent posture and bared buttocks of the figure next to her—the soldier in the *Crucifixion* and the running woman in the *Guernica*. Also, the thieves in the lower left of the *Crucifixion* and the broken warrior in the same position in the *Guernica* appear to have been inspired by the same source, the *Flood* from the *Apocalypse of Saint-Sever*... Finally, it might be mentioned that the black and white of the central portion of the *Crucifixion* becomes the color scheme of the entire *Guernica*.[180]

However, in contrast to his *Guernica*, Picasso's *Crucifixion* may have portrayed not only the immediate calamities of the Spanish Civil War but also his intuitive foreboding of the impending disasters of World War II. As the "premonition of all future catastrophes,"[181] the Crucifixion seemed an ideal ve-

---

[179] A pagan religion of Mithraism was one of Christianity's main competitors during the first centuries of the Christian era. It was based on the Persian myth about Mithras—a god of the sunlight who killed a sacred bull to initiate a new life.

[180] Kaufmann, Ruth, "Picasso's *Crucifixion* of 1930," in *The Body on the Cross*, 83.

[181] Irina Iazykova, "'Se chelovek'. *Mir Biblii*, 53.

hicle for the artistic expression of such presentiments. In his masterpiece, Picasso combines the martyrdom of Christ and the Christian promise of redemption through sacrifice with the sacrificial exorcism of pagan ritualistic processions.

As Jean Clair argues in his article "That Wonderful Thing Called Sin," "Picasso's *Crucifixion* resoundingly shows that there is no distance between Dionysus and Christ."[182] Ruth Kaufmann echoes his point. She writes: "Picasso follows the surrealist interest in primitive rites as a means of exploring men's irrational impulses by giving us a group of anguished and dehumanized figures responding to the triumvirate of idols."[183] The painting itself turns into such a primal ritual through which Picasso is trying to liberate himself and the world around him from the demons of "human irrationality in the form of hysteria, brutality, and sadism."[184]

---

[182] Clair, Jean, "That Wonderful Thing Called Sin," in *The Body on the Cross*, 66.

[183] Kaufmann, Ruth, "Picasso's *Crucifixion* of 1930," ibid, 78.

[184] Ibid, 83.

RENATO GUTTUSO (1911–1987)

*Realism today is not a school of painting,
nor an involution of taste towards this
or that moment in the history of art, but
a historical dialectical concept bound to
the present [and] strictly connected with
modern reality and culture.*

Renato Guttuso

AN ITALIAN ARTIST RENATO GUTTUSO CREATED another well-known painting of the Crucifixion accomplished in a Cubist style. Arguably, the "most 'popular' [modern] painter that Italian art produced in the twentieth century,"[185] Guttuso was born to a family of a land surveyor and amateur watercolorist. He "discovered painting early on through his father's watercolors, the studio of the painter Domenico Quattrociocchi and the workshop of the cart painter Emilio Murdolo."[186] Guttuso started signing his works—primarily copies of nineteenth-century Sicilian landscapes—when he was thirteen. In 1928 he participated in his first show—a group exhibition in Palermo, Italy. The following year the Prima Quadriennale d'Arte Nazionale in Rome accepted two of his artworks, and he decided to pursue a career in painting.

Guttuso was active in art and art criticism as well as in social issues and politics. He joined the Communist Party of Italy and took a robust anti-fascist stand, which led to his participation in the Resistance movement. In the 1930s, a "series

---

[185] *Guttuso*, eds. Andrea Buzzoni, Fabio Carapezza Guttuso and Catherine Lampert, London: Thames and Hudson, 1996, 11.

[186] Ibid, 157.

of large works[, including] Fuga dall'Etna (Flight from Etna), which won the Bergamo award in 1940, established the artist's international reputation." In the 1940s, Guttuso "founded the 'Fronte Nuovo delle Arti' (New Arts Front), a group of politically aware artists whose work dealt with the socially committed subject matter in a post-Cubist style."[187]

From the 1950s to the early 1970s, significant exhibitions of Guttuso's works were held throughout the globe, including the Venice Biennales in the 1950s, shows at the ACA-Heller Gallery in New York in 1958; at the Pushkin Museum, Moscow, and the Hermitage Museum, Leningrad in 1961; at the Musée d'Art Moderne de la Ville de Paris in 1971; along with a series of major retrospectives in Europe in the early 1970s. In 1976 he was elected a Senator of the Republic.

Renato Guttuso and Pablo Picasso were close friends. The first time, they met in a postwar Paris in 1946, and their friendship lasted from then until Picasso's death. Guttuso had a lot in common with the Spanish master. Like Picasso, he was a communist. He enrolled in the clandestine Party in 1940 and "became politically active during the German occupation of Italy as a member of a military organization of Partisans operating in Central Italy."[188] Unlike Picasso, however, Guttuso did not intend to separate his worldview from his art and to remain neutral on the safe grounds of art-for-art's sake. The evolution of Guttuso's works over the years shows a clear progression toward socially and politically charged messages—an approach to art that critics dubbed 'social realism.' Aesthetically, Guttuso was a fervent proponent of the latter in the twentieth-century dispute between abstraction and figuration. He "wanted to ensure the survival of representation [as part of] the tradition of making art a political act."[189]

---

[187] Ibid, 160.
[188] Whitfield, Sarah, "Seeing Red," in *Guttuso*, 25.
[189] Ibid, 31.

Among Guttuso's works on religious themes, critics distinguish his illustrations of *The Divine Comedy* by Dante, published in 1963, and his Crucifixion paintings. As Guttuso describes his approach to the religious subject, the "relationship between the immanent and the transcendent, between the physical, real-world and the metaphysical world must be an integral part of the lives and ideas of most of humanity." Therefore, for him, the "religious quality of a work of art is the product not so much of individual feeling or the sincerity of individual inspiration, as it is a sharing of a common view of the world, which is reflected in the work of art."[190]

Guttuso made his first Crucifixion in 1940. In this "modest-sized" *Crucifixion in a Room*—an "earlier example of [his] reworking traditional iconography... the confined space of a small interior replaces the outdoor scene of Golgotha, evoking the airless prison cell and newer equally terrible forms of dealing with religious and political dissidents."[191] Guttuso's second and most famous painting on the subject was executed a year later, in 1941. He wrote about his intentions concerning this artwork: "In 1940, I tried to paint a religious painting. Europe was at war, and I wanted to link Christ's Crucifixion to the tragedy of the war."[192]

He explained his intentions more in detail in his journal: "I want to paint the execution of Christ as a scene from contemporary life. Not in the sense that Christ dies every day on the cross to atone for our sins... but as a symbol of all those who are attacked, imprisoned, or tortured because of their ideas." In my painting of the Crucifixion, he continued, I envisioned "the crosses (the gallows) erected inside a room. Soldiers and dogs—women weeping...people coming and go-

---

[190] Crispolti, Enrico, "Guttuso, Crucifixion," *The Body on the Cross*, 108–09.

[191] Whitfield, Sarah, "Seeing Red," in *Guttuso*, 34.

[192] Crispolti, Enrico, "Guttuso, Crucifixion," *The Body on the Cross,* 110.

ing... The execution amid the crowd, acrobats, and soldiers—Circus and massacre—out in the sun with a storm approaching...".[193]

Guttuso's large *Crucifixion* resembles the one made in 1930 by his friend Pablo Picasso. Maurizio Calvesi describes in his article on Guttuso some of the similarities between the two. In Guttuso's study for the Crucifixion, he writes, "the figure on the left—a rearing horse with the rider—might correspond to the large figure with the monumental head, which in Picasso's painting is also to the left of the crucified man." He also adds that in "the final version of the Crucifixion, the animal stands out in the foreground, with its nostrils turned backward... an addition, which might derive from the other painting by Picasso which Guttuso knew [–] Guernica."[194] Another art critic, Sarah Whitfield, echoes this point by noticing that "Guttuso paid tribute to Picasso in his work by incorporating figures from his [Crucifixion] paintings, for instance, [as] a gesture of fraternal solidarity."[195]

Overall, Guttuso's *Crucifixion* leaves the impression of vital Expressionist and Cubist influences. More specifically, "references to the 'avant-garde' include a reworking of one of the most extreme gestures of grief in *Guernica* (hand beating the air) and a salute to the blue horses of Franc Marc"[196] in a figure of a naked centurion riding a blue horse himself. The parallels between Guttuso's masterpiece and other contemporary paintings and movements should not obscure, however, the originality of the Italian artist's work. His *Crucifixion* uses the Cubist technique, but rather in its "international version"—with a three-dimensional perspective instead of a flattened surface—which was in tune with Guttuso's inclination toward

---

[193] Ibid, 107.
[194] Calvesi, Maurizio, "Renato Guttuso's Journey," *Guttuso*, 16.
[195] Whitfield, Sarah, "Seeing Red," ibid, 27.
[196] Ibid, 32.

a more realistic representation. The composition of the art-work is entirely original as well.

The crucified Christ and the two thieves in the painting are not facing the viewer. Instead, the figures face each other. Maurizio Calvesi further notes that the "downward move-ment of the bodies creates a more rigid structure, drama-tized by the tension of the forms and by the red accents (the chromatically transfigured body of the thief), which contrast with the white or ashy tones."[197] The face of Christ is hidden behind the cross with one of the thieves, and Mary Magda-lene is portrayed naked while pulling toward to remove the blood from Christ's wound. These two unconventional details produced enormous religious controversy when the painting was first shown in Italy in 1942. The Vatican got so offended that it "threatened to excommunicate visitors to the exhibi-tion."[198] Since then, the *Crucifixion* "was excluded from official exhibitions in Italy up to the 1972 Venice Biennale."[199]

Finally, the vibrant colors, reminiscent of German Expres-sionism, play an essential role in conveying the painter's mes-sage. "The dominant color, red, like the clenched fists of the crucified," writes Sarah Whitfield, "is a coded reference to the defiance of the Communists under Fascism." Back in those days, the communists and the Catholics in Italy were ready to fight together against the common threat of fascism. That explains "the apparent contradiction in broadcasting a Com-munist message through a Christian image."[200] We might add that the two thieves depicted in red and the gray may as well stand for communism and fascism, the red one being the thief to whom Christ had promised salvation. .

---

[197] "Guttuso's Journey," *Guttuso*, 14.
[198] *Guttuso*, 159.
[199] "Seeing Red," *Guttuso*, 33.
[200] Ibid, 32.

JACQUES VILLON (1875–1963)

Villon's work has a special quality of reverence for the intellect—and by extension, for society's need to meditate. Thus, the work of art is defined as a vehicle for communication.

Daniel Robbins

ANOTHER INTERESTING EXAMPLE OF A CRUCIFIXION MADE in the Cubo-Futurist style comes from the French artist Jacques Villon. Born Gaston Emile Duchamp, a brother of twentieth-century art icon Marcel Duchamp, Jacques Villon (he renamed himself after French medieval poet François Villon) was a significant and prolific painter and printmaker of his time. In fact, "the extent of his graphic oeuvre, more than 600 engravings, and lithographs exceed in number that of Braque, Matisse, Picasso or Rouault."[201]

Villon's grandfather was a painter-engraver who exposed his grandson to etching in his youth and encouraged Villon's enthusiasm for art. Since "an early age [Villon] was accustomed to handling copper plates, to the smell of etching acid and the sound of melting varnish."[202] Jacques Villon produced his first etchings—the portraits of his father and grandfather—in 1891 when he was sixteen. He pursued an artistic career three years later and moved to Paris.

In Paris, Villon studied under French artist Fernand Cormon (1845–1924), a teacher of Henri de Toulouse-Lautrec

---

[201] William S. Lieberman, *Jacques Villon: His Graphic Art*, The Museum of Modern Art Bulletin: Vol. XXI, no. 1, Fall 1953, 3.

[202] Ibid, 3.

(1864–1901), and made his living as an illustrator and cartoonist for various journals. From 1904 to 1905, he attended the Académie Julian, and in 1905 he had his first show at the Galérie Legrip Rouen with his brother Raymond Duchamp Villon. In 1913, Villon participated in the famous Armory Show in New York, introducing European avant-garde artists to the American public and selling several of his works there. By the early 1950s, the artist had produced nearly a thousand canvases and prints.

Throughout his artistic career, Villon won numerous accolades and awards, including the Gold Medal for painting and engraving at the 1937 International Exhibition in Paris, the Grand Prix de la Gravure at the 1949 International Print Exhibition in Lugano, and the Grand Prix for painting at the 1958–59 Brussels World's Fair. International recognition and fame came to him in 1950 when Villon received first prize at the Carnegie Institute in Pittsburg. In 1963 Villon was elected Grand Officer of the French Legion of Honor.

Jacques Villon produced only a few explicitly religious artworks. In 1945 he made a series of etchings that illustrated Racine's *Cantiques spirituels*, including one etching of the crucifix. In 1953 he designed stained glass windows for Metz Cathedral in France. Also, in the 1950s, Villon painted a Cubist-style watercolor, *Crucified Christ*. And in 1961, he created a color lithograph of the Crucifixion.

Offering a vivid Cubist perspective, Villon's *Crucifixion* is distinguished by its brilliant and vibrant colors that may remind the viewer of another early twentieth-century movement, Futurism. An Italian art trend initiated by the poet Filippo Tomaso Marinetti in 1909, Futurism glorified the modern dynamism of life. As Marinetti proclaimed in one of his manifestos, the "world's magnificence has been enriched by a new beauty: the beauty of speed."[203] Unlike Cubism,

---

[203] F. T. Marinetti, "The Founding and Manifesto of Futurism 1909,"

which mainly focused on static analysis and dissection, Futurism emphasized a dynamic synthesis. Futurist artists applied Cubist techniques of color divisionism and decomposition of form to their own goal of portraying the world of becoming and constant transformations. They wrote: "The gesture which we would reproduce on canvas shall no longer be a *fixed moment* in universal *dynamism*. It shall simply be the *dynamic sensation* itself."[204]

The Futurist dynamism displayed two qualities. One was destructive, which aimed at eradicating the old and outdated layers of culture with its museums, libraries, and schools of learning. The second one was creative—what a French philosopher of that time, Henri Bergson, called *élan vital*, or the vital energy that creates life out of lifeless matter.

Villon's *Crucifixion* combines themes of destruction and recreation, despair, and hope. The disfigured and decomposed image of Christ suggests his suffering and death. The bright colors and the impression of the moving figure of Christ alludes to his resurrection and ascension. They also indicate the power of the Holy Spirit that permeates and animates the entire universe.

Futurist Manifestos, ed. and with an introduction by Umbro Apollonio, London: Thames and Hudson, 1973, 21

[204] Umberto Boccioni, Carlo Carrà, Luigi Russolo, Giacomo Bella, Gino Severini, "Futurist Paintings Technical Manifesto 1910," ibid, 27.

Chapter Five

THE CRUCIFIXION IN SURREALISM

ONE OF THE MAJOR TWENTIETH-CENTURY ART movements, Surrealism, is also the most significant and influential artistic development in the period between the two World
Wars. Its formal beginning dates to 1924 when a group of former Dadaist artists established the Bureau of Surrealist Research in Paris and started publishing the magazine *La Révolution Surréaliste* (Surrealist Revolution). The opening issue of
their review contained the first Surrealist Manifesto written
by the founder of the movement, André Breton. In it, Breton
defined Surrealism as "pure psychic automatism, by which it
is intended to express, verbally, in writing, or by other means,
the real process of thought. Thought's dictation, in the absence of all control exercised by reason and outside all aesthetic or moral preoccupations." Breton emphasized that
Surrealists believe "in the omnipotence of dream and in the
disinterested play of thought," which could be used "in the
solution of the principal problems of life."[205]

The Surrealist movement continued the preceding Dada—
an art trend that explored and glorified the power of the unconscious and its seemingly chaotic impulses. Methodic in-
tellectualism of the Surrealists replaced Dada's nihilistic and
absurdist attitudes. As one of the prominent Dada artists,
Hans Richter explained: "At the end of a relentless process of
destruction, there appeared a new discipline, and a philoso-

---

[205] André Breton, "What is Surrealism," in *Theories of Modern Art*, 412.

161

phy, directed towards 'positive goals.' Surrealism gave Dada significance and sense; Dada gave Surrealism life."[206]

As I previously mentioned, the philosophical inspiration for Surrealism came from a Viennese psychologist and founder of psychoanalysis, Sigmund Freud. Medically trained, Breton was familiar with Freud's psychoanalytic theories and techniques and applied them to art.

Freud's psychoanalysis, designed to be a strictly scientific endeavor, was supposed to remain neutral to anything transcending its boundaries. However, its much broader philosophical implications revealed significant concerns regarding religious matters. A self-proclaimed "godless Jew," Freud wrote several books attacking religion as an "illusion" and a "collective neurosis." The Surrealist practioners, in turn, displayed an ambiguous standing toward faith and spirituality.

One art critic pointed out that they "flirted for a time with Oriental philosophy, religion, and mysticism, and [even] believed that they had found spiritual guides in Buddha and in the Dalai Lama." Their interest in the human psyche and mainly the unconscious led them to exploit the metaphysical levels of existence in their art. [207]

However, strong resistance to organized religion and religious philosophy accompanied Surrealism's equally solid metaphysical appeal. The review *La Révolution Surréaliste* "was consciously anti-religious. [And i]n general, one could say that the Surrealists were decisively anti-clerical and non-religious in their attitudes."[208] In the 1930s, they were also attracted to communism, its class struggle theory, and laborers' libera-

[206] Hans Richter, *Dada Art and Anti-Art*, London: Thames and Hudson, 1965, 19

[207] Ibid, 15.

[208] Marianne Oesterreicher–Mollwo, *Surrealism and Dadaism. Provocative Destruction, the Path Within and the Exacerbation of the Problem of a Reconciliation of Art and Life*, Oxford: Phaidon, 1979, 15.

tion. Along with some other fellow believers, Breton became a member of the Communist Party in 1927. In 1929 the final issue of his review *La Révolution Surréaliste* came out. Between 1930 and 1933, he ventured to publish a new magazine under the revealing title *Surrealisme au Service de la Révolution* (Surrealism at the Service of Revolution). The noble ideal of the mind's inner rebellious self-disclosure was broadened to include a social revolution of the proletariat against the bourgeoisie.

The collaboration of Surrealists and communists, however, inevitably failed. Neither side was willing to sacrifice their aims for the sake of their partners. Breton was excluded from the Party in 1933, while some Surrealists—an actor and theater director Antonin Artaud, for instance—never joined the organization. Yet, the temporary alliance between the Surrealists and the communists demonstrated the anti-religious character of this twentieth-century art movement. As a result, religion and religious themes didn't play a significant role in Surrealist art *per se*, and the Crucifixion was no exception.

The earliest example of a Surrealist—or, more precisely, proto-Surrealist—Crucifixion was created by Max Ernst (1891–1976). Ernst was an artist who "exemplifies those aspects of the countervailing movements of twentieth-century art in which the mysterious and irrational predominate: first in the nihilism of Dada, then in the lyrical dream-imagery of Surrealism."[209] He painted his *Crucifixion* in 1913 in Germany—before the First World War and long before the advent of Surrealism. That is why in this painting, "the subject, and the writhing, tortured forms of the figures refer [to] Matthias Grünewald [and] his *Isenheim Altarpiece* crucifixion panel of c. 1510–15,"[210] rather than to Surrealism, properly speaking.

---

[209] Diane Waldman, "Max Ernst," *Max Ernst: A Retrospective*, New York: The Solomon R. Guggenheim Museum, 1975, 15.

[210] Ibid, 18.

SALVADOR DALÍ (1904–1989)

*Things have no meaning whatever beyond their **strictest objectivity**; herein resides, in my opinion, their miraculous poetry... More than what a horse can suggest to a painter or a poet, I am interested in the horse or kind of horse the painter and poet can invent, **or better yet, encounter.***

Salvador Dalí

THE SPANISH PAINTER SALVADOR DALÍ WAS another famous Surrealist who turned—and more than once—to the Crucifixion as a source of his artistic inspiration. Commonly regarded as the Surrealist *par excellence*, Dalí was born to a notary family in the small town of Figueres in the district of Girona in Catalonia. When he was only fourteen, Dalí had the first exhibit of his works arranged by his father in his native town. In the early 1920s, Dalí attended the San Fernando Academy of Fine Arts in Madrid, and in 1925, he had his first one-person show at the Dalman Gallery in Barcelona. In the 1930s, art curators organized Dalí's first one-person exhibitions outside his homeland in New York and London.

In his long and fruitful artistic career, Dalí produced hundreds of drawings and paintings and designed costumes and sets for ballets. He created collections of jewels, collaborated in producing films, wrote artistic manifestos, Surrealist poems, and articles, and published two autobiographical books. In recognition of his exceptional contribution to Spanish culture, the artist received one of Spain's highest decorations, the Grand Cross of Isabella the Catholic. The king of Spain, Juan Carlos, conferred on him the title of Marquis of Dalí of Pubol.

Dalí developed his unique version of Surrealism during his involvement with the movement, which was quite different from André Breton's orthodox approach. Breton insisted that artists must cultivate a passive state of mind and thus become accessible mediums whose liberated unconscious would find new expressions in the light of artistic creation. Salvador Dalí, on the contrary, believed in the active human mind that transforms or, as he put it, invents material objectivity according to its own creative impulse. Dalí called this method a 'paranoiac-critical activity' and defined it as a "spontaneous method of irrational knowledge based upon the interpretative–critical association of delirious phenomena."[211] As James Soby wrote in his book on Dalí, the Spanish painter "declared that his art sprang from a constant, hallucinatory energy. He proposed to paint like a madman rather than an occasional somnambulist. He added that the only difference between himself and a madman was that he was not mad."[212]

Raised a Catholic, the future Surrealist master made his first religious painting, *Joseph Greeting His Brethren*, before he was ten. It was "executed in the style of the nineteenth-century painters of genre scenes."[213] Dalí's mature religious works that reveal his unique spirituality were created much later, after World War II, when he was already in his late forties and fifties. By that time, he was formally excluded from membership in the movement. Still, as an art critic, Robert Descharnes, pointed out, this "'ex-Surrealist'... in fact remained more of surrealist than ever."[214]

After rediscovering his Catholic roots, Dalí decided to revive the legacy of Spanish mysticism. At that time, his religi-

---

[211] James Thrall Soby, *Salvador Dalí*, New York: Arno Press, 1968, 1st ed. 1946 by the Museum of Modern Art, 11.

[212] Ibid, 7.

[213] Soby, *Salvador Dalí*, 3.

[214] Robert Descharnes, Gilles Néret, *Salvador Dalí, 1904–1989*, Köln–Los Angeles: Taschen, 2004, 158.

osity remained controversial and paradoxically combined with past Surrealist experimentation. An extravagant showman, Dalí could say that he was "both an agnostic and a Roman Catholic."[215] He also provocatively described his understanding of God: "Eroticism, hallucinogenic drugs, nuclear science, Gaudi's Gothic architecture, my love of gold—there is a common denominator in all of it: God is present in everything...We are children of God, and the entire universe tends towards the perfection of [hu]mankind."[216]

After the first atomic bomb explosion, Dalí became fascinated by nuclear physics. In his view, science penetrated so deep into the mysteries of the universe that it approached the border that separates matter from spirit and material from the spiritual world. He went as far as to conceive "protons and neutrons as 'angelic elements.'"[217]

Dalí's newfound "nuclear mysticism" was combined with equal admiration for the Renaissance masters. He believed that the "means of pictorial expression achieved their greatest perfection and effectiveness in the Renaissance and that the decadence of modern painting was a consequence of skepticism and lack of faith, the result of mechanistic materialism."[218] In his *Diary of a Genius*, Dalí echoes his grave concerns about modern art: "Today's young painters believe in nothing. It is only normal for someone who believes in nothing to end up painting practically nothing, which is the case in the whole of modern art, including the abstract, aesthetic, and academic varieties."[219]

[215] Ibid, 166.
[216] S. Dalí and A. Parinaud, *Comment on deviant Dali*. Paris, 1973; Engl. Ed: *The Unspeakable Confessions of Salvador Dalí*, London, 1976. Quoted in ibid, 173.
[217] Ibid, 166.
[218] S. Dalí and A. Parinaud, *Comment on deviant Dali*. Quoted in Descharnes and Néret, *Salvador Dalí*, 158.
[219] S. Dalí, *Journal d'un genie*, p. 403f; Paris, 1964; Engl. Ed: *Diary of*

In this intellectual and spiritual context, "Salvador Dalí, inventor of the new paranoiac-critical mysticism and the savior of modern painting as his Christian name suggests,"[220] creates many of his religious masterpieces. *Lapis-lazuli Corpuscular Assumption* (1952) *and The Sacrament of the Last Supper* (1955) are among them. Dalí also produces a hundred illustrations for Dante's *Divine Comedy*. Between 1950 and 1955, he paints two Crucifixions—his famous *Christ of Saint John of the Cross* (1951) being one of the most striking examples of Dalí's "nuclear realism."

The painting's composition is suggested by a drawing made by St. John of the Cross and kept at the monastery at Avila. On Dalí's canvas, the crucified Christ is placed above the bay at Port Lligat, where the painter and his wife, Gala, lived. The figures beside the boat are borrowed from other artworks, including "a drawing Velázquez did for his painting *The Surrender of Breda*."[221] Dalí describes the inspiration for creating this masterpiece: "It began in 1950 with a cosmic dream I had, in which I saw the picture in color. In my dream, it represented the nucleus of the atom. The nucleus later acquired a metaphysical meaning: I see the unity of the universe in it—Christ!" After seeing the drawing of St. John of the Cross, Dalí "devised a geometrical construct comprising a triangle and a circle, the aesthetic sum total of all [his] previous experience and put...Christ inside the triangle."[222]

Another striking example of Dalí's fascination with the "threefold synthesis of classicism, the spiritual, and concern with the nuclear age"[223] is his second painting of the Crucifixion. According to Dalí's views, every particle of the uni-

---

a Genius, N.Y., 1965. Quoted in Ibid, 176.

[220] Ibid, 157.

[221] Ibid, 168.

[222] Dalí/Parinaud, *Comment on devient Dali*. Quoted in Descharnes and Néret, *Salvador Dalí*, 168–69.

[223] Ibid, 166.

verse is spiritualized. Jesus Christ is that seed of spirituality and the nucleus that holds the whole world together in its unity. In 1954 he made *Crucifixion* (*Corpus Hypercubus*), presenting his version of the central spiritual event in Christian history. Dalí painted a "hypercubic cross where the Corpus Christi acts as the ninth cube, in accordance with the rules that Juan de Herrera, the architect of El Escorial, inspired by Raimundus Lullus, laid down in his discourse on the cube."[224] In the painting, Dalí's wife, Gala, who symbolizes the Mother of God, looks above at the figure of the crucified Savior suspended in the air—a victim of and a victor over death and disintegration.

---

[224] Dalí/Parinaud, *Comment on devient Dali.* Quoted in ibid, 186.

MARC CHAGALL (1887–1985)

I try to fill my canvases in some way with objects and figures treated as forms... sonorous forms like sounds... passionate forms designed to add a new dimension which neither the geometry of the Cubists nor the patches of the Impressionists can achieve.

Marc Chagall

MARC CHAGALL IS ANOTHER FAMOUS TWENTIETH-century painter often associated with the Surrealist movement. Chagall was born to an impoverished Hassidic Jewish family in the small town of Lyozno in present-day Belarus. He studied painting in nearby Vitebsk and then in St. Petersburg and Paris. In 1913 and 1914, he exhibited his early works at the Salon des Indépendents in Paris and the *Der Sturm* Gallery in Berlin.

While those early exhibitions took place well before the formal beginning of Surrealism in the 1920s, Chagall's style of magical or fantastic realism was astonishingly close to Surrealist aspirations. According to André Breton:

> The aesthetic reversal of spatial planes and the refusal to accept the dependence of creation on gravity and the laws of nature...take their creative point of departure in Chagall both in the dream picture and in the intensive sensuousness of impression. A compelling magic emanates from his pictures, whose enchantingly prismatic colors dissolve and transmute the tortuous tensions in modern man.[225]

---

[225] André Breton, *Die Dichter verdanken ihm viel* (What Poetry Owes Him), quoted in *Marc Chagall. Origins and Paths*, ed. Roland Dosch-

The French poet and art critic Guillaume Apollinaire called Chagall's works "Peinture surnaturelle" or "supernatural paintings."[226] In the meantime, Chagall himself professed an artistic creed that was akin to Surrealist beliefs about art. His interests lay in portraying the secrets of the inner life of the human personality—of the human psyche, as Surrealists would put it later.

Chagall wrote: "I personally do not believe that scholarly endeavors serve the interests of art. Impressionism and Cubism are alien to me. Art seems to me to be primarily a condition of the soul."[227] Formally distant from both Cubism and Surrealism, Chagall was welcome to become part of the movement that significantly influenced the artistic and intellectual life of Paris, where he lived, between the two World Wars, but he chose not to do so. As Chagall remarked, "Everything in art ought to reply to every movement in our blood, to all our being, even our unconscious. [But as for the latter, for] my part, I have slept very well without Freud!"[228]

Over his long and prolific career, Chagall made hundreds of paintings, etchings, lithographs, and designs for stained glass and established himself as one of the most original twentieth-century artists. The main focus of Chagall's art is the inner life of the soul with its hopes, fantasies, dreams, love, and faith—a theme to which he remained faithful throughout his life. Chagall is also considered one of the most significant religious painters of his century. Religious and especially biblical themes remained the vital source of his art. As he wrote: "Ever since my earliest youth, I have been fascinated by the Bible, [this] greatest source of poetry of all time... I have sought its

---

ka, with contributions by Roland Doschka, Françoise Dumont, and Meret Meyer, Munich—New York: Prestel Verlag, 1998, 17.

[226] Marc Chagall, *Origins and Paths*, 16.

[227] Marc Chagall, *Mein Leben* (My Life), Stutgart, 1959, 113. Quoted in *Origins and Paths*, 16.

[228] Gill Polonsky, *Chagall*, London: Phaidon Press, 1998, 19.

reflection in life and art. The Bible is like an echo of nature, and this is the secret I have endeavored to transmit."[229]

One of the most significant differences between Chagall and most Surrealists lay in his deep and lifelong commitment to religion and religious subjects. Chagall's first paintings exploring biblical themes date back to the beginning of his artistic career. In 1913 and 1914, he exhibited his painting *Adam and Eve*, among others, at the Salon des Indépendents. In 1930, an art dealer Ambroise Vollard commissioned Chagall to illustrate the Bible, and in 1931 he traveled to Palestine to make preparatory gouaches for his Bible etchings.

In the mid-1950s, Chagall began working on a series of religious paintings called the "Biblical Message." In the late 1950s and mid-1960s, he developed a series culminating in the "Biblical Message" exhibition at the Louvre Museum. By 1969 Marc Chagall and his wife donated seventeen paintings of the series to the French government, and four years later, in 1973, the *National Museum Message Biblique Marc Chagall* in Nice opened its doors to the public. In the 1960s and 1970s, Chagall also designed numerous stained-glass windows, tapestries, and mosaics devoted to religious subjects.

Chagall's religious paintings are unique in combining Jewish and Christian imagery to show the continuity of both spiritual traditions, which convey essentially the same "Biblical message." On the painter's canvases, one finds traces of Adam and Eve, Noah's Ark, the biblical patriarchs, prophets, and kings, as well as scenes from Christ's life and death. Those that portray Christ's crucifixion and his descent from the cross parallel the paintings that depict Moses receiving the Tablets of the Law and Exodus. In many of Chagall's works, including his later masterpieces, "there is always at least one church for each synagogue, one Orthodox procession for ev-

---

[229] Polonsky, *Chagall*, 23.

ery Jewish wedding."[230] Chagall's Hassidic religious upbring-
ing did not stop him from incorporating those and other
Christian pictorial elements into his paintings. Among them,
the Crucifixion becomes one of the key themes that reflect the
inter-religious spirit of Chagall's art.

The Crucifixion appears in many of Chagall's paintings—
as one of the motifs that add symbolic complexity and depth
to the main message or as the central episode of the canvas.
In his earlier *Resistance and Resurrection* (1948), the crucified
Christ is placed at the center of the panels as a focal point
around which other pictorial elements depicting various religious and cultural symbols are arranged. In his *Creation of
Man*, made in 1958, the small crucifixion at the top of the panel reinforces the critical image of an angel carrying the first
human creature in his hands—suggesting the long and painful
journey of humanity, as well as the death and sacrifice that always accompany birth and desire.

Chagall's *White Crucifixion,* made just before the Second World War in 1938, is, perhaps, the most widely known
of his paintings on the subject. On this canvas, as one art
critic pointed out, the viewers observe a "swirling vortex
of terror...as houses, a synagogue, and Torah scroll burn,
a refugee-filled boat rows away, an armed mob comes over
the hill, and one man...on whose breast-cloth were once inscribed the words 'I am a Jew,' holds out his hands in suppli-
cation." In the above section of the panel, one also sees the
"Old Testament elders—the lamenting and helpless witnesses
to an unfolding catastrophe, which lies beyond human understanding."[231]

Here, as elsewhere in his paintings, Chagall masterfully
combines the Jewish inspiration for his art with the cultural

---

[230] *National museum Message Biblique Marc Chagall,* an album, Paris:
Réunion des musées nationaux, 2000, 14.
[231] Polonsky, *Chagall,* 32.

symbols of Western Christendom and then applies them to the events of contemporary history. Covered only by the Jewish prayer shawl, Jesus Christ in the painting is turned by the artist's power into a symbol of Jewish suffering and martyrdom. Chagall portrays Jesus as a Jew *par excellence* whose image is encircled by scenes of contemporary life events full of violence, despair, and death. "The sufferings of Jesus which continue in the sufferings of His people during the war years, in the suffering of all persecuted, wretched and impoverished of all times—that is what constitutes the genuine content of Chagall's paintings," writes Irina Yazykova in her article "*Ecce Homo.*" She continues: "To Chagall, himself a Jew, Jesus is not the God of the Christians who persecuted the Jews in the course of all history, but a man who suffers alongside the persecuted whomever they are."[232]

---

[232] Irina Yazykova, "*Ecce Homo*," 52.

ANTONIO SAURA (1930–1998)

*I have painted unrestricted joy and patches
which chance and anger have torn asun-
der, slow motion audacities and out-of-
joint accelerations… I should like to paint
fertile beings, made more of love than of
destruction, bulls without blood and true
subjects for rejoicing. Presumably, I cannot
do this, or perhaps I have done it without
knowing.*

Antonio Saura

AN IMPORTANT EXAMPLE OF SURREALIST CRUCI-
FIXION in painting comes from one of the most prominent
Spanish artists of the second half of the twentieth century,
Antonio Saura. Born in Huesca, Spain, Saura was a self-
taught young man who produced his first paintings and writings while recovering from tuberculosis. In 1950 Antonio
Saura had his first one-person show of experimental works
in the Libros bookshop in Saragossa. A year later—in Madrid,
"in the legendary Buchholtz bookshop which, together with
one or two other bookshops… represented a breath of fresh
air in the stifling climate of the time."[233] The invitation card
to his exhibition in Madrid described Saura's works as "Surrealist paintings." He considered himself a Surrealist because,
in his view, "Surrealism was the movement most closely corresponding to the anti-conformist attitude that he strove for,
a chance for evasion but at the same time a useable doctrine
of reality."[234]

---

[233] *Antonio Saura: Imagina 1956–1997*, Malmö Konsthall, 1997, 14.
[234] Ibid, 14.

In the mid-1950s, Saura came to live in Paris, where he participated in the activities of the Surrealists led by Breton, and in 1957 his first Paris exhibition was held in the Gallerie Stadler. In 1961 Saura had his first one-person show outside Europe—in the Pierre Matisse Gallery in New York.

In his long and prolific career, Antonio Saura experimented with many different genres and was involved in various artistic projects. He published books of essays and poetry and produced paintings, graphical works, lithographs, etchings, and silk-screen prints. He designed sets for opera and ballet performances and taught courses and seminars on art theory and practice at various institutions of higher learning in Spain. He was actively engaged in politics as a member of the organizing committee of the "First Democratic Spanish Pavilion" at the Venice Biennale in 1976 and the chair of the committee of the organization *Artistes du monde contre l'apartheid* in Paris from 1983 until it dissolved in 1996.

The Spanish painter enjoyed international fame and recognition for his art. He was a recipient of many prestigious prizes, including the Guggenheim Prize in New York (1960), the Carnegie Prize in Pittsburgh (1964), the Prize of Honor at the first European Print Biennial in Heidelberg (1979), and the Grand Prix des Arts de la Ville de Paris (1995). In 1982 King of Spain Juan Carlos awarded Saura with the Medalla de Oro de las Bellas Artes, and in 1990 he was made an Officer de l'Ordre des Arts et des Lettres in Paris. His works have been exhibited worldwide—in his native Spain and France, England, Germany, Italy, Switzerland, Austria, Finland, the Netherlands, Belgium, Brazil, Mexico, Argentina, and the United States.

When Antonio Saura was a child, his father took him to the Prado Museum in Madrid, where young Antonio became deeply impressed, almost mesmerized, by Velázquez's *Crucifixion*. It was "Velázquez' Christ with his black hair hanging down 'as in a female flamenco dancer' and 'feet like a bullfighter'—more precisely, a banderillero rising on his toes to thrust in his barbed darts—this, [Saura] still says, had an almost hypnotic effect on him."[235] Saura was not a Christian. Still, he turned to the theme of Crucifixion many times throughout his career. He created his first *Crucifixion* in 1957. He continued to paint "the crucified man transformed into a human"[236] through the 1980s. In the *Crucifixion*, made in 1960, and numerous others, Saura intended, unlike his much-admired Velázquez, "to create a convulsive image and a violent atmosphere of protest... In the image of the crucified figure, then, the timeless presence of suffering is implicit and the critical and religious background absent."[237] The Abstract Expressionist painters of the post-World War era expanded this approach toward Crucifixion as the symbol of suffering and rebellion faced with spiritual emptiness and crisis—even to mounting protest against religion and spirituality *per se*.

---

[235] Ibid, 27.
[236] Ibid.
[237] Christian Heck, "Between Myth and Model. Grünewald's *Crucifixions* and Twentieth Century Art," *The Body on the Cross*, 97.

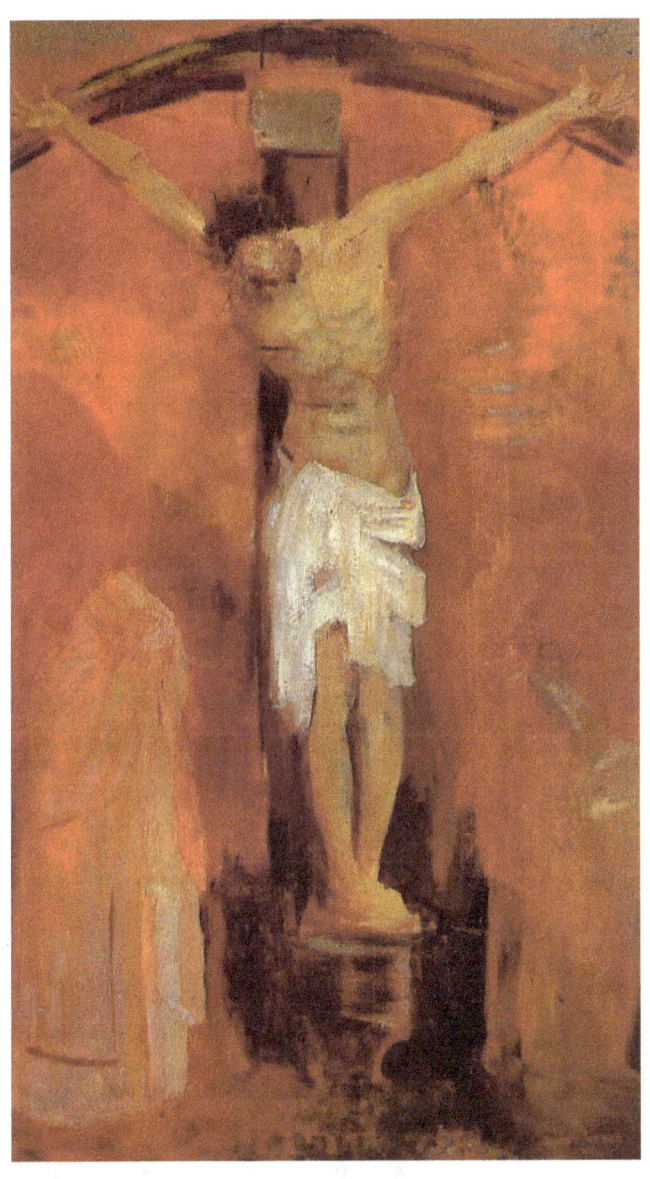

Odilon Redon (1840–1916), *The Crucifixion*, 1904,
Barber Institute of Fine Arts, Birmingham, UK.

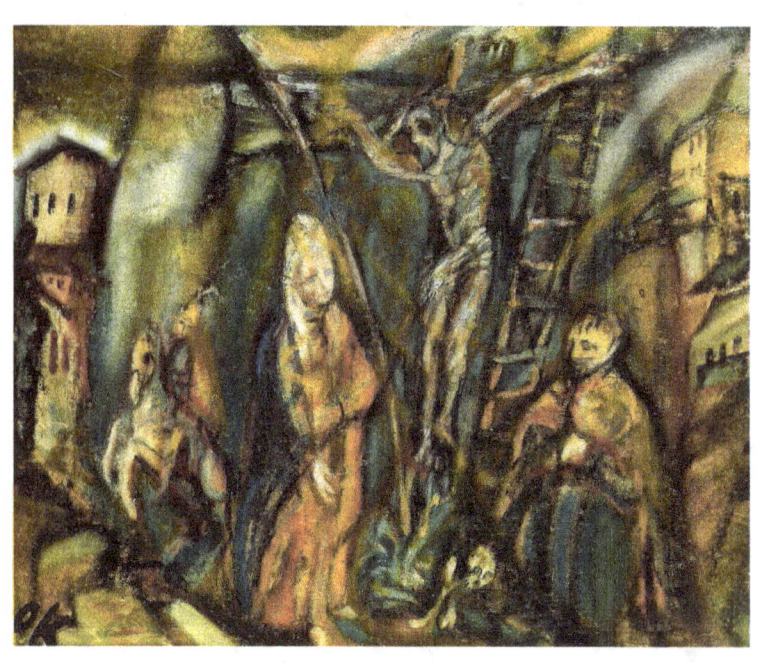

Oskar Kokoschka (1886–1980), *Crucifixion (Golgotha)*, 1912,
oil on canvas, private collection.
© 2023 Fondation Oskar Kokoschka.
Artists Rights Society (ARS), New York / ProLitteris, Zürich.

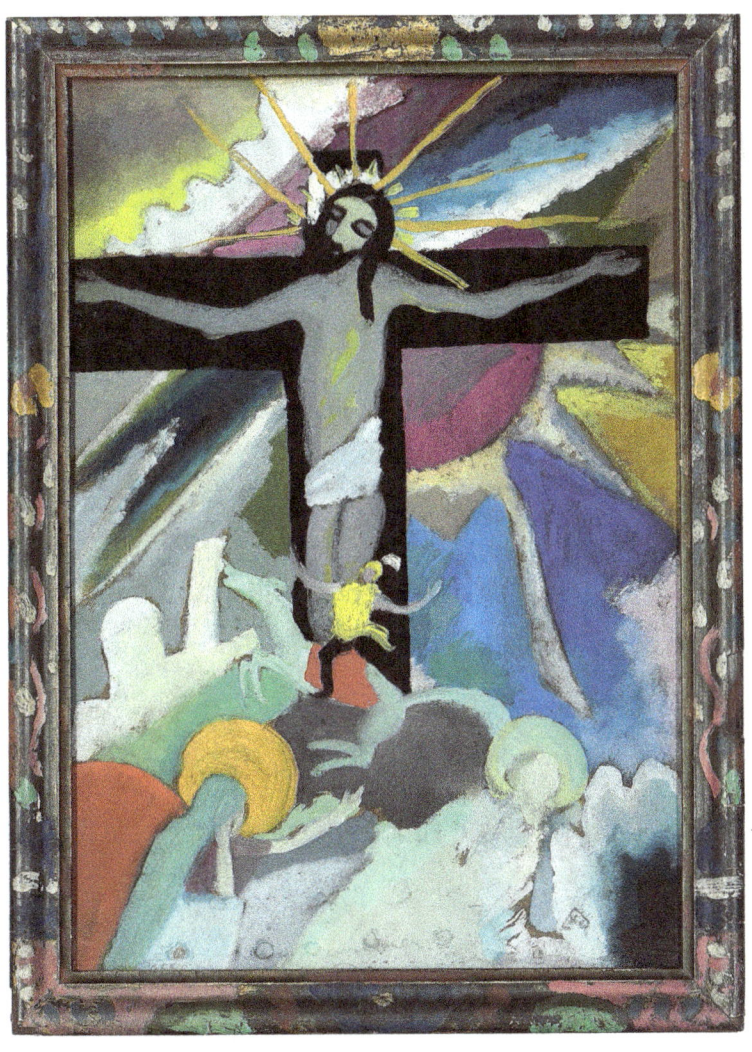

Wassily Kandinsky (1866–1944), *Crucified Christ*; Gekreuzigter Christus.
1911, private collection.
Photo © Christie's Images, London / Scala, Florence.
© 2023 Artists Rights Society (ARS), New York.

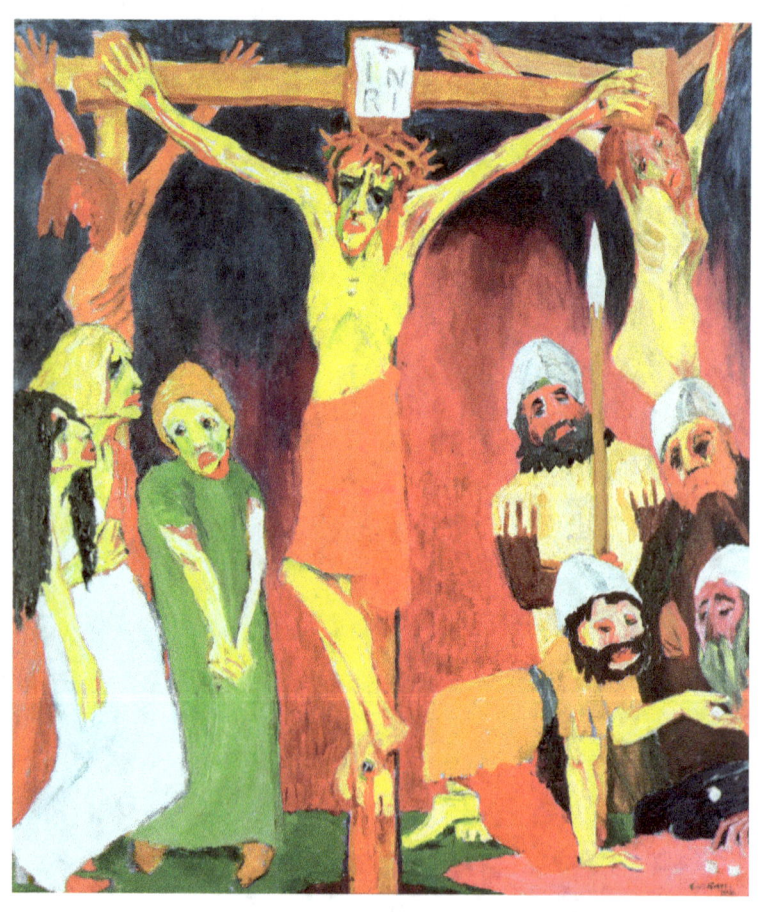

Emil Nolde (1867–1956), *Crucifixion,* 1912, painting.
Stiftung Seebüll Ada und Emil Nolde, Neukirchen, Germany.
Bridgeman Images © Nolde Stiftung Seebüll.

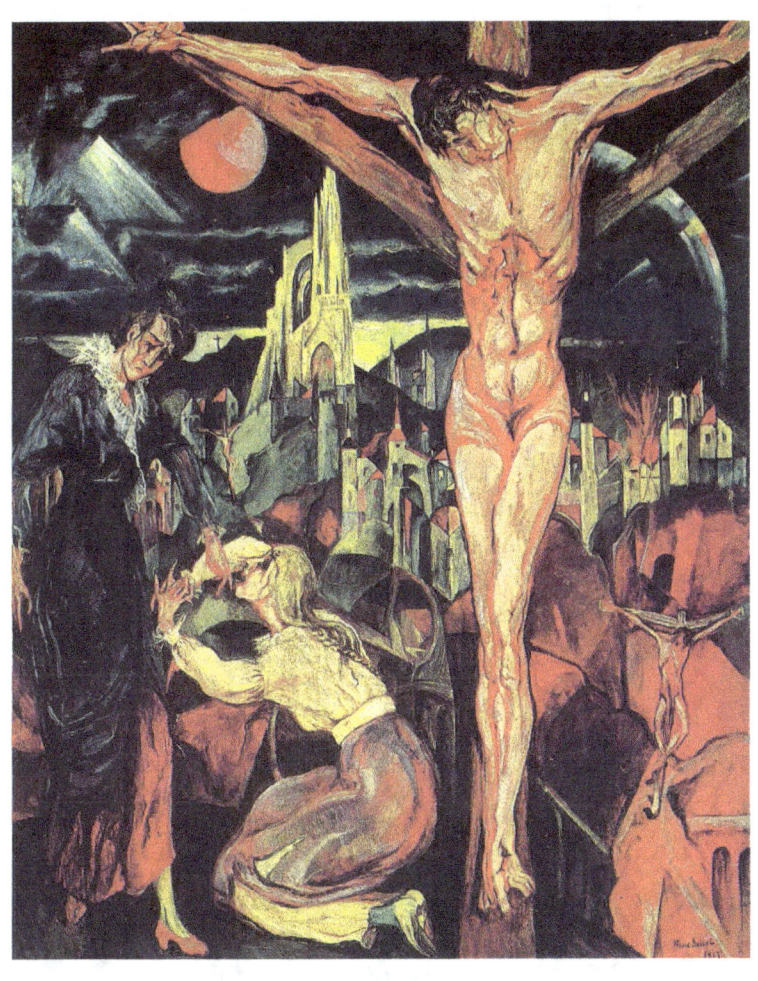

Max Ernst (1891–1976), *Crucifixion*, 1913, oil on canvas.
Museum Ludwig, Köln, Germany.
© 2023 Artists Rights Society (ARS), New York / ADAGP, Paris.

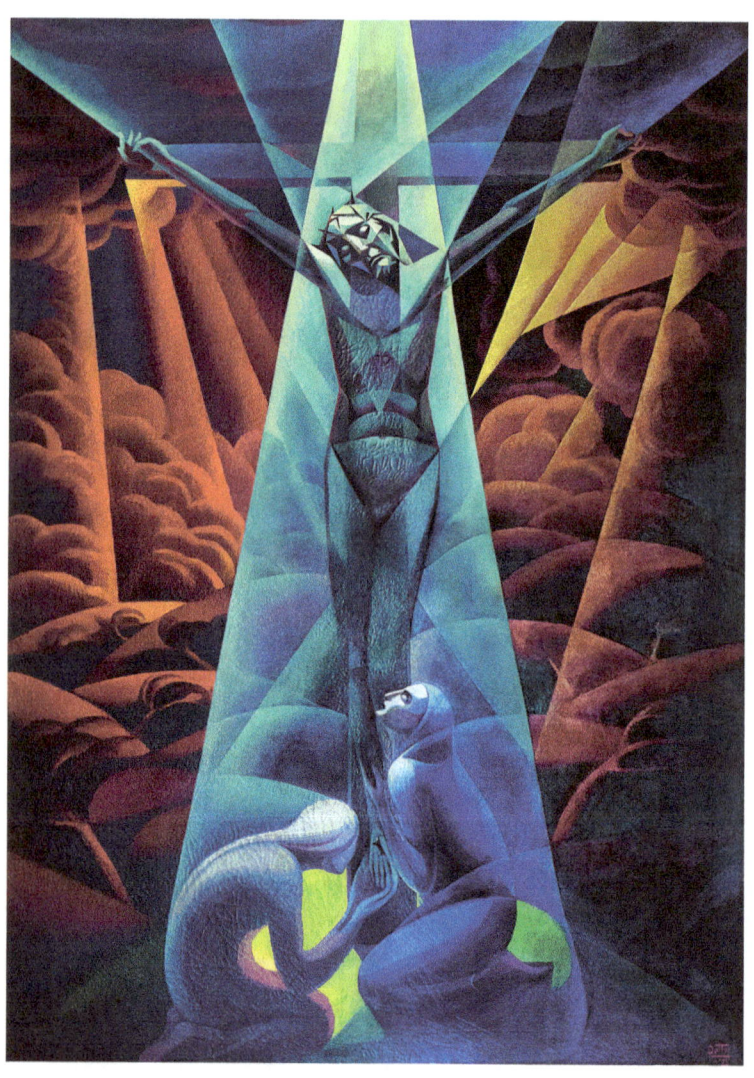

Gerardo Dottori (1884–1977), *Crucifixion*, 1927, oil on canvas,
Vatican Museums and Galleries, Vatican City.
Photo © Stefano Baldini / Bridgeman Image.
© 2023 Artists Rights Society (ARS), New York / SIAE, Rome.

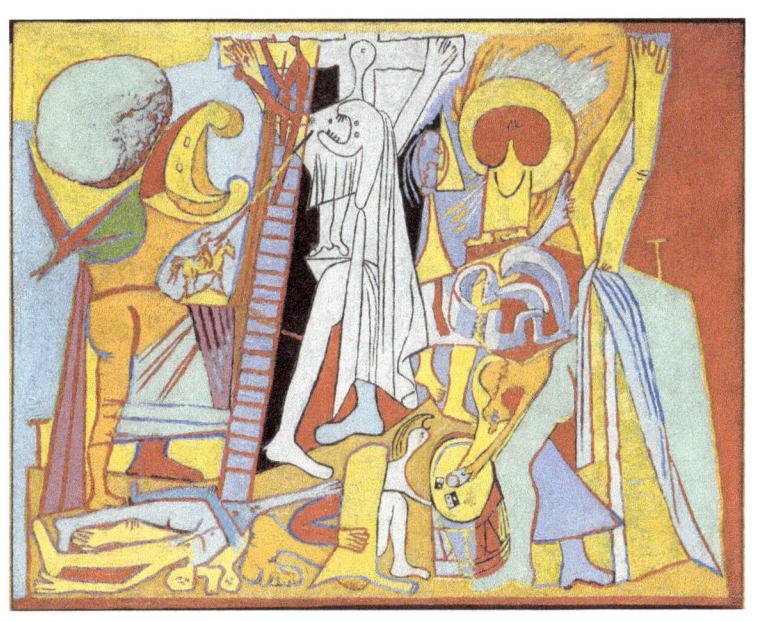

Pablo Picasso (1881–1973), *The Crucifixion*, 1930, oil on wood,
Musée National Picasso, Paris, France.
Photo: René-Gabriel Ojéda / Art Resource, NY.
© 2023 Estate of Pablo Picasso / Artists Rights Society (ARS), New York.

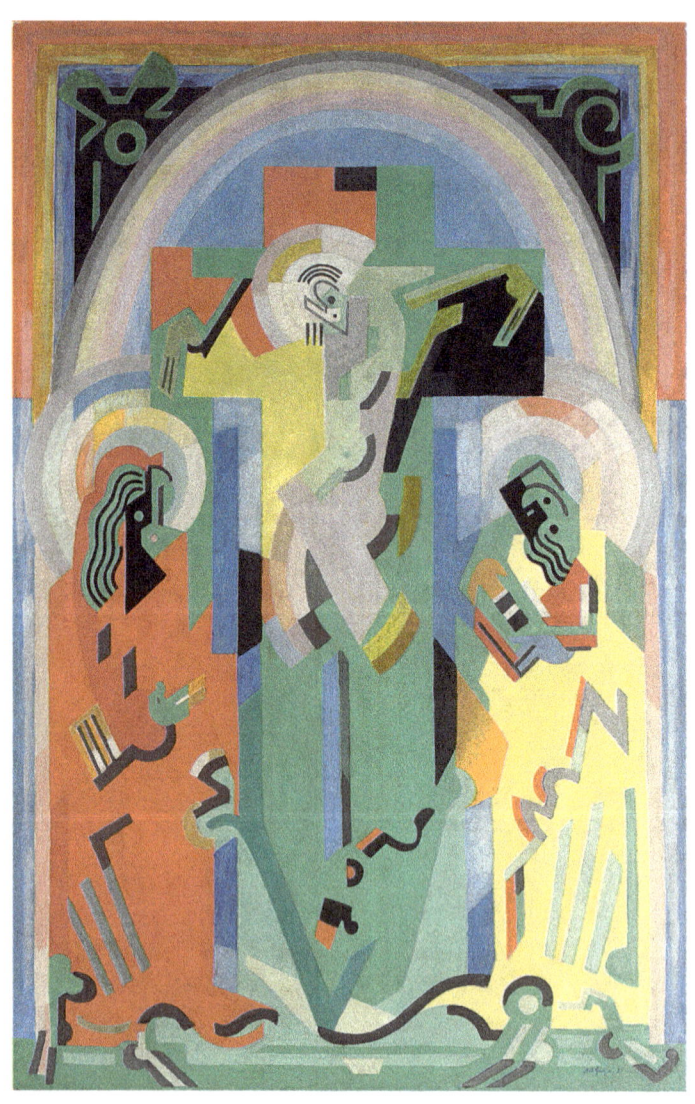

Albert Gleizes (1881–1953), *Crucifixion*, c. 1935,
oil on canvas, private collection.
Photo © Christie's Images / Bridgeman Images.
© 2023 Artists Rights Society (ARS), New York / ADAGP, Paris.

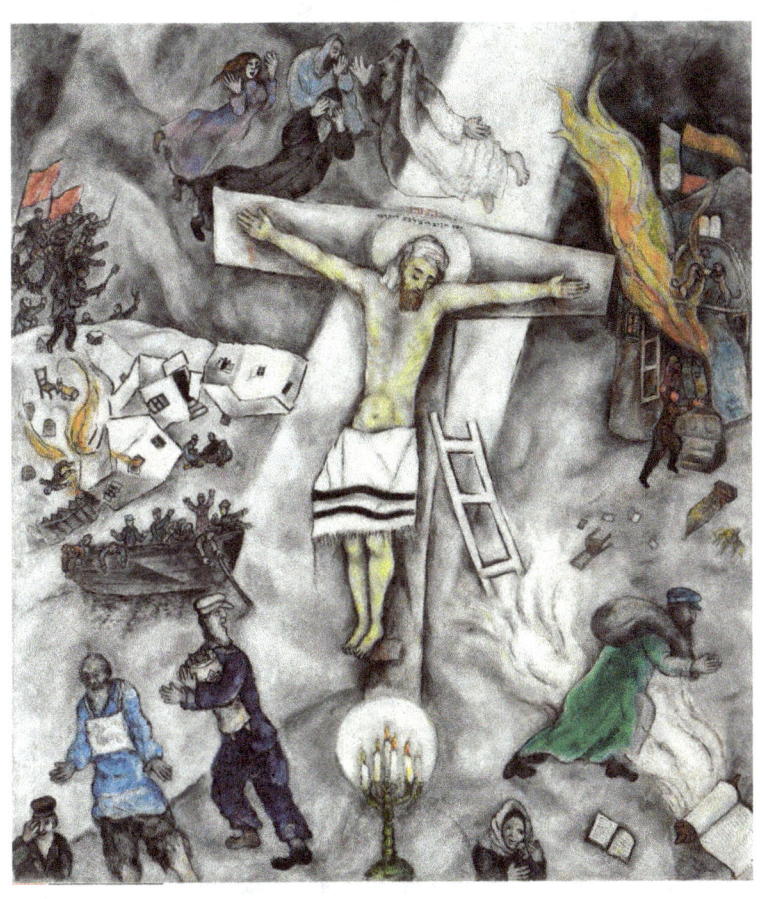

Marc Chagall (1887–1985), *White Crucifixion*, 1938, oil on canvas.
The Art Institute of Chicago, Chicago, USA / Art Resource, NY.
© 2023 Artists Rights Society (ARS), New York / ADAGP, Paris.

185

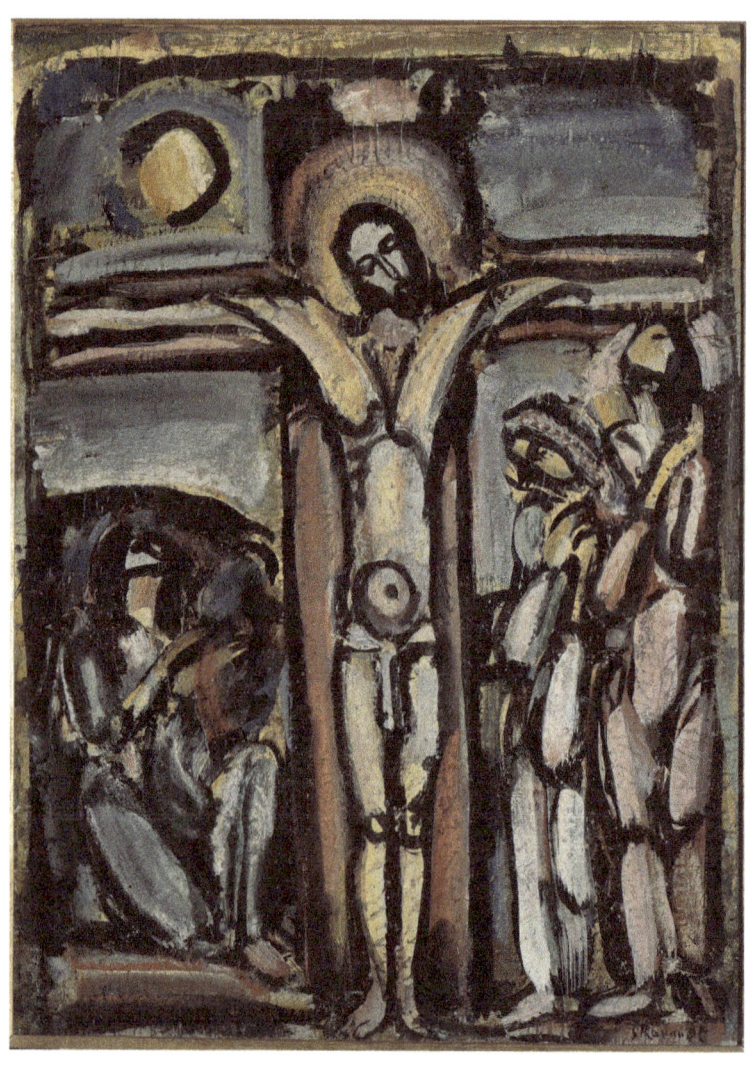

George Rouault (1871–1958), *Christ on the Cross*, 1939, oil on paper.
Musée National d'Art Moderne, Centre Georges Pompidou, Paris, France.
Photo: Christian Bahier & Philippe Migeat.
© 2023 Artists Rights Society (ARS), New York / ADAGP, Paris.

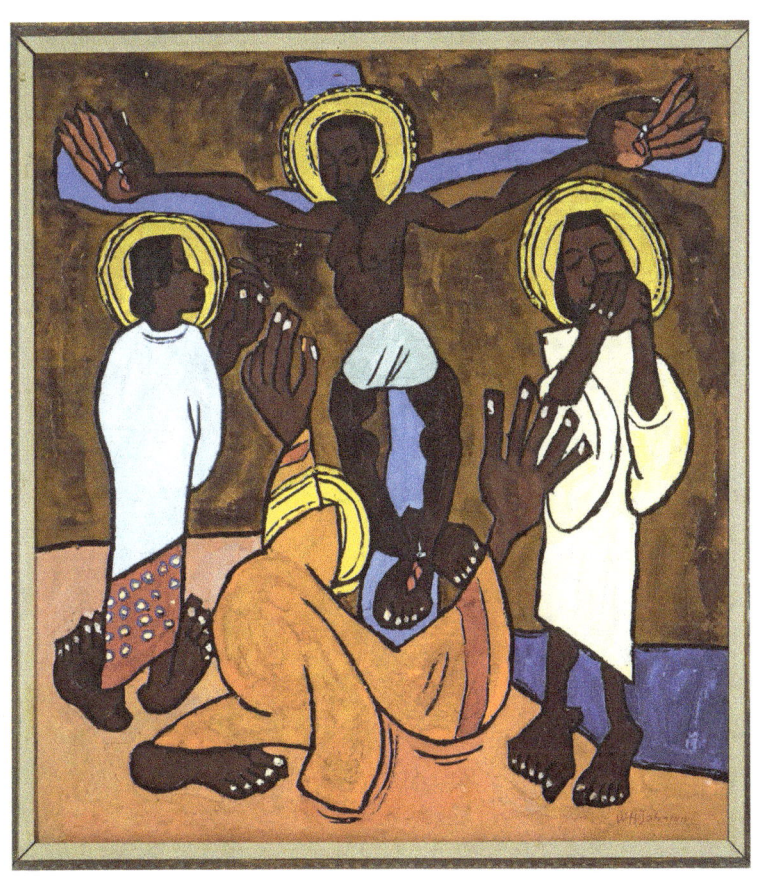

William H. Johnson (1901–1970), *Jesus and the Three Marys*, 1939,
oil on wood.
Howard University Gallery of Art, Washington, DC, USA.
Licensed by Art Resource, NY.

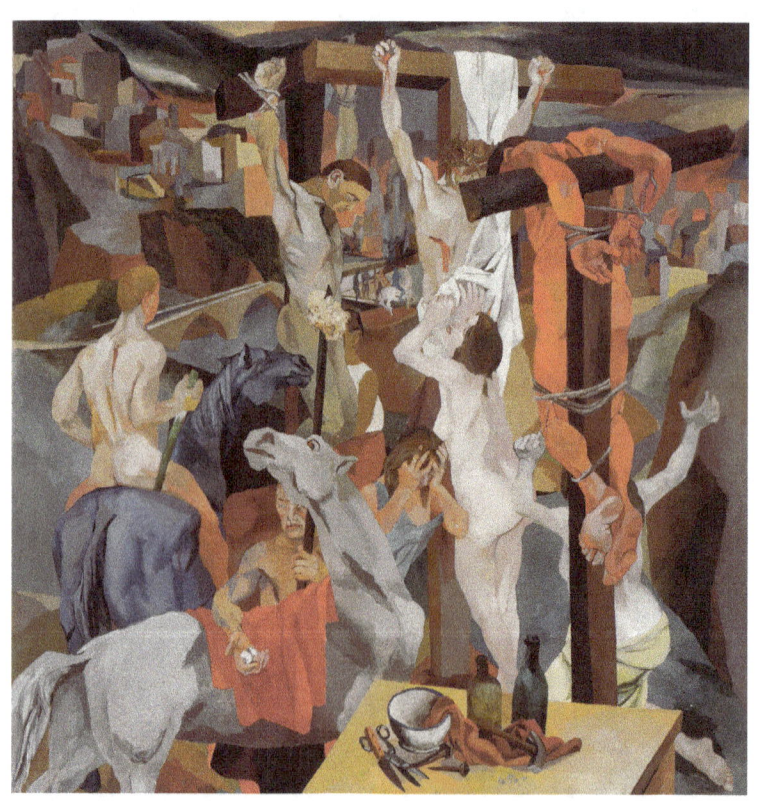

Renato Guttuso (1911–1987), *Crucifixion*, 1941, oil painting.
Galleria Nazionale d'Arte Moderna, Rome, Italy / Scala / Art Resource, NY.
© 2023 Artists Rights Society (ARS), New York / SIAE, Rome.

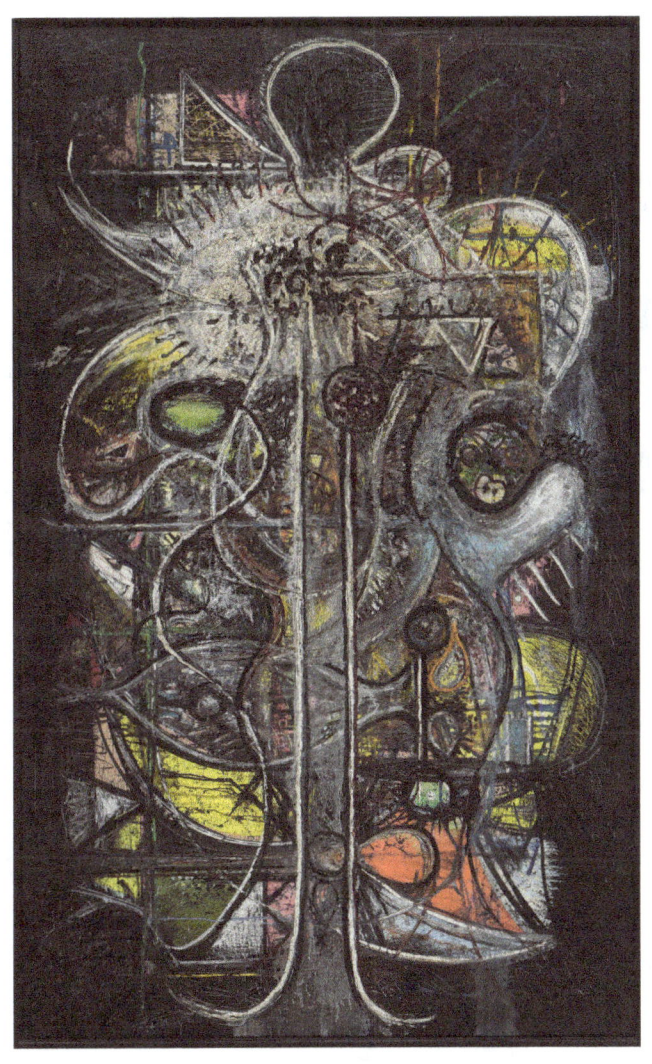

Richard Poussette-Dart (1916–1992),
Crucifixion, Comprehension of the Atom, 1944.
Oil on linen, 77 ⅝ x 49 ⅛ in. (197.2 x 124.8 cm), collection of the artist.
© 2023 Estate of Richard Pousette-Dart /
Artists Rights Society (ARS), New York.

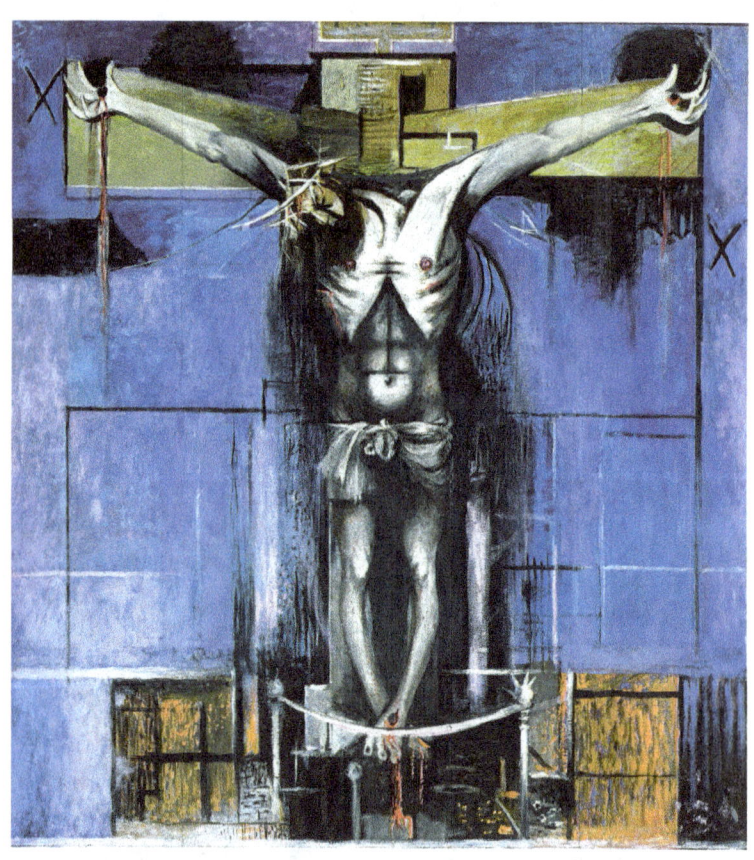

Graham Sutherland (1903–1980), *The Crucifixion,* 1946, oil on hardboard.
St. Matthew's Church, Northampton, Northamptonshire, United Kingdom.
© Gordon Roberton Photography Archive / Bridgeman Images.
© 2023 Artists Rights Society (ARS), New York / ProLitteris, Zurich.

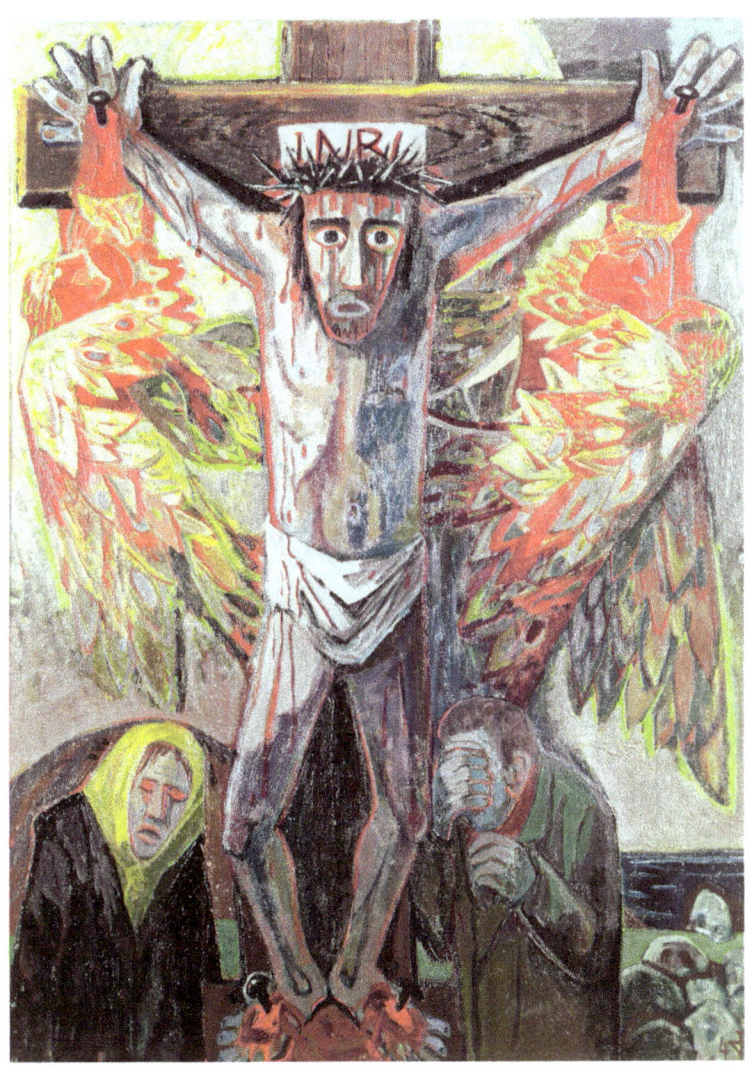

Otto Dix (1891–1969), *The Crucifixion*, 1948, painting.
Staatsgalerie, Stuttgart, Germany / Bridgeman Images.
© 2023 Artists Rights Society (ARS), New York / VG Bild-Kunst, Bonn.

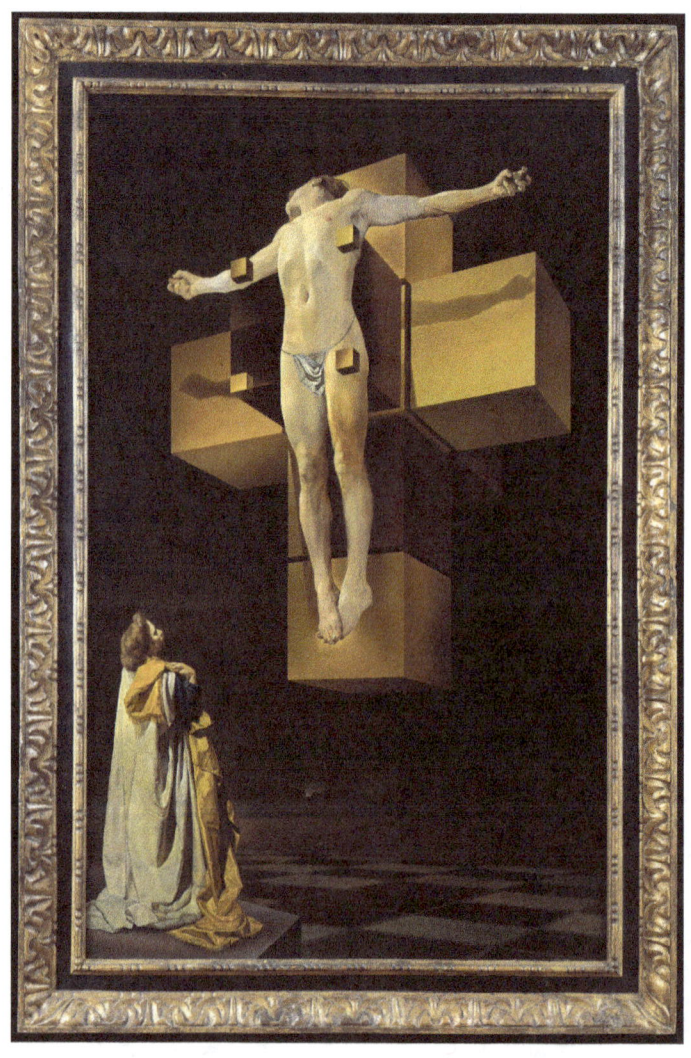

Salvador Dalí (1904–1989), *Crucifixion (Corpus Hypercubus)*,
1954, oil on canvas.
The Metropolitan Museum of Art, New York, NY, USA / Art Resource, NY.
© 2023 Salvador Dalí, Fundació Gala-Salvador Dalí, Artists Rights Society.

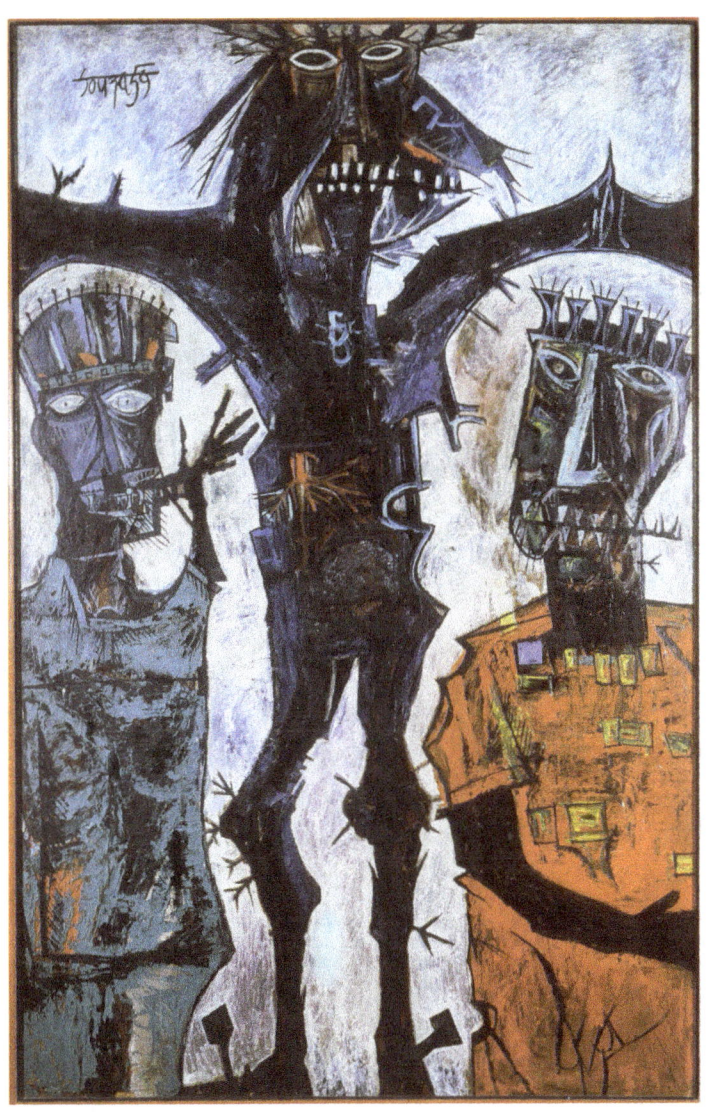

Francis N. Souza (1924–2002), *Crucifixion*, 1959, oil on board.
Tate Gallery, London, Great Britain / Art Resource, NY.
© Estate of F N Souza. All rights reserved, DACS / ARS 2023.

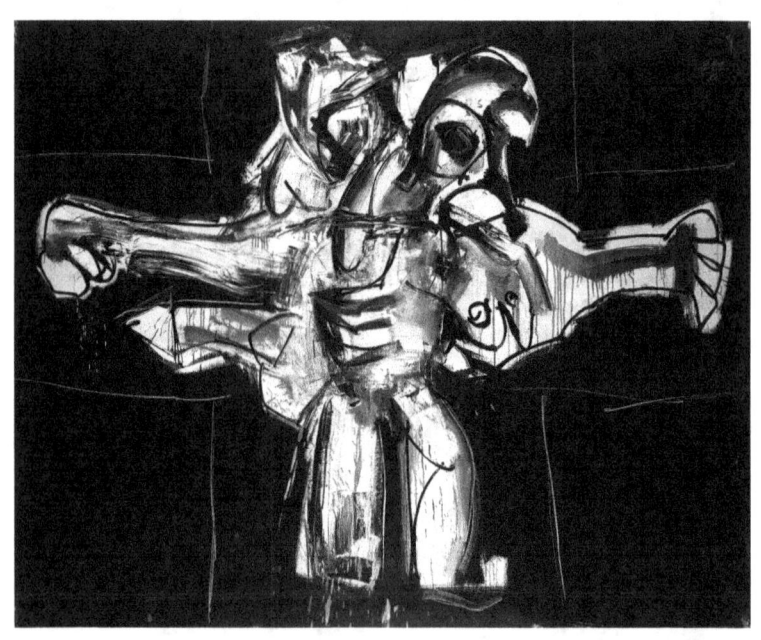

Antonio Saura (1930–1998), *Crucifixion*, 1961, oil on canvas,
private collection.
Photo © Christie's Images / Bridgeman Images.
© Succession Antonio Saura / www.antoniosaura.org / ADAGP, Paris, 2023.

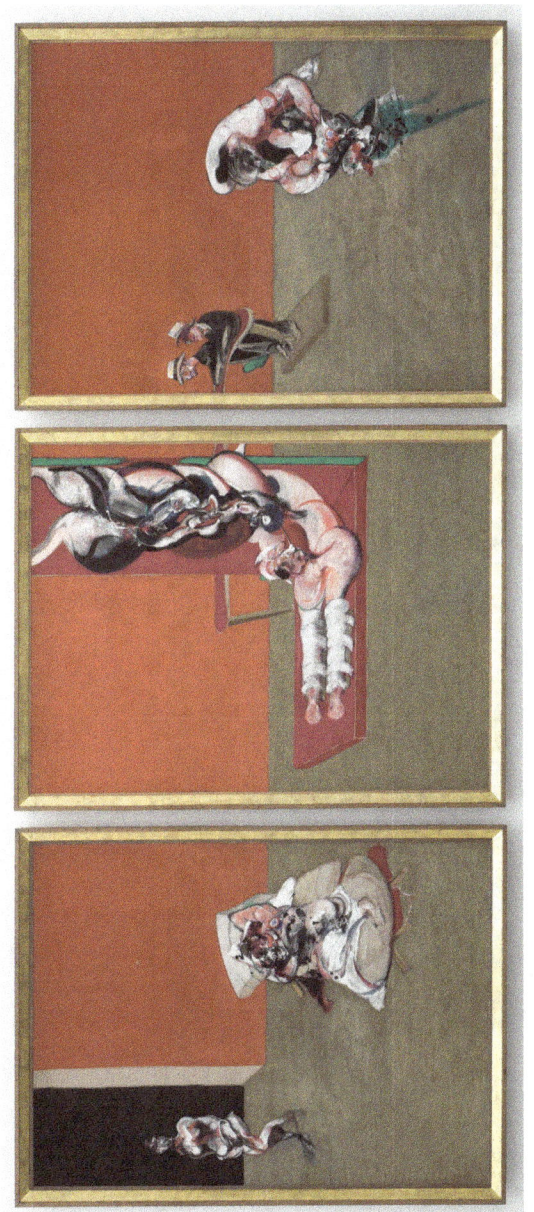

Francis Bacon (1909–1992), *Crucifixion*, triptych, oil on canvas, 1965, CR number 65-01, Bayerische Staatsgemäldesammlungen Pinakothek der Moderne, Munich, Germany.

Photo: Hugo Maertens

© The Estate of Francis Bacon. All rights reserved. / DACS, London / ARS, NY, 2023.

Barnett Newman (1905–1970)
The Station of the Cross — Twelfth Station, 1965.
National Gallery of Art, Washington, DC.
© 2023 The Barnett Newman Foundation /
Artists Rights Society (ARS), New York.

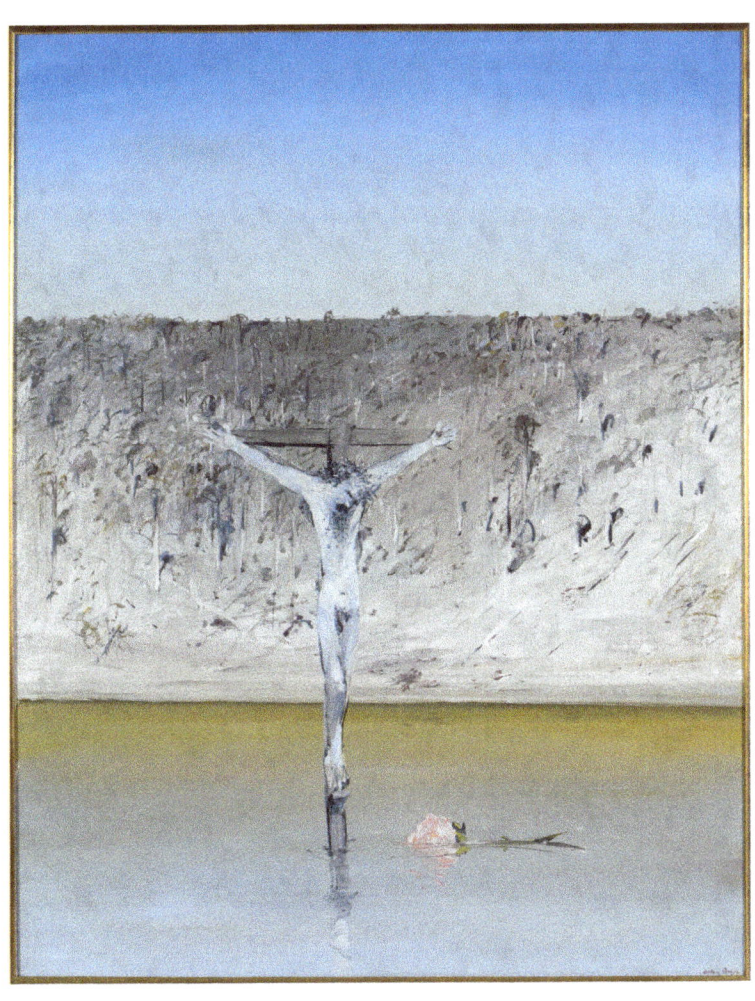

Arthur Boyd (1920–1999), *Crucifixion and Rose*, 1979-80.
Oil on canvas, 1525 x 1220 mm, Bundanon Collection, bundanon.com.au.
© Bundanon Trust, Australia / Copyright Agency.
Licensed by Artists Rights Society (ARS), New York, 2023.

197

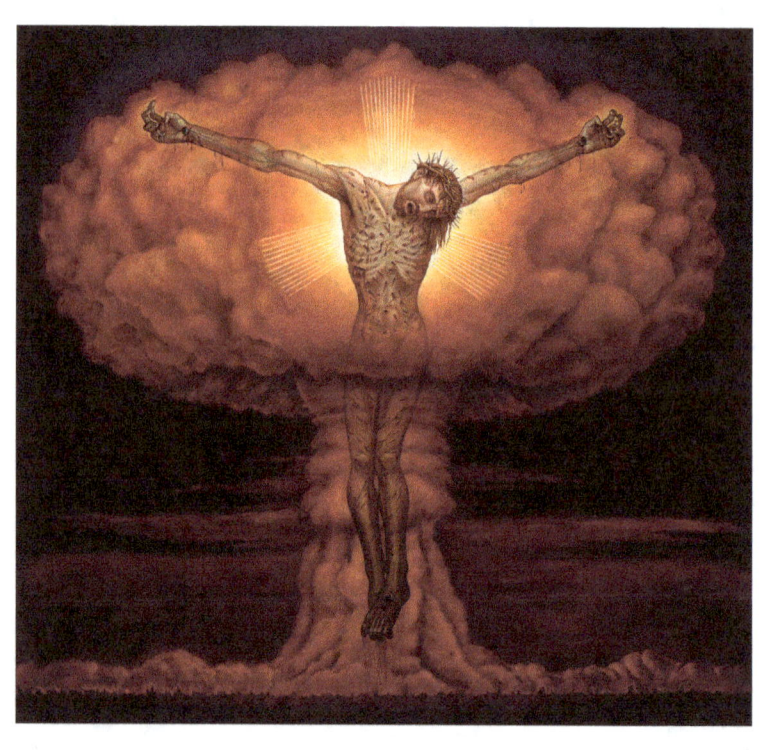

Alex Grey (b. 1953), *Nuclear Crucifixion*, 1980, oil on linen.
© Alex Grey, New York, NY, USA.

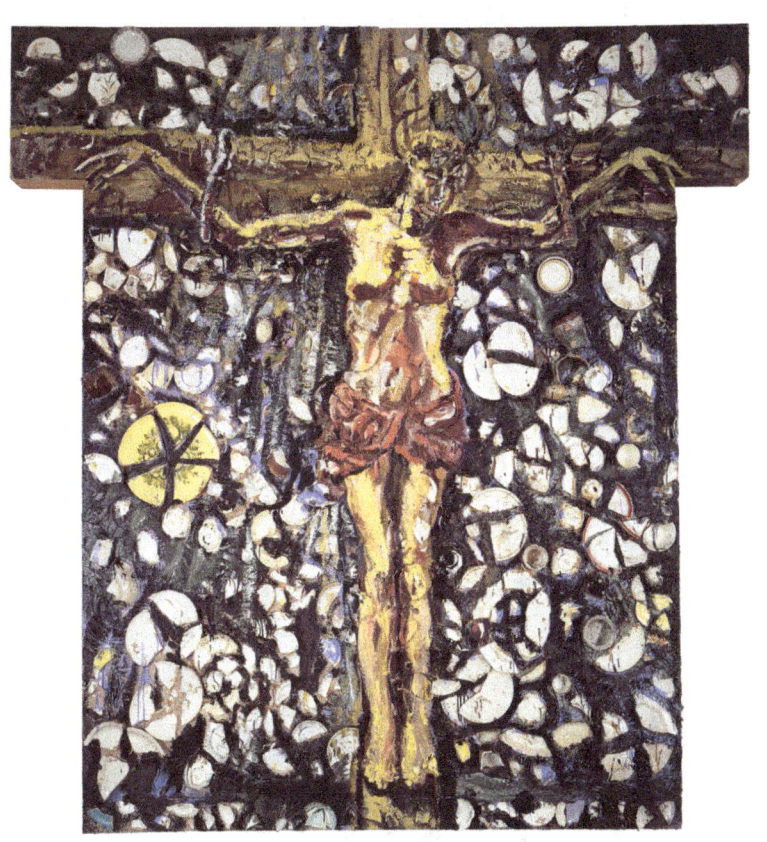

Julian Schnabel (b. 1951), *Vita*, 1983, oil, plates, and bondo on wood, private collection.
© 2023 Julian Schnabel / Artists Rights Society (ARS), New York.

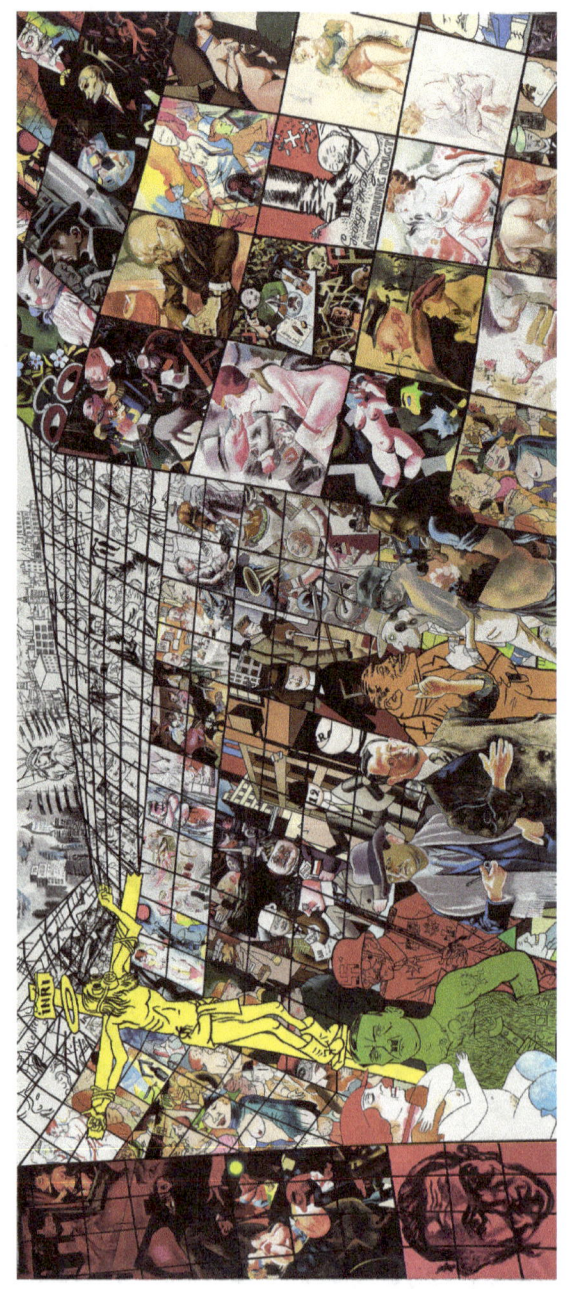

Gudmundsson Erró (b. 1932), *George Grosz*, 1997,
Museum Ludwig, Köln, Germany.
Photo: © Rheinisches Bildarchiv Köln, Germany.

Chapter Six

THE CRUCIFIXION IN ABSTRACTION

ABSTRACT ART WAS, ARGUABLY, THE MOST radical innovation Western artists have embarked on in Modern times. Cubism had challenged the five-hundred-year-old tradition of Renaissance painting and redefined its representational principles. Abstraction has rejected the very notion of representation or imitation of nature and broke away from the previous history and practice of Western art. This new twentieth-century artistic approach's far-reaching significance and consequences manifested at least in two interrelated tendencies.

First, abstraction did not become yet another in a countless series of art movements that sprang like mushrooms after the rain on the artistic fields of the prolific century. From the beginning, abstract art crystallized into a broader trend of an already rich creative landscape. This trend united such diverse early and late-twentieth-century movements as Suprematism and De Stijl, Vorticism and Abstract Expressionism, Minimalism and Optical art.

Second, from the very first decades of the century, abstraction transcended the confined limitations of painting and visual arts. It asserted itself as art's universal language by producing experimentation in dance, film, and even poetry. A Russian choreographer Michel Fokine (1880–1942), created the first abstract ballet in 1909. In architecture, the new abstract style of the famous Bauhaus School of Art and Design in Germany became so widespread and influential worldwide that it acquired the title of the International Style. In the second half of the twentieth century, abstract art became known as 'High Modernism.' It epitomized the completion and fruition of the project of artistic modernity when art became fully autonomous and independent from anything but itself.

The beginning of modern abstract painting dates to the first decades of the twentieth century. In the 1910s, there appeared in various parts of Europe—almost simultaneously but entirely independent from each other—several groups of artists that were moving away from figurative art. In Paris between 1911 and 1914, painters as different as Robert Delaunay (1885–1941), Frank Kupka (1871–1957), and Fernand Léger (1881–1955) exhibited works that displayed such an inclination. A French poet and art critic Guillaume Apollinaire characterized the new tendency as "Orphic Cubism" or simply Orphism. By that term, he described "an art which would dispense with the recognizable subject matter and rely on form and color to communicate meaning and emotion (just as Orpheus has done through the pure forms of music)."[238]

In England, painters like Wyndham Lewis (1882–1957), William Roberts (1895–1980), Edward Wadsworth (1889–1949), and others—also before World War I—have ushered in the abstract movement dubbed Vorticism. Its name came from the poet Ezra Pound, "a close associate of Lewis," who argued that in contrast to "Futurism [which] is essentially an acceleration of successive images, seen simultaneously, across a very shallow plain... Vorticism did... extend this acceleration into depth, creating an intense, inrushing perspective—a vortex."[239] Windham Lewis also edited the magazine *BLAST* and reproduced many works of these early English abstract painters and the publication of which "was one of the most important events in English art of the time."[240]

---

[238] Virginia Spate, "Orphism," *Concepts of Modern Art,* 85.
[239] Paul Overy, "Vorticism," ibid, 107.
[240] Ibid, 106.

The founder of abstract painting, the Russian artist Wassily Kandinsky (1866–1946), started working on his first abstract composition in 1909 and completed it by the following year. Kandinsky's pioneering *Composition I* was destroyed during Second World War and exists now only in black-and-white reproductions.[241] From those initial days, modern abstraction developed along the two lines of either expressionism or geometricism. Kandinsky was devoted to expressionist conception, especially in the first Munich period of his artistic activity. The Russian painter formulated the basics of abstract art in his seminal book *On the Spiritual in Art*, published in Munich in 1911. He then applied his creative vision to conveying spiritual emotions and feelings onto his groundbreaking pre-World War I canvases.

Another Russian painter, Kazimir Malevich (1878–1935), pioneered geometric abstraction. Malevich initiated his artistic movement called Suprematism around 1913 in Russia. He rejected any representation or imitation in art as a form of creative dependence on nature, religion, or the state. As an art critic, Aaron Scharf wrote in his article "Suprematism," "Malevich believed [that art] was meant to be useless. It should never seek to satisfy material needs. The artist must maintain his spiritual independence in order to create."[242]

In 1915 in St. Petersburg (then Petrograd), Malevich exhibited his programmatic canvas with a black square on a white background—a notorious emblem of geometric abstraction. Scharf explains: "Malevich's geometry was founded on the straight line, the supremely elemental form, which symbolized man's ascendancy over the chaos of nature." The straight line gave rise to the square, which does not exist in the natural world. Thus, the square became "the basic suprematist element: the

---

[241] See: Mikhail Sergeev, "Apocalyptic Themes in Twentieth-Century Painting: Wassily Kandinsky's *Last Judgment*," *ARTS: The Arts in Religious and Theological Studies*, vol. 16, 2 (2004), 14.

[242] Aaron Scharf, "Suprematism," *Concepts of Modern Art*, 139.

fecundator of all other suprematist forms. The square was a repudiation of the world of appearances and of past art."[243]

The first wave of abstraction, initiated by Wassily Kandinsky and developed by Kazimir Malevich, Piet Mondrian (1872–1944), and many others, flourished after World War I. It reflected the profound crisis of European culture and traditional aesthetic values but also expressed the unwavering optimism and high spiritual aspirations of the early generation of abstract painters. Those "artists found support for their ideas and techniques in different versions of idealist philosophy—from Neo-Platonism to modern mysticism."[244] They believed that by transcending the world of appearances and objects, by immersing themselves in the realm of pure relations and abstract forms, they could explore and partake of genuine and universal spirituality.

Kandinsky outlined this position in his work *On the Spiritual in Art*. A "Dutch artist Piet Mondrian, the leading figure in the most influential and long-lasting early twentieth-century abstract movement, De Stijl,"[245] also shared those convictions. Like Kandinsky, he believed that by "removing completely from the work all objects, 'the world is not separated from the spirit,' but, on the contrary, put into a balanced opposition with the spirit, since the one and the other are purified."[246]

In addition to such Platonist-style spirituality, Wassily Kandinsky engaged various religious themes and symbols in his painting. He was a practicing Orthodox Christian and applied the tradition of the Orthodox sacred art of iconography to his creative endeavors. Many of Kandinsky's early works, especially his pre-war compositions, were devoted to biblical subjects, precisely the apocalyptic narrative. Art historians

---

[243] Ibid, 138.
[244] Sergeev, "Apocalyptic Themes in Twentieth-Century Painting," *ARTS*, 12.
[245] Ibid, 13.
[246] Piet Mondrian, "Plastic Art and Pure Plastic Art" ("Figurative Art and Nonfigurative Art"), *Theories of Modern Art*, 359.

suggest that those compositions turned again and again to the themes of "the three horsemen of the Apocalypse...the flood or deluge, with reference to the Biblical narrative of Noah and his Ark [while the] last in a sequence, *Composition VII*, combined several religious themes, including the Last Judgment and Resurrection."[247]

Despite abundant religious imagery, Kandinsky rarely focused on Crucifixion in his artworks. The same is true regarding his fellow artists of the first wave—at least generally. The Crucifixion theme paved its way into the abstract canvases only with the second wave of abstraction that originated in the United States after World War Two.

There are many similarities between those two phases of twentieth-century abstract art. Both flourished around the wars and expressed a profound disillusionment with the established forms of culture. Kandinsky's friend Paul Klee once noted that the "more fearful this world becomes... the more art becomes abstract."[248]

The abstract artists of both periods also believed in pure idealism and spirituality. However, after the Second World War, American painters were "confronting a more developed condition of the same alienation of man from the world." There was nothing they "could affirm with the confidence with which [they] could affirm [their] own existence and [their] own mortality."[249] They were more open to the tragic experience in life. In art, the most familiar and suitable vehicle for its expression in the Christian tradition had long been the Crucifixion.

In addition, post-war American artists assimilated the theories and practices of Surrealism with their interest in the human unconscious. However, unlike their French predecessors,

---

[247] Sergeev, "Apocalyptic Themes in Twentieth-Century Painting," *ARTS*, 14.

[248] Norbert Lynton, "Expressionism," *Concepts of Modern Art*, 44.

[249] Charles Harrison, "Abstract Expressionism," ibid, 201.

they were more attracted to a Jungian rather than a Freudian version of psychoanalysis. American artists searched for the exploration of mythological dimensions of primitive Native American lifestyle, for the subconscious depth of 'collective archetypes'—the Crucifixion being the ultimate manifestation of one of them, namely, the archetype of the righteous sufferer.

American Abstract Expressionism started in the 1940s in the aftermath of the Second World War that became a significant catalyst for the movement. The war proved to be a disaster due to the immense loss of human lives, cultural and material devastation, and the emergence of the Soviet Union as a superpower. Europe was lying in ruins, and for the first time in history, American artists found no European model in the art to follow.

At the dawn of the Cold War, the United States responded to the challenge by transforming itself into a political, military, and economic super-state. In these new circumstances, the American cultural elite needed to counteract the Soviet totalitarian approach to art by defending American values of freedom and individualism.

All these factors have contributed to the emergence of Abstract Expressionism—the first American-born art movement of international significance. The movement reflected the horrors of the war, including the invention and use by the United States of weapons of mass destruction. It asserted the freedom of artistic expression by turning to archaic symbolism and primitive mythologies as lasting solutions to the madness of modern civilization.

The painting *Crucifixion, Comprehension of the Atom,* was a vivid example of addressing those cultural concerns in a novel stylistic fashion. It was created in 1944 by one of the pioneers of the new American school Richard Poussette-Dart (1916–1992). Poussette-Dart was born to a family of American artists. His father, Nathaniel Poussette, was a painter and writer; his mother, Flora Louis Dart, was a poet. Richard had a first solo exhibition of his works in 1941 at the Artists' Gallery in New York. Three years later, in 1944, he was included in the inaugural exhibition *Forty American Moderns* at Howard Putzel's 67 Gallery. Since then, he has participated—solo or along with his fellow Abstract Expressionists—in numerous exhibitions of modern American art.

"A founding member of the New York School that came into being in the 1940s and was generally known as Abstract Expressionism in the 1950s,"[250] Richard Poussette-Dart shared his fellow artists' interest in abstract myth-making and tribal, ritualistic art. Unlike many Abstract Expressionists, however, he focused in his painting not only on the tragic dimensions of human experience but also on the life-affirming and eternal creative impulse by "emphasizing creation as a primal act of self-definition."[251]

With its death camps and atomic bomb horrors, the Second World War dramatically impacted the development of the Abstract Expressionist School. Poussette-Dart's *Crucifixion, Comprehension of the Atom* (1944) was one of his works that reflected the enormity of human suffering during the war. Still, in this "crucial world moment," he pointed out, art "must have heart, mind, body, and spirit; a sweep inclusive of true atomic comprehension and a realization that in the truest sense chaos is impossible and man is whole." Thus, for the painter, the atomic age that runs parallel to the 'atomization of the form' in abstract art has both destructive and constructive potential.[252]

---

[250] Robert Hobbs and Joanne Kuebler, *Richard Poussette-Dart*, Indianapolis: Indianapolis Museum of Art, 1990, 80.

[251] Ibid.

[252] Notebook B 4, 1946–51, ibid, 18.

BARNETT NEWMAN (1905-1970)

> *To the extent that my painting was not*
> *an arrangement of objects...of spaces...*
> *of graphic elements, [it] was an open*
> *painting... and I still believe that my work*
> *in terms of its social impact does denote*
> *the possibility of an open society.*
>
> Barnett Newman

ANOTHER PROMINENT ABSTRACT EXPRESSIONIST WHO EXPLORED religious subjects and imagery in his contribution to the movement was Barnett Newman. One of the pioneering artists of Abstract Expressionism in the United States, Newman was born to a family of Jewish immigrants from Russian Poland. He studied at the Art Students League and City College of New York, majoring in philosophy. Barnett Newman worked as an art teacher in New York high schools and, from 1962 onward, as an instructor at various American universities.

The first solo exhibition of Newman's paintings occurred in 1950 at Betty Parsons Gallery in New York. In 1958 the Museum of Modern Art exhibition "The New American Painting," shown in Europe, included his works, and in 1965 his paintings were exhibited at the eighth São Paulo Art Biennial in Brazil. In 1970, Brandeis University in Waltham, Massachusetts, awarded Barnett Newman a Creative Arts Medal in Painting. In the same year, Newman died of a heart attack. The first retrospective exhibition of Barnett Newman's works, planned by the painter since 1969, opened posthumously in 1971 at the Museum of Modern Art in New York and then traveled to the Stedelijk Museum in Amsterdam, the Tate Gallery in London, and Galeries Nationales du Grand Palais in Paris.

In his theoretical essays written in the 1940s, Barnett New-man reasserts the unique importance of art in human life but decidedly redefines its character and purpose. In "The First Man Was an Artist," he argues that their artistic vocation dis-tinguishes humans from animals. He writes: "Man's first cry was a song [and the] myth came before the hunt. The purpose of man's first speech was an address to the unknowable. His behavior had its origin in his artistic nature."[253]

The aim of traditional art was the expression of beauty. "The impulse of modern art," Newman continues in his second programmatic essay, "The Sublime Is Now," "was this desire to destroy beauty."[254] It is not beauty but the sublime that is the proper subject matter of art. The classical European tradi-tion embodied the sublime content of the Christian religion in beautiful images and figures of heroic characters. Modern art-ists, on the contrary, lack the sublime message and are turning away from the notion of beauty.

Newman argues that modern art's last bastion of beauty is a contemporary biomorphic and geometric abstraction that creates beautiful forms, shapes, and patterns. "The question that now arises," he states, "is how, if we are living in a time without a legend or mythos that can be called sublime if we re-fuse to admit any exaltation in pure relations, if we refuse to live in the abstract, how can we be creating a sublime art?"[255]

According to Newman, contemporary artistic narrative stems from the notion of "terror (before the 'unknowable') and [from] the acknowledgment of terror [as] tragedy (the cogni-zance of the 'unknowable'; the awareness of the hopelessness of action in the face of ignorance and chaos)."[256] The essence

---

[253] Barnett Newman, "The First Man Was an Artist," *Theories of Modern Art*, 551.

[254] Newman, "The Sublime Is Now," ibid, 552.

[255] Ibid, 553.

[256] Harrison, "Abstract Expressionism," *Concepts of Modern Art*, 191.

of the artistic act, this "action in chaos," in its turn, aims to manifest the "tragedy of the unknown" by employing what Newman calls an 'ideograph'—a symbol that points to an idea without giving its name. These 'pure ideas,' as Newman argues, reveal the sublime in its most original form when "instead of making *cathedrals* out of Christ, man, or 'life' we are making it out of ourselves, out of our own feelings."[257]

Newman's *Stations of the Cross: Lema Sabachthani,* made between 1958 and 1966, provides a vivid example and a practical application of his artistic program. The series of fourteen paintings are all accomplished using color-field (in this case, black-and-white) and zip format that, according to Newman, unravel the naked sublimity of the human condition of terror and loneliness. The *Stations* were not commissioned to Newman but expressed his unorthodox spirituality freely. Indeed, the painter considered all his works, including the *Stations,* deeply spiritual. As an art critic, Ann Temkin pointed out:

> As was true for many American Jews of his generation, Newman's strong ethnic identification as Jewish did not often extend to religious observance at a synagogue. Instead, artists and writers of the postwar era hypothesized that the moral and ethical basis of Judaism could survive, and even be expressed through, secular cultural modernism. For these cosmopolitan Americans, modernism provided something in which to believe in the most profound way possible in the twentieth century. The museum was the place for that belief.[258]

In tune with Newman's informal approach to religion, his *Stations of the Cross* breaks entirely from traditional Christian

---

[257] Newman, "The Sublime Is Now," *Theories of Modern Art,* 353.
[258] Ann Temkin, "1966—*The Stations of the Cross: Lema Sabachthani* Solomon R. Guggenheim Museum," *Barnett Newman,* Philadelphia: Philadelphia Museum of Art, 2002, 64.

iconography. The technical characteristics of the series emphasize the trans-cultural and inter-religious nature of Newman's art. *The Twelfth Station* or the Crucifixion epitomizes the painter's "preoccupation with the heroic or tragic assertion in total solitude." It represents the visual referent of the series' subtitle "Lema Sabachthani"—the Hebrew rendering of Jesus' cry from the Cross: "My God, My God, why hast Thou forsaken me!" Ann Temkin explained: "The Stations of the Cross present a virtuoso demonstration of the qualities Newman's art generally displays: restricted formal means, cross-referencing between paintings, and spiritual ambitions."[259]

---

[259] Ibid.

FRANCIS BACON (1909–1992)

> *I believe that realism has to be re-invent-*
> *ed [by making] changes in reality, which*
> *become lies that are truer than the literal*
> *truth. This is the only possible way the*
> *painter can bring back the intensity of the*
> *reality which he is trying to capture.*

Francis Bacon

LIKE THOSE OF ANOTHER MEMBER OF the Abstract Expressionist group, Mark Rothko (1903–1970), Barnett Newman's paintings are purely abstract and lack expressionist qualities. The artworks of other movement participants—Willem de Kooning (1904–1997) and Robert Motherwell (1915–1991)—are highly expressionist but retain the vestiges of figuration. The paintings of their contemporary English artist Francis Bacon, representing a European version of post-war Existentialist art, are also more expressionist than abstract.

Francis Bacon was born in 1909 in Dublin to the family of an English racehorse trainer who "claimed to be a descendant of the philosopher Sir Francis Bacon (1561–1626)."[260] Because of his health problems—Bacon suffered from acute asthma—he did not receive a formal education. In the late 1920s, Bacon made his first drawings, watercolors, and oil paintings—to be shown at the first exhibition of his works in 1929. The first exclusive exhibit of Bacon's art occurred at the Hanover Gallery in London in 1951.

In the 1950s, Bacon's works were exhibited for the first time outside England—in 1950 in the United States, in 1957 in

---

[260] *Francis Bacon and the Tradition of Art*, ed. Wilfred Seipel et al., Milano: Skira Editore, 2003, 357.

France, and in 1958 in Italy. In the 1960s, Francis Bacon enjoyed wide recognition for his art. In 1962 the Tate Gallery in London held a retrospective exhibition that included ninety-two of his paintings. In 1963 the Guggenheim Museum in New York followed suit. Its retrospective displayed sixty-four of Bacon's works, and it later traveled to the Art Institute of Chicago and the Contemporary Arts Association in Houston. In 1967 Francis Bacon was given "two international prizes; the Carnegie Institute Award in Painting of the Pittsburgh World Exhibition, which he refused, and the Rubens Prize [which he donated] for the restoration of artworks in Florence following the severe flooding of the city."[261] In 1978 he was awarded the Max Beckmann Prize by the city of Frankfurt, which he also rejected.

Bacon's artistic fame has expanded internationally in the last two decades of his life. In 1977 an exhibition of his art was organized in Mexico; a year later—in Spain. In 1983 the first exhibition of his works was held in Japan, and in 1988 in Soviet Russia. Francis Bacon died in 1992 of a heart attack during his visit to Madrid, Spain.

Throughout his painterly career, Francis Bacon emphasized in his art reality over what he perceived as an escape from the truth of life. In one of his interviews, he says: "Anything in art seems cruel because reality is cruel. Perhaps that's why so many people like abstraction in art because you can't be cruel in abstraction."[262] In another conversation, he reinforces the same point: "Man is haunted by the mystery of his existence and is therefore much more obsessed with the remaking and recording of his own image on his world than with the beautiful fun of even the best abstract art."[263]

---

[261] Ibid, 360.

[262] David Sylvester and Michel Archimbaud, "Interviews with Francis Bacon," *Francis Bacon and the Tradition of Art*, 349.

[263] Michael Peppiatt, "Three Interviews with Francis Bacon," *Francis Bacon. A Retrospective,* guest curator Dennis Farr, New York: Harry N. Abrams Publishers, 1999, 42.

Like Pablo Picasso, Francis Bacon deconstructs, decomposes, and distorts the reality of sensual experience, but he never reaches a point of complete abstraction in his devolution of figuration. Bacon is the true spiritual heir of Picasso in the same way Samuel Beckett is the natural inheritor of the legacy of Franz Kafka. In one of his interviews, Bacon himself recognized the unique importance the Spanish master had for his artistic development. He says: "It was after staying in Paris, where I saw an exhibition of Picasso, that I said to myself that I was going to paint... Certain works of Picasso have not only unlocked images for me, but also ways of thinking, and even ways of behaving."[264]

One theme that runs consistently throughout Bacon's artistic career is that of the Crucifixion. He painted his first *Crucifixions* as early as 1933. One of the three canvases "became the best-known of Bacon's early paintings." And all three were bought "by Sir Michael Sadler...the foremost collector of contemporary art in England [and] the first private collector to buy the artist's pictures [which] marked his first success as a painter."[265]

In 1944 Bacon returned to the subject by painting his famous *Three Studies for Figures at the Base of a Crucifixion*. The triptych aimed to blend Christian and pagan mythological motifs by depicting the "chthonic forces of the Furies" in the Christian context.[266] However, "the only relatively strong reference in the picture itself [to the Crucifixion] is the white cloth that one of the figures wears as a blindfold and which points to Christ's loincloth."[267]

---

[264] "Interviews with Francis Bacon," *Francis Bacon and the Tradition of Art*, 351–52.

[265] Dennis Farr, "Catalogue," in *Francis Bacon. A Retrospective*, 52.

[266] Sally Yard, "Francis Bacon," ibid, 11.

[267] Verena Gamper, "The Motif of the Crucifixion in Triptych Format," *Francis Bacon and the Tradition of Art*, 330.

In the 1960s, Francis Bacon created several Crucifixions—*Three Studies for a Crucifixion* (1962) and yet another triptych *Crucifixion* (1965) that displays "colors and motifs of Nazism [possibly] as a type of shorthand for alarm and terror... as a ready means to shock and provoke."[268] A professed atheist, Bacon explained in his interviews that Crucifixion did not hold a religious connotation for him but symbolized the cruelty of men toward their fellow men and the inevitability and raw agony of suffering and death. His *Three Studies for a Crucifixion*, made in 1962, are quite revealing in this respect.

As an art critic Verena Gamper explained, in the painting, "the crucified Christ has been displaced from the central panel. Instead, the right panel is occupied by a figure reminiscent in its raw carnality of a slaughtered animal."[269] On the central panel, as she continues, "instead of a Crucifixion scene, we find...a completely shattered figure lying on a bed in frontal view. It almost seems as though the chunk of meat from the center black surface had slid directly onto the bed."[270]

It looked like by "the 1970s, the possibilities of the crucifixion had been exhausted for Bacon." Bacon wrote that he "would never use it or could never use it again."[271] Nevertheless, in 1988, he produced the *Second Version of 'Triptych 1944'*, a painting "over twice the size of the 1944 triptych" with "a blood-red background [instead of] the orange-red of the earlier work."[272]

In many of his Crucifixion paintings, Francis Bacon used the classical Christian art format of the triptych. He did it for the first time in *Three Studies for a Crucifixion* in 1962. Howev-

---

[268] Margarita Cappock, "'The Chemist's Laboratory' Francis Bacon's Studio,'" ibid, 91.

[269] Gamper, "The Motif of the Crucifixion in Triptych Format," in *Francis Bacon and the Tradition of Art*, 331.

[270] Ibid.

[271] Sally Yard, "Francis Bacon," *Francis Bacon. A Retrospective*, 16.

[272] "Second Version of 'Triptych 1944'," ibid, 217.

er, Bacon's triptychs reveal more of a 'serial principle' than the traditional hierarchical structure when the central panel occupies the critical position to which the left and right pictures are subordinate. Bacon pointed out that his "triptych corresponds more to the idea of a succession of images on film."[273] He said in another place: "I see images in series. And I suppose I could go on long beyond the triptych and do five or six together, but I find the triptych is a more balanced unity."[274]

Similarly, the title of Crucifixion should not confuse the viewer, who may ascribe a traditional religious interpretation of the subject to the painter. As mentioned earlier, Francis Bacon was not a believer. The symbol of Crucifixion represented for him the inhumanity of men and the inevitability of death rather than the divine gift of salvation.

Crucifixion, for him, "epitomized mutilation of the flesh, pain, butchery, and ultimately, death in a horrific manner." Bacon's Crucifixions evoke the images of slaughterhouses and meat that fascinated him and represented the triumph of everlasting decay over eternal life. As one art critic shrewdly noted, "Bacon's paintings [of Crucifixion] are ironic subversions of the tragic image of sacrifice at the core of Christianity," from which the Crucifixion *per se* disappears, and only hybrid forms of half-human and half-animal nature remain on the canvas.[275]

---

[273] Michel Archimbaud, *Francis Bacon. In Conversation with Michel Archimbaud*, London: Phaidon Press, 1993, p. 165. Quoted in *Francis Bacon and the Tradition of Art*, 330.

[274] *Francis Bacon and the Tradition of Art*, 350.

[275] Margarita Cappock, "'The Chemist's Laboratory' Francis Bacon's Studio,'" ibid, 311.

GRAHAM SUTHERLAND (1903–1980)

Painting, it is true, can often be the equivalent of lyric poetry...which enlightens the significance and nature of things... which makes things hold more than their original meaning, and which defines their essence.

Graham Sutherland

IN CONTRAST TO BARNETT NEWMAN AND Francis Bacon, the English painter Graham Sutherland has produced more traditional, Christian-oriented Crucifixion artworks using Abstract Expressionist techniques and style. Graham Sutherland was born in London to the family of a civil servant. In 1926 he graduated from Goldsmiths College School of Art at the University of London. He later worked as a teacher at the Chelsea School of Art (1928–39) and Goldsmiths' College (1946–47).

Sutherland's first one-person drawings and engravings exhibition occurred in 1925 at the XXI Gallery. Thirteen years later, he had his first one-person exhibition of paintings at the Rosenberg and Helft Gallery. The first international one-person show of Sutherland's artistic works occurred in 1946 in New York. Since then, his paintings have been exhibited all over Europe, including Germany, Austria, France, Italy, the Netherlands, and Switzerland.

Graham Sutherland was awarded the Order of Merit in 1960 and received an Honorary Degree of Doctor of Literature in 1962 at the University of Oxford. He was also elected Honorary Fellow of the American Academy of Arts and Letters in 1972, appointed Commandeur des Arts et des Lettres in France, and Honorary Fellow of the Accademia di San Luce in Rome in 1973, as well as awarded the Shakespeare Prize in Hamburg in 1974.

Graham Sutherland's approach to art consists of transcending appearances and penetrating the metaphysical depth of reality, uncovering its essential nature. His idea of painting is not "strictly abstract...concerned with the display of pure and absolute forms and colors in space." Although his artwork "seems abstract or partially so, [it] is essentially bound to reality, and concerned with seeing reality in a new way."[276]

Throughout his career, Sutherland painted plenty of landscapes. He was also a brilliant portraitist, and when appointed an official War Artist during the Second World War, he worked on the war scenes. Although he converted to Catholicism in his youth and remained devoted to his faith, Sutherland rarely addresses religious themes in his art. His most famous ecclesiastical commissions are the painting of *The Crucifixion* for St. Matthew's Church in Northampton (1946) and the design of the excellent tapestry for the new Coventry Cathedral (1962).

The idea of the Crucifixion attracted Sutherland because, as he put it himself, "it has a duality, which has always fascinated me." He continued: "It is the most tragic of all themes, yet inherent in it is the promise of salvation. It is the symbol of the precariously balanced moment, the hair's breadth between black and white."[277] Art critics highly praised his Northampton Crucifixion as "one of the finest religious works of the twentieth century [in which] the spectator is drawn into the tragedy, enveloped and hypnotized by the anguished yet noble figure of the Redeemer."[278]

---

[276] Martin Hammer, *Graham Sutherland: Landscapes, War Scenes, Portraits 1924–1950*, London: Scala Publishers, 2005, 142.

[277] Ibid, 144.

[278] John Hayes, *The Art of Graham Sutherland*, New York: Phaidon Press, 1980, 26.

Chapter Seven
THE CRUCIFIXION IN POST-MODERNISM

THE LAST THREE DECADES OF THE twentieth century saw the rise of a new cultural and artistic paradigm in Western societies that is now summarily called "postmodernism." The definitions of this novel trend can vary, but the change itself "is often said to begin in 1977, with the publication of Charles Jencks' *The Language of Post-Modern Architecture.*" In this book, Jencks "sought to supplant the minimalism of International style design with more eclectic approaches."[279]

To understand the nature and evolution of postmodernism and postmodern art, we must recollect the basics of modern thought against the background of which its ideological successor rose to prominence. As the term "postmodern" suggests, the rising movement aimed to overcome the limitations of modernity by constructing a more progressive alternative. The new way of thought was supposed to rebel against the premises and surpass the accomplishments of its historical and cultural predecessor.

However, before we can dwell on the succession of art movements, we should also clarify specific terminological ambiguities that arise using the words (post)modernity and (post)modernism. Modern times or modernity is a cultural period in the history of European and Western civilization that began with the eighteen-century Enlightenment and

---

[279] Christopher Reed, "Postmodernism and the Art of Identity," in *Concepts of Modern Art*, 271.

continues to the present day. Modernism, in turn, represents a series of movements in visual arts, music, and literature that emerged in the last quarter of the nineteenth century through the first half of the twentieth century. Associated with the era of "industrialization, the nearly global adoption of capitalism, rapid social change, and advances in science and the social sciences," modernist art reflected "a growing alienation incompatible with Victorian morality, optimism, and convention."[280]

In contrast to modernism, the "postmodern world" or postmodernity, as explained by an American historian Frederick Jameson, is characterized by an ideology of a post-industrial society, "also designated [as an] information society, or high tech, and the like."[281] Postmodern thinkers accepted some of the basic premises of the Enlightenment, but they strongly argued against others, especially the absolutization of science and scientific discourse.

At the center of the "postmodern condition" stands the question of the legitimacy of knowledge. The Enlightenment philosophers challenged the validity of tradition in favor of purely rational ideas and theories. However, according to Enlightenment thought, those theories still had absolute legitimacy and delivered the universal truth. In turn, the defenders of postmodern views questioned the notions of universality and legitimation *per se*.

They argued that claims about absolute truth are, by definition, impossible. Their pre-modern or modern versions produced the so-called "Grand Narratives" that legitimized the thirst for power rather than the search for truth. Instead of sliding down the path of either traditional religious or mod-

---

280 "Modernism," Encyclopedia Britannica,
https://www.britanni-ca.com/art/Modernism-art.
281 Frederick Jameson, *Postmodernism or Cultural Logic of Late Capitalism*, Durham: Duke University Press, 1991, 3.

ern secular versions of despotic rule, post-industrial democracies should first de-absolutize knowledge. Those societies must renounce ideologies based on absolute truth by equalizing various knowledge systems or, in postmodern terms, "language games"—science, religion, magic, or mythology. The resulting eclectic socio-cultural milieu will serve as a more appropriate vehicle for developing and promoting the values of democracy, tolerance, and multiculturalism all over the globe.

In that sense, postmodernity does not entirely reject the modern worldview but radicalizes and extends it to encompass the latest social experiments and philosophical reflection. As one of the prominent advocates of the "postmodern condition," French philosopher Jean-François Lyotard has put it, a "work can become modern only if it is first postmodern. Postmodernism thus understood is not modernism at its end but in the nascent state, and this state is constant."[282]

If modernism represents the culmination and completion in the arts of the project of modernity, then postmodernism or postmodern artistic practices express the contemporary worldview at the age of postmodernity. As such, postmodernism replaced the "High Modernism" of abstract art in the post-World War era. And since its beginning, it proclaimed to inherit and deconstruct the modernist legacy.

The application of postmodern ideology into the art world was twofold. First, postmodern artists returned to figuration and rejected abstraction as the ultimate expression of modernism in the arts. One might say that postmodern art is the non-abstract art of the post-Second World War era. The first movement to proclaim its return to figuration was Pop art that arose in the late 1950s—early 1960s, almost simultaneously in Britain and the United States.

---

[282] Jean-François Lyotard, *The Postmodern Condition: A Report on Knowledge,* Minneapolis: University of Minnesota Press, 1991, 79.

Born out of discontent with abstraction, the spirit of Pop was essentially the same in both countries. Pop artists turned to the real life and culture of contemporary cities—to science fiction and Hollywood movies, TV commercials, and popular music—to all that the elite despised and deemed unworthy of being represented as an art form.

Pop artists approached the consumer environment and its mentality with irony and satirical humor—but also with sympathy and acceptance. They created direct parodies of cultural artifacts of Western societies, but those were parodies of what artists loved and have been part of. One famous American pop icon, Roy Lichtenstein, once noted: "In parody, the implication is the perverse, and I feel that in my own work, I don't mean to be that. Because I don't dislike the work that I'm parodying... The things that I have apparently parodied I actually admire."[283]

Unsurprisingly, Pop artists rarely used Crucifixion images in their paintings. The agony of Crucifixion seemed incompatible with and even opposite to Pop's 'take-it-easy' message. The parody of religious subjects, especially the Crucifixion, remained taboo in the English-speaking world, where the movement predominantly evolved.

---

[283] Lucy Lippard, *Pop Art*, London: Thames and Hudson, 1970, 87.

GUDMUNDUR GUDMUNDSSON (ERRÓ, B. 1932)

> *Painting is the laboratory of what is pos-*
> *sible: a place where you can experiment...I*
> *paint because painting is a private form of*
> *utopia, the pleasure of contradicting, the*
> *bliss of being alone against everybody, the*
> *joy of being provocative.*

> Erró

A SERIES OF CRUCIFIXION DRAWINGS COMPLETED IN the mid-1960 by "one of the giants of Abstract Expressionism, [and] a major influence on [the] work"[284] of many American Pop artists, Willem de Kooning, represents a rare example of the provocative combination of Christ's crucified body and a joyous smile on his face. An Icelandic painter and a leading figure of European Pop art, Gudmundur Gudmundsson provides another case of a viable Pop art Crucifixion.

Known in the art world under the pseudonym Erró, Gudmundur Gudmundsson was born on July 19, 1932, in Olafsvik, Iceland, to a manual worker Soffia Kristinsdóttir. At an early age, Gudmundur developed an interest in art and painting. Pursuing his vocation, he studied at the College of Art and Crafts in Reykjavik and the Art Academy in Oslo, Norway. He continued his education and research abroad by traveling to Europe—Spain, Germany, Paris, and Italy, where he studied at the Academy of Art in Florence. It was also in Italy, at the Galleria Santa Trinitá in Florence in 1955, that he had his first solo exhibition. Since then, Erró has had over two hundred solo exhibitions of his artworks in all parts of the world, es-

---

[284] Edward Lucie-Smith, "Pop Art," in *Concepts of Modern Art, 225.*

pecially in the countries of Western and Eastern Europe, but also in his native Iceland as well as in the Middle East (Israel), America (the United States and Venezuela) and Asia (Japan). Several television films devoted to the art and artistic personality of the famous Icelandic painter have also been produced in France and Iceland.

In addition to his thorough and systematic training in the classical tradition of European art, Erró, in his youth, was heavily influenced by the Surrealist movement and the Western counterculture of the post-Second World War period. In the mid-1950s, he met Jean-Jacques Lebel, the "son of the most important auction expert for modern art in Paris, Robert Lebel," and a future artist himself. Jean-Jacques was a young art restoration student who had first-hand knowledge of post-war modernism and "'converted' Erró... to avant-garde art."[285]

In the 1960s, Erró developed an enduring fascination with Pop art's painterly techniques, centering on the perpetual recycling of cliché images that dominated the media space of industrial consumer societies. The following three decades of prolific artwork turned an aspiring Icelandic painter into "a leading representative of Pop art approaches in Europe."[286] Erró's artistic vision and inclinations significantly differed from those on the American art scene since his transatlantic colleagues projected an ironic but well-conformist, non-ideological, enjoyable picture of popular Western culture.

Erró's "critical collages," his "anti-compositions," as art critic Robert Fleck labeled them,[287] reflected, on the contrary, a profoundly satirical and politically engaged position toward contemporary societies. Another art critic Lorand Hegyi point-

---

[285] *Erró: Von Mao Bis Madonna*, catalogue, ed. Uli Todoroff, Museum moderner Kunst Stiftung Ludwig Wien, 1996, 62.
[286] Ibid, 59.
[287] Ibid, 65.

ed out that in Erró's paintings, "genuine emotions are distorted into ridiculous, kitsch-laden and degenerate pseudo-emotions." He added that Erró's "true aesthetic drama, the grappling to resolve conflicts, and the battle to change the world degenerate into pitiful pseudo-activity Hollywood-style."[288] In his 1997 kitsch-like painting *George Grosz* Erró delivers a satirical portrayal of the Crucifixion scene—more specifically, of how it engages popular culture that commercializes and vulgarizes all of its objects, including the most sacred ones.

---

[288] Ibid, 29.

WILLIAM H.JOHNSON (1901–1970) ET AL.

I have had one absorbing and inspiring idea and have worked towards it with un-yielding zeal: to give—in simple and stark [artistic] form—the story of the Negro as he has existed.

William Johnson

STYLISTICALLY, POSTMODERN ART RETURNED TO FIG-URATION. In terms of the content, it expressed, among other things, a profound concern for the rights of minorities. The 'minority art' directly connects with the ideological relativity of postmodern thought, which postulates that competing me-ta-narratives have equal claims to truth and, hence, to social legitimacy.

Many of those narratives serving the interests of under-privileged classes and controversial socio-political causes be-come suppressed. They fall victim to the competing influence of powerful societal groups that have, firmly on their side, the privileges of wealth, state hierarchy, and social convention. It is imperative to advance and protect the under-represented communities whose rights have been traditionally neglected to counteract those advantages and change the status quo. Postmodern artists do so by focusing in their art on the iden-tity issues, problems with racial, gender, and sexual minorities, and the work of the activists who promote progressive social causes, such as environment and consumer protection, help for people living with AIDS, defense of animal rights, and so on.

In this context, the readers should be reminded of one of the first modern paintings that radically challenged the ca-nonical depiction of a crucified Christ—Gauguin's famous *Yel-*

low Christ, made in 1889. A post-Impressionist and Symbolist painter, Paul Gauguin (1848–1903) spent his artistic career searching for new ways to uncover the essentials behind appearances and assert the eternal in the primal and primitive over the artificiality of modern industrial life. In pursuit of his vision, Gauguin left the city for the province—to live among the peasants at Pont-Aven in western France—and then moved to the South Pacific, the dwelling place of aboriginal people. Gauguin's painterly innovation consisted in emancipating color from direct visual perception.

In his masterpiece *The Vision After the Sermon*, made in 1888 at Pont-Aven, "for the first time, Gauguin really grants color a full autonomy... and he would spend the remainder of his life exploring its implications."[289] His *Yellow Christ* painted a year later, represents another step in this direction. The portrayal of the Savior on this canvas reminds the viewers of the native inhabitants of Haiti rather than of the classical white and good-looking male often encountered in traditional Christian iconography. In the twentieth century, such a stance toward Crucifixion found its successor in an African American painter William H. Johnson.

William Henry Johnson was born to an African American family—an elder brother to two brothers and two sisters. He studied painting at the School of the National Academy of Design. At twenty-six, he traveled to Paris for a year of independent study, where he had his first solo exhibition at the Students and Artists Club. Three years later, in 1930, William Johnson had the first solo exhibition of his artworks in the country of his birth—in Michigan and his native South Carolina. The same year he married a Danish woman Holcha Krake and settled with his wife in Denmark. In the coming decade, Johnson had numerous exhibitions of his artwork in the Scandinavian countries—Denmark, Sweden, and Norway.

---

[289] Michael Gibson, *Paul Gauguin*, New York: Rizzoli, 1992, 14.

Upon returning to the United States at the end of 1938, Johnson taught painting at the Harlem Community Arts Center. He got actively involved as a participant in various art exhibitions across the U. S. In 1942 he was awarded a Certificate of Honor for his "distinguished service to America in art." After the death of his wife Holcha in 1944, Johnson's health declined, and three years later, he was diagnosed with paresis. He spent the remainder of his life—unable to paint—at the Central Islip State Hospital in Long Island, New York, where he died in 1970. The three decades that followed his death were marked by the resurgence of interest in his painting. Today William Johnson is recognized as one of the most significant African American artists of the century.

Religious themes have found expression in William Johnson's paintings since the early 1940s. Circa 1942–43—under the title *Ezekiel Saw the Wheel*—he painted his version of the Old Testament prophet Ezekiel's encounter with God. In 1944 after the death of his wife from cancer and suffering from unbearable pain caused by the terrible loss, he created two Crucifixions—*Jesus and the Three Marys* and *Mount Calvary*—and the concluding painting of his "Passion cycle" *Lamentation*. Johnson returned to the inspiration of biblical stories in *Climbing Jacob's Ladder*, which he painted the same year.

Johnson not only shared Paul Gauguin's fascination with primitive cultures but also directly identified with them as of African descent. As he said in one of the interviews, "I myself feel like a primitive man, like one who is at the same time both a primitive and a cultured painter."[290] Johnson idealized Africa and Africans whose civilization may have been primitive but whose spirituality, he believed—for the very reason of indigenous lifestyle and simple, uncorrupted hearts—was higher, purer, and more authentic than in the West. As he explained in

---

[290] Richard J. Powell, *Homecoming: The Art and Life of William H. Johnson*, New York: Rizzoli, 1991, xix.

another interview, "All of the darker races are far more primitive—these are the people who are closer to the sun... [the sun] is closer to us dark people."[291]

Convinced of the compelling confluence of spirituality and primitivism, Johnson explores it in his art, especially in his Afro-centric Crucifixions. One of those canvases, *Jesus and the Three Marys*, completed in 1940, depicts a black crucified Christ who is mourned by the women sharing the racial features of the Savior. According to Johnson's intentions, portraying Jesus as a black man reveals the indissoluble bond between divinity and the indigenous spirit.

Richard Powell, an art historian and scholarly authority on Johnson's works, also noted in his study that *"Jesus and the Three Marys*, a brilliant Afrocentric folk version of the Crucifixion... demonstrated Johnson's... serious attempt at creating a black analog for a standard biblical theme."[292] When discussing the origin and influences of *Mount Calvary*—the second Crucifixion of the painter whose own religious affiliation remains unknown—Powell further wrote that "Johnson's inspiration for [this work] was the intuitive, fundamentalist spirit of black religiosity." He compared it to "black folk tradition, in which biblical imagery and an unconscious African mode of cultural articulation reign supreme."[293]

In the 1950s and 1960s, the presentation of Jesus in art underwent significant transformations that reflected the signs of the times and the new wave of social change in America. The civil rights and black power movements, racial violence, and forced desegregation have led to a significant shift in identifying Christ with black spirituality and the suffering of African Americans in the white-dominated society.

---

[291] Ibid, 69.
[292] Ibid, 182.
[293] Ibid, 183.

In this new social and artistic context, the 'black Messiah' would now become 'brother Jesus' who partakes in the agony and pain of millions of blacks in America, having been looked down upon, ignored, and exploited in their own country. One of the well-known examples of this ever-evolving approach to Crucifixion is the painting *Behold Thy Son* (1956) by an African American painter and art collector, David C. Driskell (b. 1931).

A tragic incident inspired his artwork. In 1955 in Mississippi, "Emmett Till, the black youth...was lynched after having been accused of whistling at a white woman." On his canvas, Driskell depicted "Till's mother presenting her son in death to the church. The outstretched arms and bruised body of the young man recall the crucifixion of Christ and signify the sacrifice of many young lives for freedom."[294]

Around the same time, in 1959, Indian painter Francis Souza (1924–2002) made another black Crucifixion, which continued the controversial tradition of transforming the image of Christ into its latest postmodern reincarnations. Souza was raised Catholic, and he wrote in his autobiographical work "Words and Lines" that the "Roman Catholic Church had a tremendous influence over [him], not in its dogmas but its grand architecture and the splendor of its services." He was deeply impressed by the priest's "vestments...symbolizing the accouterment of Christ's passion [and by] the enormous crucifix with the impaled image of a Man supposed to be the Son of God, scourged and dripping, with matted hair tangled in plaited thorns."[295]

Later in life, Souza grew disappointed by the Catholic clergy's perceived hypocrisy and became a member of the Com-

---

[294] *Narratives of African American Art and Identity: The David C. Driskell Collection*, ed. Juanita Maria Holland, San Francisco, CA: Pomegranate Communications, 1998, 123.

[295] Aziz Kurtha, *Francis Newton Souza, 1924–2002: Bridging Western and Indian Modern Art*, Ahmedabad, India: Mapin Publishing, 2006, 203.

munist Party for some years. Despite his anti-clerical senti-
ments, Souza produced many religious paintings, including
a series of Crucifixions. His famous 1959 piece received mixed
critical acclaim—due to a provocative depiction of Christ in
the form of a wooden figure crowned by a tribal African mask.
While some critics compared Souza's neo-expressionist style
to "Graham Sutherland's treatment of the subject," others,
like an Indian art critic Geeta Kapur dismissed the painting
as totally irreverent. She wrote that Souza "turns Christ into
a caricature, an effigy made of crooked pieces of thorny wood
and a face like a primitive mask, all whiskers, and teeth. His
figure... invites neither pity nor fear [and is] so bitterly con-
temptuous."[296]

---

[296] Ibid, 83.

ARTHUR BOYD (1920–1999) ET AL.

I'd like to feel that through my work, there is a possibility of making a contribution to a social progression or enlightenment. The creative effort or impulse [should be] connected with a conscious contribution to society, a sort of duty or service.

Arthur Boyd

IN ADDITION TO STANDING UP FOR and giving voice to racial minorities, postmodern art focuses on other critical social problems, including the liberation of women from the male-dominated social order and the dangers posed to civilization by weapons of mass destruction. In his Crucifixion paintings, Arthur Merric Bloomfield Boyd, who belongs to an Australian dynasty of artists, provides an excellent example of the artistic depiction of those issues. While having no formal training in painting, Boyd studied the craft under his grandfather, the landscape painter Arthur Merric Boyd, and the Australian sculptor Merric Boyd. Many of Arthur Boyd's relatives were painters, sculptors, or architects.

Arthur Boyd created his first paintings in adolescence, and many accomplishments marked his long and prolific artistic career. In 1979 he received the honorary Order of Australia, and in 1995 he was named the Australian of the Year for his service and contributions to the arts. In 1958, 1988, and 2000, Boyd represented his native country at the Venice Biennale.

Within the large body of Boyd's artworks, some paintings involve religious and, more specifically, biblical subjects. As one Australian art critic Rosemary Crumlin pointed out, "before 1940, there was little religious art in [that country because

232

colonial] Australia was born out of skepticism and pessimism as a penal colony."[297] In 1950, a Jesuit priest Michael Scott and a Jewish businessman Richard Morley established the Blake Prize for Religious Art, which would motivate many Australian painters to engage scriptural themes in their creative activities. As a result, the following generation of artists in Australia grew more accustomed to religion and religious subject matter. They approached it not only because of concerns for career, prestige, or financial security but also from personal faith and social commitment.

Much of the art of Arthur Boyd, who "has stood throughout his life on the side of peace over war and justice over various forms of injustice," is likewise characterized by the "subject matter [that] is explicitly religious and has its roots in biblical narratives."[298] In many religious paintings, Boyd explores the biblical narrative as a point of departure for commenting on contemporary social and cultural issues. By juxtaposing Christian and modern symbols, the Australian painter makes a powerful statement about the ambiguities of today's struggle between traditional Christianity and modern secularism, eternal spirituality and social progress.

Arthur Boyd's *Crucifixion, Shoalhaven*, provides a striking example of such an artistic strategy. In this painting, he places "the crucifix, Christianity's most powerful symbol, against the Australian landscape [where the cross stands], not on the hill of Golgotha, but in the still waters of the Shoalhaven River."[299] He also rebels against a two-thousand-year tradition of Christian art by painting a lady, instead of a man, on the cross. In one of his interviews, Arthur Boyd commented on this decision: "I do not believe it is enough to say he rep-

---

[297] Rosemary Crumlin, *Images of Religion in Australian Art*, Kensington, Australia: Bay Books, 1988, 14.
[298] Ibid, 18.
[299] Ibid, 158.

resented all of us. I do not wish to separate the idea of suffering by allowing just the male to be seen. There has been an awakening consciousness of the potential and force of women in our time."[300] To emphasize this progressive trend, Arthur Boyd revitalized the eternal Christian message of love through sacrifice by applying it to the advance of the modern feminist cause that struggles for women's social and spiritual liberation.

A Crucifixion painting by Julian Schnabel (b.1953), called *Vita*, is another demonstration of feminist concerns in postmodern art. An American artist Julian Schnabel "first gained recognition in 1978, as he restored the panel painting to a position of importance in contemporary art, combining painting with unusual materials which he nailed, glued, or screwed onto his pictures."[301] In 1979 all of Schnabel's paintings at his first one-person show at the Mary Boone Gallery in New York were sold before the exhibition's opening. Since then, Julian Schnabel has remained one of the most talked-about and commercially successful postmodern artists whose work is widely discussed in the art world and beyond.

Schnabel's artistic creed involves "a heroic feeling for life, full of longings and exaltations, anxieties and presentiments of death." For him, "a work of art always signifies a revolt against the transitoriness of being."[302] Throughout his career, Schnabel drew and painted many crosses and Crucifixions as a symbolic gesture of victory over death, the triumph of eternity over all-consuming time. In his *Vita*, made in 1983, he depicts a crucified female body—thus making another powerful statement about the various facets of sacrificial suffering since, as he writes, "agony has many faces: violent, passive,

---

[300] Ibid.
[301] *Julian Schnabel: Works on Paper 1975–1988*, ed. Jörg Zutter, Munich: Prestel-Verlag, 1990, 5.
[302] Ibid.

loud or quiet, making possible readings that go forwards and backwards in time."[303]

Finally, a *Nuclear Crucifixion* by another American painter Alex Grey (b. 1953), provides a striking example of contemporary postmodern art that expresses deep concerns with the rise of modern weaponry and its deadly capabilities. A former Artistic Anatomy and Figure Sculpture instructor at New York University, Alex Grey taught Visionary Art courses at The Open Center in New York City and other institutes in New York, Colorado, and California. Grey developed his unique style of 'x-ray paintings' that aim to depict "the multiple layers of reality and reveal the interplay of anatomical and spiritual forces."[304]

Since the autumn of 2004, Grey placed fifty such artworks in the Chapel of Sacred Mirrors (CoSM) that he co-founded with his wife, Alyson, in New York City. As an art critic Virginia Maksymowicz writes, the "mission of the Chapel is to awaken higher potential through art and to inspire the global community by building sacred architecture as an enduring symbol of the universal spirit."[305] The artworks that Alex Gray exhibited in the Chapel, as Maksymowicz continues, "are a series of paintings depicting the self in body, mind, and spirit; they include a range of spiritual archetypes such as Jesus and Buddha."[306] Grey's *Nuclear Crucifixion* is part of that exhibition. It warns its viewers of the devastating effects of nuclear weapons that can be counteracted only by the divine power of redemption.

---

[303] *Julian Schnabel: Paintings 1975–1986*, London: Whitechapel, 1986, 3.

[304] Alex Grey: http://alexgrey.com/

[305] Virginia Maksymowicz, "Reimagining Religious Art," *Arts: The Arts in Religious and Theological Studies*, 19(1) 2007, 26.

[306] Ibid.

Remarks in Conclusion

MODERNITY HAS OPENED A NEW CHAPTER IN the history of Christianity and, eventually, all of humanity. From the standpoint of religion, it represented the systemic crisis of the Christian faith that resulted in the radical questioning of sacred scriptures and the newfound emphasis on the power of human rationality. From the social sciences perspective, modern Western civilization originated during the Renaissance and matured since the European Enlightenment. Its characteristic features include industrial might, democratic values, and secular culture.

European civilization served as the cradle of this new historical and cultural epoch. For several centuries European nations were spreading the project of modernity throughout the globe. The twentieth century bore witness to the brilliant successes and, at the same time, often ambiguous, even tragic, results of that enterprise. In the canvas *Crucifixion and Rose*, completed in 1980, Australian painter Arthur Boyd recaptures the dramatic tension between modern and traditional cultures in visual and symbolic terms.

The rose in the artwork "can indicate purity, virginity, or even celestial happiness. But in [Boyd's] paintings...it [carries] another meaning; it is the English rose, the symbol of an English culture, which cannot take root in the ruggedness of the Australian climate."[307] In one of his interviews, Arthur Boyd pointed out that the English rose in his Shoalhaven paint-

---

[307] Crumlin, *Images of Religion in Australian Art*, 160.

ings "represents the desperate attempts of the Europeans to impose their culture on an essentially primitive landscape. It floats because it cannot take root. If it does, it destroys, like lantana."[308]

Modernity is the ultimate product of Christian civilization. It is hardly surprising that the image of the Crucifixion—the central event in Christian history—remains so widespread in apparently secular and frequently atheistic twentieth-century art. Professional critics have spotted "two crucial components" in contemporary Crucifixion paintings—"a desire to de-emphasize the religious content [and] to identify with the body on the cross, even to the extent of self-portraiture."[309] While this observation is undoubtedly accurate, twentieth-century Crucifixions, as our study demonstrates, exhibit a much greater variety and complexity.

On the one hand, there are atheistic Crucifixions by painters like Picasso, Guttuso, Bacon, and Saura, each using the body on the cross for their distinct iconoclastic causes. On the other, we find more traditional Crucifixions by Dalí, Sutherland, and Rouault that differ in how painters apply modern techniques to this centuries-old subject. In the middle of the spectrum, modern Crucifixions exploring a wide range of social and spiritual concerns are situated.

Paintings by Newman and Poussette-Dart, Nolde, and Kokoschka are existential canvases that each peculiarly reflect the anxieties of modern times. The artworks by Johnson and Boyd identify Christ's agony with the suffering of African Americans and women—thus addressing the issue of discrimination concerning minorities and other oppressed social groups. Chagall's Crucifixions can also be viewed as part of this group as they emphasize the Jewishness of Jesus and his

---

[308] Ibid.

[309] Christian Heck, "Between Myth and Model. Grunewald's *Crucifixions* and Twentieth Century Art," *The Body on the Cross, 96.*

martyrdom as a symbolic sacrifice of the long-persecuted Jewish nation.

Christ was crucified repeatedly on the canvases of painters who brought a new dimension and modern perspective to the death of the Savior two thousand years ago in one of the corners of the Roman Empire. What is the common denominator behind the incredible diversity of contemporary painters' depictions of Jesus on the cross? In my view, it consists of the transformation that the perception of the Crucifixion underwent in the twentieth century—from a religious event with crucial dogmatic and theological implications to a primary cultural archetype that symbolizes righteous suffering. As such, it has become the ideal vehicle for rendering the existential and social realities of the century's tragic, often unbearable history.

Artworks Discussed and their Present Locations

Historical Background

1. Painted ceiling of a cubiculum in the Catacomb of Saints Peter and Marcellinus, early fourth century, Rome, Italy.
2. Ivory relief, c. 420–30. North Italy. Casket. Crucifixion, Death of Judas. London, Great Britain.
3. *The Crucifixion*, mosaic in the monastery church in Daphne, Greece, 1090–1100.
4. School of Pisa: *Crucifix with Episodes from the Passion*, the second half of the 13th century, Uffizi, Florence, Italy.
5. Rafael, *Crucifixion*, 1503, National Gallery, London, Great Britain.
6. Masaccio, *Holy Trinity*, c. 1428, Santa Maria Novella, Florence, Italy.

Expressionism

7. El Greco, *Christ on the Cross*, c. 1580, Louvre, Paris, France.
8. Hieronymus Bosch, *Calvary*, Musées Royal des Beaux-Arts, Brussels, Belgium.
9. Matthias Grünewald, *Crucifixion*, c. 1510, Öffentliche Kunstsammlung, Basel, Switzerland.
10. Oskar Kokoschka, *Crucifixion (Golgotha)*, 1912, collection Hans C. Bechtler, Zurich, Switzerland.
11. Emil Nolde, *Crucifixion*, 1912, Stiftung Seebüll Ada und Emil Nolde, Neukirchen, Germany.

12. Georges Rouault, *Crucifixion*, c. 1918, collection Henry P. McIlhenny, Philadelphia, USA.

13. Georges Rouault, *Christ on the Cross*, 1939, Musée National d'Art Moderne, Centre Georges Pompidou, Paris, France.

14. Otto Dix, *The Crucifixion*, 1948, Staatsgalerie, Stuttgart, Germany.

CUBISM

15. Pablo Picasso, *The Crucifixion*, 1918, Musée Picasso, Paris, France.

16. Pablo Picasso, *The Crucifixions,* Boisgeloup drawings, 1932, Musée Picasso, Paris, France.

17. Pablo Picasso, *The Crucifixion*, 1930, Musée National Picasso, Paris, France.

18. Renato Guttuso, *Crucifixion in a Room*, 1940, private collection Mario Grimaldi, Salermo, Italy.

19. Renato Guttuso, *Crucifixion*, 1941, Galleria Nazionale d'Arte, Rome, Italy.

20. Jacques Villon, *Crucifixion*, 1961, color lithograph.

SURREALISM

21. Max Ernst, *Crucifixion*, 1913, Museum Ludwig, Köln, Germany.

22. Salvador Dalí, *Christ of St. John of the Cross*, 1951, Glasgow Art Gallery, Great Britain.

23. Salvador Dali, *Crucifixion (Corpus Hypercubus)*, 1954, The Metropolitan Museum of Art, New York, USA.

24. Marc Chagall, *Resistance, Resurrection*, 1948, National Museum Message Biblique Marc Chagall, Nice, France.

25. Marc Chagall, *White Crucifixion*, 1938, Art Institute of Chicago, USA.

26. Antonio Saura, *Crucifixions*, 1959–1985, private collection.

ABSTRACTION

27. Richard Poussette-Dart, *Crucifixion, Comprehension of the Atom*, 1944, collection of the artist.

28. Barnett Newman, *The Stations of the Cross—Twelfth Station,* 1965, National Gallery of Art, Washington, D.C, USA.

29. Francis Bacon, *Crucifixion*, 1933, private collection.

30. Francis Bacon, *Three Studies for Figures at the Base of a Crucifixion*, 1944, Tate Gallery, London, Great Britain.

31. Francis Bacon, *Crucifixion*, triptych, 1965, Pinakothek der Moderne, Munich, Germany.

32. Francis Bacon, *Second Version of "Triptych 1944,"* 1988, Tate Gallery, London, Great Britain.

33. Graham Sutherland, *The Crucifixion*, 1946, St. Matthew's Church, Northampton, Great Britain.

POSTMODERNISM

34. Willem de Kooning, *Untitled (Crucifixion)*, a series of drawings, 1966, Xavier Fourcade, New York, USA.

35. Erró, George *Grosz*, 1997, Museum Ludwig, Köln, Germany.

36. Paul Gauguin, *Yellow Christ*, 1889, Albright-Knox Art Gallery, Buffalo, N.Y., USA.

37. William Johnson, *Jesus, and the Three Marys*, 1939, Howard University Gallery of Art, Washington, D.C., USA.

38. William H. Johnson, *Mount Calvary*, c. 1944, Smithsonian American Art Museum, Washington, D.C., USA.

39. David Driskell, *Behold Thy Son*, 1956, The David Driskell Collection, USA.

40. Francis Souza, *Crucifixion*, 1959, Tate Gallery, London, Great Britain.

41. Arthur Boyd, *Crucifixion, Shoalhaven,* 1980, collection of the artist, Australia.

42. Julian Schnabel, *Vita,* 1983, private collection.

43. Alex Grey, *Nuclear Crucifixion,* 1980, Chapel of Sacred Mirrors (CoSM), New York, USA.

CONCLUSION

44. Arthur Boyd, *Crucifixion and Rose,* 1980, Bundanon Collection, Australia.

CHRONOLOGY OF MODERN ART MOVEMENTS

1755

In his book *Thoughts and Imitation of Greek Works in Painting and Sculpture* (1755), the German theorist Johann Joachim Winckelmann (1717–1768) popularized a memorable slogan for the Neoclassical approach to art — "noble simplicity and calm grandeur."

1780

A Spanish Romantic painter and printmaker, Francisco De Goya Y Lucientes (1746–1828), made his *Christ Crucified* (1780), now located at the Museo del Prado in Madrid, Spain.

1781

In sculpture, Neoclassicism was explored by Jean-Antoine Houdon (1741–1828), who specialized in portraiture. His *Voltaire Seated* (1781) displayed all the features of Neoclassicism and was rightly acclaimed as a "modern classic."

1784

In architecture, England was the birthplace of the Neoclassical style. The spirit of Neoclassicism manifested in the first half of the eighteenth century in the so-called "Palladian revival." Initiated by Lord Burlington (1694–1753) in Great Britain, Palladianism spread abroad to the American colonies, branded as the Georgian style. Thomas Jefferson's House in Monticello, Charlottesville, Virginia (1784) represents a magnificent example of the Neoclassical style in the United States.

1793

The leading Neoclassical painter of the time, Jacques-Louis David (1748–1825), followed the French Baroque painter Nicolas Poussin (1594–1665) in his style, favoring clarity and order and preferring line over color. David's accomplishments served as the foundation for our understanding of the movement. In his masterpiece, *The Death of Marat* (1793), David immortalized a historical figure as a secular hero and revolutionary martyr.

1809

A French Neoclassical painter Jean-Auguste-Dominique Ingres (1780–1867), created *The Crucifixion*, now located at the Musée Ingres, Montauban, France.

1800–1850

The flourishing of Romanticism in visual arts, literature, and music. Romantic painters rediscovered and thoroughly explored the richness of landscape artworks as a distinctive genre of modern art.

1819

Focusing on emotional intensity and colorful palettes, Romantics loved to portray people in extreme circumstances — revolutionary wars, mass executions, massacres, miraculous rescues, and so on. *The Raft of the "Medusa"* (1819) by a French painter and lithographer, Théodore Géricault (1791–1824), readily comes to mind.

1848

A French Romantic artist Eugene Delacroix (1798–1863) painted his *Crucifixion*, now located at the Museum Boijmans Van Beuningen, Rotterdam, Netherlands.

1849

A French Realist painter Gustave Courbet (1819–1877), exhibited his first programmatic canvas, *The Stone Breakers*.

1850s

Realism rose to prominence in the second half of the nineteenth century as a new movement in art and literature. Great Realist writers — Honoré de Balzac (1799–1850) in France, Charles Dickens (1812–1870) in England, Henrik Ibsen (1828–1906) in Norway, and Leo Tolstoy (1828–1910) in Russia — rejected the conventions of Romanticism and turned their attention to the reality and truth of contemporary societies.

1857

A French Symbolist poet Charles Baudelaire (1821–1867), published his infamous collection of poetry, *Flowers of Evil*.

1862

A French Symbolist artist Gustave Moreau (1826–1898), created a series of artworks, *The Stations of the Cross*, which included the *Twelfth Station: Christ Dying on the Cross*.

1875

A new cultural and artistic movement called Symbolism flourished in Europe in the last quarter of the nineteenth century. Having rejected the social criticism of Realist artworks, the Symbolist writers and artists turned their attention to the inner world of humanity with its evil passions and forbidden desires.

1888

A Belgian Symbolist painter and printmaker, James Ensor (1860–1949), made his *Christ in Agony*, now located at the Galerie Bellier in Paris, France.

1889

A French Post-Impressionist artist Paul Gauguin (1848–1903), painted his *Yellow Christ*, now located at the Albright–Knox Art Gallery in Buffalo, N.Y., USA.

1893

A Norwegian Symbolist artist Edvard Munch (1863–1944), created his famous painting *The Scream*.

1904

A French Symbolist artist Odilon Redon (1840–1916), painted *The Crucifixion*, now located at the Barber Institute of Fine Arts in Birmingham, United Kingdom.

1905

Les Fauves (Wild Beasts), including Henry Matisse (1869–1954), André Derain (1880–1954), and Maurice Vlaminck (1876–1958), exhibit together at the Salon d'Automne in October.

The Dresden group of expressionist artists Die Brücke (The Bridge) is formed. The group, including such painters as Ernst Ludwig Kirchner (1880–1938), lasted till 1913.

1906

At the Salon des Indépendants, Matisse exhibits his programmatic painting *Joie de Vivre* (Joy of Life).

Ernst Kirchner publishes an expressionist Manifesto.

1907

Pablo Picasso (1881–1973) paints *Les Demoiselles d'Avignon*, which, according to some critics, is the most critical single pictorial document of the century.

1909

The First Futurist Manifesto, written by the founder of this movement, an Italian poet Filippo Tommaso Marinetti (1876–1944), appears in the French newspaper *Le Figaro*.

1910

Pablo Picasso (1881–1973) and George Braque (1882–1963) developed an analytic form of Cubism.

Wassily Kandinsky (1866–1944) makes the first non-objective watercolor.

1911

Two exhibitions of the Munich group of Expressionist artists, Der Blaue Reiter (The Blue Rider), were organized by Wassily Kandinsky and Franc Marc (1880–1916) from December 1911—February 1912.

Kandinsky published his book *On the Spiritual in Art*, and created his painting of the Crucifixion: *Crucified Christ*; Gekreuzigter Christus. 1911.

The first significant showing of Futurist paintings takes place in Milan.

Crucifixion by Oskar Kokoschka (1886–1980).

1912

Picasso and Braque invent collage.

Emil Nolde (1867–1956) paints *The Life of Christ*.

1913

The Armory Show, which introduces America to European avant-garde art, is held in New York.

Beginning of the synthetic phase of Cubism which lasts till the death of its primary representative Juan Gris (1887–1927).

Kazimir Malevich (1878–1935) launched his abstract art movement called Suprematism.

1914

Marcel Duchamp (1887–1968) designated one of his first "ready-made"—a bottle rack.

1916

Cabaret Voltaire opened in Zurich, Switzerland, marking the beginning of the Dada movement that would last till 1921.

1917

The beginning of the De Stijl abstract art movement that lasted until 1931. The primary representative of De Stijl was Piet Mondrian (1872–1944).

1918

The First De Stijl manifesto is published in the De Stijl magazine.

1924

The first Surrealist manifesto, written by André Breton (1896–1966), is published in the opening issue of the Surrealist review *La Révolution Surréaliste*.

1925

Max Ernst (1891–1976) discovers "frottages,"—an automatic technique in painting.

1927

An Italian Futurist painter Gerardo Dottori (1884–1977), one of the signatories of the 1929 "Aeropainting Manifesto," created a Futurist representation of the *Crucifixion* (1927), which is now housed in the Vatican Museum.

1930

Pablo Picasso paints his *Crucifixion*.

1935

A French artist and theoretician, one of the founding fathers of Cubism, Albert Gleizes (1881–1953), painted a Cubist representation of the Crucifixion (c. 1935).

1938

The International Exhibition of Surrealism in Paris marks the acme of the movement between the World Wars.
White Crucifixion by Marc Chagall (1887–1985).

1939

Georges Rouault (1871–1958) paints his *Christ on the Cross.*

1941

Crucifixion by Renato Guttuso (1911–1987).

1944

Richard Poussette-Dart (1916–1992), paints *Crucifixion, Comprehension of the Atom.*
William Johnson (1901–1970), *Mount Calvary.*
Three Studies for Figures at the Base of a Crucifixion by Francis Bacon (1909–1992).

1946

The Northampton Crucifixion by Graham Sutherland (1903–1980).

1948

A group of Abstract Expressionist artists founded a school called "The Subject of the Artist." Abstract Expressionist movement, also called "Action painting" or "American-type painting," dominated in the 1950s.
The Crucifixion by Otto Dix (1891–1969).

1951

Salvador Dalí (1904–1989) paints his *Christ of St. John of the Cross.*

1954

Crucifixion (Corpus Hypercubus) by Salvador Dalí.

1956

Richard Hamilton's collage "Just What is it that Makes Today's Homes so Different, so Appealing?" brings about the beginning of Pop-Art.

1960

Pierre Restany wrote the first manifesto of the Nouveaux Réalistes.

1961

Crucifixion by Jacques Villon (1875–1963).
Antonio Saura (1930–1998), paints *Crucifixion.*

1965

The Responsive Eye Exhibition at the New York Museum of Modern Art became the first international exhibition with a predominance of Op-Art paintings.
An exhibition, "Pop Art and the American Tradition," at the Milwaukee Art Center, USA.
Crucifixion, triptych by Francis Bacon (1909–1992).
Barnett Newman (1905–1970), paints *The Stations of the Cross—Twelfth Station.*

1966

"Primary Structures"—one of the first exhibitions to present Minimalism as an accomplished body of work.

1970s

Rise of Postmodern ideology and art.

1980

Crucifixion and Rose by Arthur Boyd (1920-1999), now stored in the Bundanon Collection, Australia.

Nuclear Crucifixion, by Alex Grey, Chapel of Sacred Mirrors (CoSM), New York, USA.

1997

Gudmundsson Erró (b. 1932), paints *George Grosz,* which incorporates a Pop-Art parody image of the Crucifixion.

Selected Bibliography

General Sources

Books

Art After Modernism: Rethinking Representation, ed. And with an Introduction by Brian Wallis, Foreword by Marcia Tucker, New York: The Museum of Contemporary Art, 1996.

Bainton, Roland H. *Here I Stand: A Life of Martin Luther.* New York: Penguin, 1995.

Berdyaev, Nicholas. *Philosophy of Creativity, Culture, and Art* [Filosofiya nvorchestva, kul'tury i iskusstva], two volumes, Moscow: "Iskusstvo," 1994.

Brown, Stephanie. *Religious Painting: Christ's Passion and Crucifixion*, New York: Mayflower Books, 1979.

Chipp, Herschel B. *Theories of Modern Art: A Source Book by Artists and Critics*, with contributions by Peter Selz and Joshua C. Taylor, Berkeley: University of California Press, 1968.

Chong, Alan, De Appolonia, Giovanna, et al., *The Art of the Cross: Medieval and Renaissance Piety in the Isabella Stewart Gardner Museum*, Boston, MA: Isabella Stewart Gardner Museum, 2001.

Crumlin, Rosemary. *Images of Religion in Australian Art*, Kensington, Australia: Bay Books, 1988.

Concepts of Modern Art: From Fauvism to Postmodernism, ed. Nikos Stangos, 3rd ed., (original ed. 1974), London: Thames and Hudson, 1994.

Crowther, Paul. *The Language of Twentieth Century Art: A Conceptual History*, New Haven and London: Yale University Press, 1997.

Dada Artifacts, Iowa City: The University of Iowa Museum of Art, 1978.

Dillenberger, Jane. *Style and Content in Christian Art*, New York: Crossroad, 1986.

Dube, Wolf-Dieter. *The Expressionists,* trans. from German Mary Whittall (original printing 1972), London: Thames and Hudson, 1985.

Fry, Edward F. *Cubism*, London: Thames and Hudson, 1978, (1st ed. 1966).

Futurist Manifestos, ed. and with an introduction by Umbro Apollonio, London: Thames and Hudson, 1973.

Grubb, Nancy. Revelations: *Art of the Apocalypse*, New York—London—Paris: Abbeville Press, 1997.

Habermas, Jürgen. *The Anti-Aesthetic: Essays on Postmodern Culture*, ed. Hal Foster, Bay Press, 1983.

Harris, Stephen L. *Understanding the Bible*, 4th ed., (1st ed. 1980), Mountain View, CA—London—Toronto: Mayfield Publishing Company, 1997.

Henkes, Robert. *The Crucifixion in American Art*, Jefferson, NC–London: McFarland Publishers, 2003.

Hippolytus of Rome, Treatise on Christ and Antichrist, Early Christian Writings, **www.earlychristianwritings.com/text/ hippolytus-christ.html**.

Hobbs, Robert Carleton and Levin, Gail. *Abstract Expressionism. The Formative Years*, Ithaca—New York: Herbert F. Johnson Museum of Art / Whitney Museum of American Art, 1978.

Hunt, J. Eric. *English and Welsh Crucifixes: 670–1550*, London: S.P.C.K., 1956.

Jameson, Frederick. *Postmodernism or Cultural Logic of Late Capitalism*, Durham: Duke University Press, 1991.

Janson, H. W. with Dora Jane Janson. *A History of Art: A Survey of the Visual Arts from the Dawn of History to the Present Day*, 3rd ed., (1st ed. 1962), London: Thames and Hudson, 1981.

Jencks, Charles. *What Is Post-Modernism?* London: Academy Editions, 1996.

Jencks, Charles. *Post-Modernism: The New Classicism in Art and Architecture*, New York: Rizzoli International Publications, 1987.

Lippard, Lucy R. *Pop Art*, London: Thames and Hudson, 1970.

Livingstone, Marco. *Pop Art: A Continuing History*, New York: Thames & Hudson, 2000.

Lyotard, Jean-François. *The Postmodern Condition: A Report on Knowledge*, trans. from the French by Geoff Bennington and Brian Massumi, Minneapolis: University of Minnesota Press, 1991.

MacGregor, Neil with Erika Langmuir. *Seeing Salvation: Images of Christ in Art*, New Haven—London: Yale University Press, 2000.

Modernism: An Anthology of Sources and Documents, ed. Vassiliki Kolocotroni, Jane Goldman, and Olga Taxidou, Chicago: The University of Chicago Press, 1998.

Narratives of African American Art and Identity: The David C. Driskell Collection, ed. Juanita Maria Holland, San Francisco, CA: Pomegranate Communications, 1998.

Oesterreicher–Mollwo, Marianne. *Surrealism and Dadaism. Provocative Destruction, the Path Within and the Exacerbation of the Problem of a Reconciliation of Art and Life*, Oxford: Phaidon, 1979.

Perkins, Pheme. *Reading the New Testament: An Introduction*, 2nd rev. ed., (1st ed. in 1978), New York, N.Y. / Mahwah, N.J.: 1988.

Pop, ed. Mark Francis, London—New York: Phaidon Press, 2005.

Porter, J. R. *The Illustrated Guide to the Bible*, New York—Oxford: Oxford University Press, 1995.

Richter, Hans. *Dada Art and Anti-Art*, London: Thames and Hudson, 1965.

Sandler, Irving. *Art of the Postmodern Era. From the Late 1960s to the Early 1990s,* New York: IconEditions, 1996.

Schiller, Gertrud. *Iconography of Christian Art*, vol. 2, *The Passion of Jesus Christ*, trans. Janet Seligman, Greenwich, Connecticut: New York Graphic Society, 1972.

Selz, Peter. *Art in Our Times. A Pictorial History: 1890–1980*, New York: Harcourt Brace Jovanovich—Harry N. Abrams, 1981.

Sergeev, Mikhail. *Theory of Religious Cycles: Tradition, Modernity, and the Bahá'í Faith*, Leiden–Boston: Brill, 2015.

Tansey, Richard. G., Kleiner, Fred. S. *Gardner's Art Through the Ages*, 10th ed., (1st ed. 1926), New York: Harcourt Brace College Publishers, 1996.

Taylor, Brandon. *Contemporary Art: Art Since 1970*, Upper Saddle River, N.J.: Pearson Prentice Hall, 2005.

Taylor, Brandon. *Avant-Garde and After: Rethinking Art Now*, New York: Harry N. Abrams, Inc., 1995.

The Body on the Cross: Picasso, Bacon, Dix, De Kooning, Guttuso, Sutherland, Saura, a catalogue, Paris: Réunion des musées nationaux, 1992.

The Oxford Study Bible. Revised English Bible with the Apocrypha, ed. M. Jack Suggs, Katharine Doob Sakenfeld, and James R. Mueller, New York: Oxford University Press, 1992.

The Postmodern Moment. A Handbook of Contemporary Innovation in the Arts, ed., with an Introduction, by Stanley Trachtenberg, Westport, Connecticut—London, England: Greenwood Press, 1985.

The Documents of Vatican II with Notes and Comments by Catholic, Protestant, and Orthodox Authorities, gen. ed. Walter M. Abbott, trans. ed. Very Rev. Msgr. Joseph Gallagher, Geoffrey Chapman, 1966.

Tillich, Paul. *On Art and Architecture,* ed. with an Introduction by John Dillenberger, trans. from the German Robert. P. Scharlemann, New York: Crossroad, 1989.

Variations Autour de la Crucifixion: Regards Contemporains sur Grünewald, a catalogue, Colmar: Musée d'Unterlinden, 1993, v. I.

Viladesau, Richard. *The Beauty of the Cross: The Passion of Christ in Theology and the Arts, from the Catacombs to the Eve of the Renaissance*, Oxford: Oxford University Press, 2006.

ARTICLES

"Cross/Purpose: A New CIVA Exhibition (The Edward and Dianne Knippers Collection)—Lenten Devotional Images," *SEEN: The Journal of CIVA (Christians in Visual Arts)*, Vol. VI.1 2006, pp. 3–17.

Iazykova, Irina. "'Se chelovek'. Iisus Khristos v izobrazitel'nom iskusstve XX veka" ['*Ecce Homo*'. Jesus Christ in 20th Century Visual Art], *Mir Biblii* [*The World of the Bible*], an illustrated almanac of St. Andrew's Biblical-Theological College, 10(2004), pp. 47–65.

Maksymowicz, Virginia. "Reimagining Religious Art," *Arts: The Arts in Religious and Theological Studies*, 19(1) 2007, pp. 24–30.

Mikhail Sergeev. "Crucifixion in Twentieth-Century Painting," *Transactions of the Association of Russian-American Scholars in the U.S.A.*, vol. XXXVII, New York, 2011–2012, pp. 395–416.

————. "Crucifixion in Twentieth-Century Art: The Paintings of Marc Chagall," *Symposion: A Journal Russian Thought*, Vol. 15 (2010), pp. 47–56.

————. "Crucifixion in Painting: Historical Considerations and Twentieth-Century Expressionism," *ARTS: The Arts in Religious and Theological Studies*, vol. 18, 1(2006), pp. 26–36.

————. "Biblical Themes in Twentieth-Century Painting: Wassily Kandinsky's Apocalyptic Abstractions," *Transactions of the Association of Russian-American Scholars in the U.S.A.*, vol. XXXIII, New York, 2003, pp. 323–332. Reprinted in *ARTS: The Arts in Religious and Theological Studies*, vol. 16, 2(2004), pp. 12–18.

————. "Iskusstvo moderna: osnovnye tendentsii v 20-m veke" [Modern Art: Main Trends in the Twentieth Century], *The Coast* almanach, Philadelphia, 2000.

Yates, Wilson. "To the Margins of the Sea Where Furies Dwell: Reflections on Bacon and Sutherland," *Arts: The Arts in Religious and Theological Studies*, 18(2) 2007, pp. 40–44.

INTERNET SITES

"Arianism," *Encyclopedia Britannica*, www.britannica.com/topic/Arianism.

"Athanasius of Alexandria," *The Development of the Canon of the New Testament*, http://www.ntcanon.org/Athanasius.shtml.

"Ecumenical Councils," *Theopedia*, https://www.theopedia.com/ecumenical-councils.

"Diet of Worms," *New World Encyclopedia*, http://www.newworldencyclopedia.org/entry/Diet_of_Worms#cite_note-bainton-0.

"Filioque clause," *Theopedia*, https://www.theopedia.com/filioque-clause.

"Modernism," *Encyclopedia Britannica*, https://www.britannica.com/art/ Modernism-art.

"Nicene Creed," *Encyclopedia Britannica*, www.britannica.com/topic/Nicene-Creed.

"Passion Cycle," *The Free Dictionary*, https://encyclopedia2.thefreedictionary. com/Passion+cycle.

"Praying The Stations of the Cross" by Louise Merrie, *Catholic Exchange*, https://catholicexchange.com/praying-the-stations-of-the-cross/.

"Protestant Reformation Art," *Encyclopedia of Art History*, http://www.visual-arts-cork.com/history-of-art/protestant.htm.

PAINTERS

BOOKS

Antonio Saura: *Imagina 1956–1997,* Malmö Konsthall, 1997.

Arcangeli, Francesco. *Graham Sutherland,* trans. from the Italian by Helen Barolini and H. Joseph Narks, New York: Harry N. Abrams Publishers, 1975.

Barnett Newman, ed. Ann Temkin, Philadelphia: Philadelphia Museum of Art, 2002.

Bradbury, Kirsten. *The Essential Dalí,* London: Dempsey Parr, 1999.

Calvocoressi, Richard. *Kokoschka: Paintings,* New York: Rizzoli International Publications, 1992.

Courthion, Pierre. *Georges Rouault,* New York: Harry N. Abrams Publishers, 1977.

Descharnes, Robert, Néret, Gilles. *Salvador Dalí, 1904–1989,* Köln—Los Angeles: Taschen, 2004.

Descharnes, Robert. *The World of Salvador Dalí,* New York: Harper and Row, 1962.

Diary of a Genius. Salvador Dalí, trans. from the French by Richard Howard, notes by Michel Déon, New York: Prentice Hall, 1965.

Erró: Von Mao Bis Madonna, catalogue, ed. Uli Todoroff, Museum moderner Kunst Stiftung Ludwig Wien, 1996.

Fabre, Josep Palau I. *Picasso,* New York: Rizzoli, 1981.

Ferrier, Jean-Louis. *Picasso,* Paris: Terrail, 1996.

Francis Bacon and the Tradition of Art, ed. Wilfred Seipel et al., Milano: Skira Editore, 2003.

Francis Bacon. A Retrospective, guest curator Dennis Farr, New York: Harry N. Abrams Publishers, 1999.

Francis Newton Souza, 1924–2002: Bridging Western and Indian Modern Art, ed. Aziz Kurtha, Ahmedabad, India: Mapin Publishing, 2006.

Gibson, Michael. *Paul Gauguin,* New York: Rizzoli, 1992.

Guttuso, eds. Andrea Buzzoni, Fabio Carapezza Guttuso and Catherine Lampert, London: Thames and Hudson, 1996.

Hammer, Martin. *Graham Sutherland: Landscapes, War Scenes, Portraits 1924–1950*, London: Scala Publishers, 2005.

Hayes, John. *The Art of Graham Sutherland*, New York: Phaidon Press, 1980.

Hobbs, Robert and Kuebler, Joanne. *Richard Poussette-Dart*, Indianapolis: Indianapolis Museum of Art, 1990.

Jacques Villon, ed. Daniel Robbins, Cambridge, MA: Harvard University, 1976.

Julian Schnabel: Works on Paper 1975–1988, ed. Jörg Zutter, Munich: Prestel-Verlag, 1990.

Julian Schnabel: Paintings 1975–1986, London: Whitechapel, 1986.

Karcher, Eva. *Otto Dix, 1891–1969*, London—New York: Taschen, 2002.

Léal, Brigitte, Piot, Christine, Bernadac, Marie-Laure. *The Ultimate Picasso*, New York: Harry N. Abrams, 2000.

Lieberman, William S. *Jacques Villon: His Graphic Art*, The Museum of Modern Art Bulletin: Vol. XXI, no. 1, Fall 1953.

Marc Chagall. Origins and Paths, ed. Roland Doschka, with contributions by Roland Doschka, Françoise Dumont, and Meret Meyer, Munich—New York: Prestel, 1998.

Maritain, Jacques. *Georges Rouault*, New York: Harry N. Abrams Publishers, 1952.

Max Ernst: A Retrospective, New York: The Solomon R. Guggenheim Museum, 1975.

National Museum Message Biblique Marc Chagall, an album, Paris: Réunion des musées nationaux, 2000.

PhoenixArt 2003: Erró, Fahlström, Kópcke, Lebel, ed. Claus Mewes, Hamburg: Christians Verlag, 2003.

Picasso, eds. Patrick McCaughey and Judith Ryan, Sidney: International Cultural Corporation of Australia, 1984.

Polonsky, Gill. *Chagall*, London: Phaidon Press, 1998.

Powell, Richard. J. *Homecoming: The Art and Life of William H. Johnson*, New York: Rizzoli, 1991.

Richard Poussette-Dart: The New York school and beyond, ed. Sam Hunter and Joanne Kuebler, Milano: Skira Editore, 2005.

Russell, John. *Max Ernst: Life and Work*, New York: H. N. Abrams, 1967.

Selz, Peter. *Emil Nolde*, New York: The Museum of Modern Art, 1968.

Sims, Lowery Stokes and Polcari, Stephen. *Richard Poussette-Dart (1916–1992)*, New York: The Metropolitan Museum of Art, 1998.

Soby, James Thrall. *Salvador Dalí*, New York: Arno Press, 1968, 1st ed. 1946 by the Museum of Modern Art.

The Living Edge: Richard Poussette-Dart, 1916–1992. Works On Paper, ed. Ingrid Ehrhardt and Katja Hilbig, Frankfurt Schirn Kunsthalle Frankfurt, 2001.

The Salvador Dalí Museum Collection, foreword by A. Reynolds Morse, introduction by Robert S Lubar, Boston: Bulfinch Press, 1991.

Venturi, Lionello. *Chagall: Biographical and Critical Study*, trans. S. J. C. Harrison and James Emmons, Geneva: Editions d'Art Albert Skira, 1972, (1st ed. 1956).

Viladesau, Richard. *The Beauty of the Cross. The Passion of Christ in Theology and the Arts, from the Catacombs to the Eve of the Renaissance*, Oxford—New York: Oxford University Press, 2006.

William De Kooning: Drawings, Paintings, Sculpture, eds. Paul Cummings et al., New York: Whitney Museum of American Art, 1983.

Zweite, Armin. *Barnett Newman*. Paintings, Sculptures, Works on Paper, trans. From the German by John Brogden, Ostfildern-Ruit, Germany: Hatje Cantz Publishers, 1999.

INTERNET SITES

Alex Grey: http://alexgrey.com/.

Links to Images of the Crucifixion of Jesus:
http://www.textweek.com/art/crucifixion.htm.

www.ingramcontent.com/pod-product-compliance
Lightning Source LLC
Chambersburg PA
CBHW071252220526
45468CB00001B/97